CATALOGUING IN THE NEW ERA
Gazing through the Bodleian Catalogues to RDA

CATALOGUING IN THE NEW ERA

Gazing through the Bodleian Catalogues to RDA

Subhankar Biswas
University of Calcutta

Assisted by
Durga Sankar Rath
Vidyasagar University

Ess Ess Publications
New Delhi

CATALOGUING IN THE NEW ERA
Gazing through the Bodleian Catalogues to RDA

ISBN: 978-81-933597-6-1

First Published 2017

Published by:
Ess Ess Publications
4831/24, Ansari Road,
Darya Ganj,
New Delhi-110 002.
INDIA
Phones: 23260807, 41563444
Fax: 41563334
E-mail: info@essessreference.com
www.essessreference.com

Cover Design by *Patch Creative Unit*

Printed and bound in India at Salasar Imaging Systems.

Dedicated

to

DR. SHIB SANKAR DATTA
(Beloved Abolokiteswar, Babunda)

Contents

Introduction

Descriptive Cataloguing is a dynamic concept. Dynamism is the ever flowing life-blood of descriptive catalogues and of a cataloguing code. Like the descriptive catalogues, the code also changes consistently to survive with the changes all around. History has shown that the moment a descriptive cataloguing code loses its momentum, decay starts. Several renowned cataloguing codes have perished in the long legacy of Anglo American Cataloguing Codes, and the only cause of their abolition that was common to all was lack of dynamism. Thus, dynamism plays the pivotal role to keep descriptive catalogues and the code effective.

This book is centered round the concept of exploring the presence or absence of dynamism in the Anglo American Cataloguing Codes and its impact on the effectiveness of these codes. The descriptive and analytical study made throughout almost all the renowned cataloguing codes and catalogues (like the Bodleian Catalogues) of Anglo-American origin has shown a lot of twists and turns of cataloguing history which have enriched the study with new dimensions. It is found that despite frequent revisions and updates, AACR2 failed to adapt with the technology driven fast changing information world because hardly any fundamental changes took place during the revision process; rather the cosmetic changes overcrowded every revision. They were not effective enough to address the most problematic issues of AACR2. Secondly, Ranganathan's Principles and Canons of cataloguing were followed in AACR2 and RDA in a stray and sporadic manner. But if they were used in an organized way as the basic guidelines for the cataloguing rules, it could offer better strength and stability to both the codes. Third important finding that must be mentioned here is that, the effectiveness of RDA to library catalogues found not very impressive one, as well as its chances of immediately being widely implemented in the libraries seems very rare.

This work is a re-examination and re-evaluation of the origin, growth and development; policy for the designing, updating and revisions of descriptive cataloguing codes along with their implementations in the practical cataloguing. The increasing e-resources, the changing information seeking behavoiur of the users and the changing means of access to the resources have brought the cataloguers in front of huge challenges now-a-days that can not be countered only through routine revisions like the previous century. Rather, it has made the cataloguers more cautious about the impending danger they may face in document description and access due to the uncalled for hostilities created by the online search engines which produces thousands of hits within a few seconds. Metadata element sets are also another threat that concerns the present-day cataloguers about the future role of catalogues to the coming generations. Dynamism, guided by the principles and canons of cataloguing is the only saviour which may indicate the right path keeping the torch ablaze at the top of the lighthouse amidst unprecedented turbulence created by the explosive outburst of information, development of Information and Communication Technology (ICT) and the fast changing nature of the resources in the electronic era.

Kolkata **S. Biswas**

1

Catalogue and Cataloguing

1.0. INTRODUCTION

Revision has a vital role to keep the descriptive cataloguing viable. The information world is ever changing. To keep it relevant, library catalogues also need to be revised according to the changing context. This capability of revision or dynamism is the most significant part of descriptive cataloguing. Cataloguing is a practice, adopted since the inception of library itself. But the conception of cataloguing code is of recent origin. It's a contribution of the modern period. Cataloguing code is a tool that provides explicit guidelines to cataloguers about how to do practical cataloguing with a clear rationale for why it is to be done that way. Therefore, a cataloguing code cannot be static; it must be revised with the changing needs. History shows that if a cataloguing code fails to adjust itself with the changing context or to adapt with the changing environment, it would automatically perish. This changing necessity has given birth to new cataloguing codes with better adaptability from time to time. The new codes always appear with the intention to make amicable solution of the emerging unresolved issues in the changing context.

1.1. RECENT DEVELOPMENTS IN CATALOGUING

Since the introduction of AACR2 (1978), numerous revisions were made. Revisions become necessary because of the fast changing needs in the bibliographic world. Several efforts have been made to accommodate the changes in the existing structure of the code. This is quite justified because dynamism is the essence of descriptive cataloguing. But how far these efforts fulfilled the expectations of the cataloguers is a matter that invites much debate.

The explosive outburst of information technology has brought sea changes to the nature of documents and library holdings, as well as the information seeking behaviour of the users. With the multiplication of web-literature within a very short period, some mechanism became essential to catalogue and manage them along with the conventional library-materials. But AACR2, despite its frequent revisions seems unable to satisfy the needs of the cataloguing community. Obviously, demand for a new code emerged to cope up with the situation. *International Conference on the Principles and Future Development of AACR* held in Toronto in 1997 advocated strongly in favour of a new cataloguing code. Thus, the Joint Steering Committee for Revision of AACR (JSC) decided to introduce a new code Resource Description and Access (RDA) in place of revised AACR2. Questions arising from many corners whether it was a daring effort on the part of JSC to make up the difficulties it caused due to inadequate revisions of AACR2.

Some experts opined that, it is atonement for the Joint Steering Committee for Revision of AACR (JSC). According to them, it's the huge deficiency on the part of JSC in the design and revision of AACR2 that has led the cataloguing community to rethink about the future use of the code in its present form. JSC is doing penance for the gross injustice it did to the erstwhile cataloguing tradition coming down from the 16th century. The very idea of using the 'literary unit' concept (on which the new code RDA is built) in cataloguing began as early as 1595 by Andrew Maunsell. It was very much in practice in the later cataloguing of Bodleian, and to some extent in Panizzi's famous *91 Rules*, Jewet's Code, as well as in Cutter's RDC. It's very difficult to determine now why and how JSC dropped or over-looked this significant concept whenever designing AACR2. There was a huge debate in the *International Conference on Cataloguing Principles, ICCP* 1961 on this concept where stalwarts like Lubetzky voiced strongly in its favour. Even JSC paid no heed to this during so many revisions when it was struggling to cope up with the unfulfilled demands of the cataloguing communities.

The same JSC has to turn its eyes towards its forefathers again to full fill their unsatisfied desires through the use of 'literary unit' concept by means of a thorough revision of the existing code AACR2. The initial effort was to bring out a revised code named *AACR3: Resource Description and Access,* although revised decision later distanced itself from the AACR part and renamed it as *RDA (Resource Description and Access). RDA*, which is based on *FRBR* concept propounded by IFLA is based on the same 'literary unit' concept introduced by the then cataloguers of 16th and 17th century.

RDA (Resource Description and Access) is a content standard, a set of guidelines for describing a resource. RDA is based on FRBR model- a conceptual entity relationship model designed by *IFLA Study Group on Functional Requirements for Bibliographic Records (FRBR),* for the bibliographic universe, intended to be independent of any cataloguing code. FRBR deals with entity relationship concept that identifies the relationship among entities of a bibliographic record, i.e., relationship between the works, their creators and their subjects to assemble and organize literary units. The book in hand here is considered not as a single item but as a representative of literary unit. Although IFLA has designed it very recently for the versatile bibliographic universe of 21st century, the root of FRBR can be traced far back in the cataloguing of the 16th century.

JSC's decision to introduce a completely new code is not accepted unquestionably by the cataloguing experts. Many of them raised voices questioning the justification of the decision. They are in favour of a thorough revision of AACR2 instead of a brand new code. Some even says that AACR2 provides an infinitely expandable framework to accommodate new media which will be able to deal with the problems such new media may pose. In a variant opinion it is said that some of the issues that are strongly projected these days as reasons behind the introduction of the new code were highlighted by different critics of AACR2 years ago, but they were mostly overlooked during the previous revisions of the code. But what is most interesting is that these issues are dealt in a peculiar manner in RDA. Most of them have reappeared in the new code (RDA) also but in different names, or in different forms keeping the concept almost the same. Therefore, it would not be absurd to explore how much dynamic the new initiative of JSC is.

AACR2 has been dominating the bibliographic world for more than three long decades and surviving for such a long period despite having under tremendous pressure of unprecedented technological advancement. But with the fast changing nature of documents, changing information seeking behaviour of the users and the increasing pressure of electronic documents in the libraries and information centers, AACR2 has begun to show its age. A thorough revision of the code became very urgent. According to Joint Steering Committee for Revision of AACR (JSC) *The International Conference on the Principles and Future Development of AACR* that was held in Toronto in 1997 identified substantive problems with AACR2. Although the updates issued in the years following that conference that addressed some of these problems, it became clear that a fundamental rethinking of the code was required to respond fully to the challenges and opportunities of the digital world.

Initially, it was decided to publish a revised AACR2, i.e., AACR3. JSC began working on the new set of rules according to the strategic plan developed in 2002. In December 2004, the first draft of *AACR3* was released. Based on the comments from the constituency review the JSC decided that a completely new approach was needed and work began in that direction. In April 2005 meeting, the working title was changed to *RDA: Resource Description and Access.*

Finally, the new code RDA was published in June 2010 and after a lot of controversy and hesitation, the implementation process started in April 2013 starting from Library of Congress. In-between, revision process of the code is also going on. The latest of it released in 2015. RDA is basically a web based cataloguing tool, unlike the previous AACR2, but a printed version of the same is also published and updates are circulated at regular intervals.

1.2. DESCRIPTIVE CATALOGUING

Descriptive cataloging refers to the kind of cataloging process that is concerned with the identification and description of books and non-book reading materials to assist the users to find out the most suited document to fulfill their demand of information. It may not be irrelevant to mention here that in today's information world almost all the libraries emphasizing for maximum descriptions in the catalogues. Descriptive cataloging can be defined as that phase of the process of cataloging which concerns itself with the identification and description of books (Thompson, 1943: 45). Descriptive cataloguing, as contrasted with other forms of cataloguing, such as subject cataloguing, analytical cataloguing etc, refers to the process of describing a book or other document in a catalogue entry (Tait & Anderson, 1971: 9). In a descriptive catalogue the cataloguer is principally concerned providing within the array of entries in the catalogue, a statement sufficient in description to identify a copy of a book or document, to distinguish one edition of it from another, and to show its bibliographical relation to other books and documents (Hunter, 1974: 91).

It (descriptive cataloging) involves several levels of work. The first level is concerned with the choice of a main entry and of added entries and references by which to provide points of access for the library user. The second involves the construction of headings fixing the place of the names or titles in the catalog. The third step involves the identification and description of the physical item often by transcribing specified elements from the item itself to aid the user in selecting or rejecting one item from the others in the file (Henderson, 1976: 227).

A precise concept of descriptive cataloguing can be indicated by stating what a bibliographic description is and meant for. A detailed description of a book, with an accurate transcription of the title-page and full collation of the contents, is likely to reveal unsuspected variations in other 'copies' when they are compared with it; some copies may prove to be a different edition, a reprint from the same type with or without alterations, or they may contain insertions or cancellations (Foxon, 1955: 5). When we speak of descriptive cataloguing, we refer to the description of the book or document which comprises the main part of the catalogue entry, i.e., all the entry except the heading (Tait & Anderson, 1971: 13). Although this view has changed with the recent developments of the descriptive cataloguing codes that put major emphasis on different kinds of headings along with descriptive part of the catalogue.

1.3. THE OBJECTIVES AND PURPOSES OF DESCRIPTIVE CATALOGUING

In 1697 the curators of the Bodleian requested from the staff of that library any suggestions they might have for its own improvement. In answer to this request, one member of the staff, Humphrey Wanley, included with his suggestions an account of the questions which he thought needed to be solved before a new catalogue could be attempted. Some of these questions were:

i. whether the catalogue should be classified or alphabetical

ii. whether titles and dates of books should be recorded in the language of the book

iii. whether the size of a book should be recorded

iv. whether author and title analytics should be included

v. whether the name of the publisher should be included in the imprint

vi. whether there should be mention of the fact that a book lacks place or date

vii. whether the first or best edition of a book should be so indicated

viii. whether a book's rarity or costliness should be noted

Wanley made no mention of any problem concerning entry, although this whole area was still in a very undeveloped state (Strout, 1956: 265). Wanley through his brilliant questions about the problems he faced during practical cataloguing had given birth of the very concept 'Descriptive Cataloguing'. Although 'Author Title Catalogue' reigned in the cataloguing world for another century, the areas of descriptions to be considered for inclusion in a descriptive cataloguing entry was probably fixed by Humphrey Wanley in 1697.

What Piggot said is significant here. According to her to identify a work, author and title are usually sufficient. To identify a book it is usually necessary to add the number of the edition and/ or the place and date of publication. To enable comparison to be made with other appearances of the same work, it is necessary to add (where relevant) variations in the title, the name of the editor, translator etc., the name of the publisher, the pagination, illustrative matter, size, the name of the series of which the book forms the part. The nature and extent of further information will depend partly on the publishing history of the book, partly on the purpose of the catalogue (Piggot, 1963: 47).

1.4. GENERAL FUNCTIONS OF DESCRIPTIVE CATALOGING

According to Library of Congress (1946: 25) general functions of cataloguing are:

i. To describe the significant features of the book which will serve
   a) to distinguish it from other books and other editions of this book, and
   b) characterize its content, scope and bibliographical relations;
ii. To present the data in an entry which will
   a. fit well with the entries of other books and other editions of this book in the catalogue, and
   b. respond best to the interest of the majority of readers.

The objective of description of a bibliographic entity (a book in a catalogue entry) is to enable the user of the catalogue to distinguish one work from another and also one edition from another edition of the same work available in the library's collection. The details given in the description should be determined on this basis. If the information on the title page, and elsewhere in a book is inadequate to achieve this object, brief annotation, stating the credentials of the author, the scope and the purpose of the work and its context among other related works is necessary (Viswanathan, 1990: 74).

According to Lubetzky, an effective catalogue must serve:

- First, to facilitate the location of particular book, or item which the library has, and
- Second, to reveal to the catalogue user what other editions, translations, or representations the library has of the work, and what it has of the author (Lubetzky, 1969: 4).

Tait & Anderson (1971: 13) describes that the purpose of Descriptive Cataloguing are two fold:

i. To identify a book, so that it is easily recognizable from its catalogue entry;

ii. To distinguish the work from other works having similar features, and even to distinguish different editions of the same work.

It is important for a cataloger always to keep in mind the users of a particular catalog and the functions of that catalog in providing the descriptive cataloging data. The cataloger has found it increasingly necessary to do this within the larger context of being able to cooperate with other libraries- either to use all or some of the data from those libraries, or to contribute data for the use of other libraries. In order to cooperate most effectively, codes have become important tools for the descriptive cataloger.

1.5. NECESSITY OF A CATALOGUING CODE

The origin of catalogue can be traced back to the origin of book itself. The ancient form of library catalogue indicates that it was compiled to serve as a simple inventory or lists of library resources. It is really very difficult to determine what purpose they served or which of them were actually catalogues and which were mere inventory lists or even just book labels. In due course of time, gradual changes take place in the form, style and techniques of catalogues. The physical features of book and other reading materials, the users' approach to these reading materials and the advances made in the field of classification have all had their impact on the library catalogue. But it has taken a longer period to come to its present shape. According to Shera and Egan, "The modifications however, have been unnecessarily slow, and sometimes inadequate, because of incomplete understanding of the nature and functions of the catalogue and its place in the system as a whole" (Shera and Egan, 1956:1).

Modern library cataloguing has been influenced little by the ancient cataloguing. Whatever developments there may have been in the compilation of catalogues in antiquity, no remains of them survived. There was no carry over into the middle ages, for during that period cataloguing as we conceive it today did not even exist; neither did the Renaissance turn up anything about cataloguing from classical periods except the barest and most conjectural evidence. Therefore, with the exception of the fact that the Greeks taught us to refer to books by their authors, it is not far wrong to maintain that the art, the technique, of cataloguing is a completely modern development (Strout, 1956: 274).

In the Medieval Age the catalogue was more a record for the keeper or custodian of the books than one for the users. In most of the medieval libraries in most cases there was only a rough inventory only to keep track of the holdings because books were treated as valuable property and had to be protected and enumerated among the treasures of a house. Some of the monastic libraries used to keep lists of the books to keep a track of the donations received or to check loss or theft. Still again, there was 'catalogues' written in metrical form, which suggests that the young monks were required to commit the lists to memory. Only in the larger monasteries do we find real catalogues, i.e. guides to the content and location of books available for use. Thus, the earlier medieval catalogues were primarily shelf lists. True author subject records were a later development (Thompson, 1957: 613).

A cataloguing code is a set of rules framed for the preparation of catalogue entries and rendering information about a document in the catalogue. Cataloguing codes are the set of rulers framed to be followed whenever preparing catalogue entries of a document and rendering the information about it. Codes are complied in an attempt to ensure that in turn a catalogue will be compiled to be as efficient as possible in whatever approaches and details its users require. The word 'consistency' always crops up when the why of code compilation is discussed (Horner, 1970: 30). Catalogue has been as old as book itself. But still about the latter half of the nineteen century, most catalogues were based on a set of rules framed by individual libraries in a casual way to suit their respective conditions. Such a set of rules was often drafted by the cataloguer of a library on the basis of tradition, evaluated through years and transmitted first orally and later in some written form (Ranganathan, 1955: 14). *91 Rules* prepared by Panizzi, the then librarian of British Museum in collaboration with Edward Edwards, J. W. Jones, John H. Parry and adopted by the British Museum in 1841 embodying the practice of the British Library.

Most of the twentieth century catalogue codes are either joint venture or committee codes. And the tradition is still going on in our time also. Modern cataloguing theory sees again to an extent respectively two schools of thought: a) the 'case' code, which enumerates all types of documents likely to be enumerated, which rules for how to enter and describe them, and b) the 'conditions' code, which first identifies underlying author and title characteristics in document, irrespective of the 'case' or category to which they belong; and second, outlines general rules on how to deal with them (Horner, 1970: 33). Whatever may be the type, the codes are complied to ensure that it will help the cataloguers as an efficient tool to prepared catalogues maintaining utmost uniformity and consistency in whatever approaches and details its users require.

1.6. CONCLUSION

In general it can be said that in descriptive cataloguing, code plays a pivotal role in shaping the modern library catalogue. A detailed study of the origin, growth and development of important cataloguing codes along with their significant characteristics like dynamism will follow this chapter to get a clear picture about the descriptive cataloguing codes starting right from Panizzi's 91 Rules through RDA.

REFERENCES

Foxon, David. (1955). *The Technique of Bibliography*. London. National Book League.

Henderson, K.L. (1976). Treated with a degree of uniformity and common sense: descriptive cataloging in the United States 1876-1975. Library Trends, *25*(1), 227-71.

Horner, John. (1970). *Cataloguing*. London: Association of Assistant Librarians.

Hunter, Eric J. (1974). *Cataloguing: a guide book*. London: Clive Bingley.

Library of Congress. (1946). *Studies of Descriptive Cataloging*. Library of Congress: Washington D.C.

Lubetzky, Seymour. (1969) *Descriptive Cataloging: problems and principles: report 3 of a series on the principles of cataloguing*. Los Angeles: California University.

Pettee, Julia. (1936). The Development of authorship entry and the formulation of authorship rules as found in the Anglo-American Code. *Library Quarterly, 6*(3), 270-90.

Piggot, Mary. (1963). *Uniformity in descriptive cataloguing*. Libri, 13(1), 45-54.

Ranganathan, S. R. (1955). *Heading and canons: comparative study of five catalogue codes*. Madras (India): S. Viswanathan.

Shera, J. H & Egan M. E. (1956) *The Classified Catalogue*. Chicago: American Library Association.

Strout, Ruth Frence (1956). Development of the Catalog and Cataloguing Codes. *Library Quarterly, 26*(4), 254-275.

Tait, James A. and Anderson, Douglas (1971). *Descriptive Cataloguing: a students' introduction to the Anglo-American cataloguing rules*. 2nd. revd. & enl. ed. London: Clive Bingley.

Thompson, Elizabeth H.(comp.). (1943). *A.L.A. Glossary* of *Library Terms*. Chicago, ALA, 1943, p. 45.

Thompson, James Westfall. (1957). *The Medieval Library*. New York: Hafner Club.

Viswanathan, C.G. (1990). *Cataloguing theory and practice*. 6th ed. New Delhi: Ess Ess Publications.

2

Origin, Growth and Development of Cataloguing Codes

2.0. INTRODUCTION

Anglo American Cataloguing Rules, Second Edition *(AACR2)* has been dominating the cataloguing world for last three decades. Despite being a code of English speaking countries, it is followed almost throughout the world. Even, it got translated in different languages and fulfilled the needs of the cataloguing communities almost satisfactorily decades after decades. It is truly a catalogue code that has influence internationally. The aim and objective of the study in this chapter is to find out how AACR2 developed and dominated the bibliographic world for three long decades. To study the background of AACR2, some of its predecessors are also discussed here.

Sir Anthony Panizzi was the pioneer of modern cataloguing, by whose diligence and consistent persuasion the year 1841 is marked as the beginning of a new phase in the evolution of cataloguing rules. Due to his tireless effort, the rudimentary methods of cataloguing slowly evolved and the need of rules to systematize the work generally came to be recognized.

Although it was Cutter, who very successfully introduced the objectives, functions and principles of cataloguing explicitly in his *Rules for a Dictionary Catalogue (RDC)*, Panizzi's code embodied many of the cataloguing principles upon which other subsequent codes were drawn up. *Rules for a Dictionary Catalogue* has become a classic in cataloguing. In fact, theory of cataloguing was born with the publication of this revolutionary work of Charles Ammie Cutter.

Before Cutter and Panizzi, the worth mentioning catalogues were that of Bodleian Library where Sir Thomas Bodley took the initiative to systematize the catalogue of Oxford University Library. But his thoughts and ideas about cataloguing can be known from his letters to the librarian only. Although they have enriched modern cataloguing, they fail to make a mark as theory of cataloguing.

Earlier catalogues were made by the librarians largely for their own use, just to perform single function that of an inventory or a collection of lists showing the holdings. As long as libraries were small and very few books were published, this method well served their purpose. But with the increase of collection this method becomes inadequate. It was first felt by Sir Thomas Bodley when he set out to buy books for the Oxford University Library.

As the holdings increased and the production of books rose, new functions were imposed and the old improvised methods became in-adequate. When Sir Thomas Bodley set out to buy books for the Oxford University Library, and sought to find from its catalog whether certain books were already there in the library's holdings, he found that the entries were often vague in their descriptions and sometimes the records could not be found at all.

The catalogues of that time was simply a list or lists of the holdings of the library made without any well defined rules or principles. It was well for inventory purposes, for example, to list a book bound with another book under the title of its companion; but when Bodley failed to find it under its own author's name he could escape buying another copy only by recollecting that it was already on hand. His letters to the librarian on the failings of the Oxford catalog of that time were probably among the earliest practical lessons in cataloging from the viewpoint of the user other than the librarian. They demonstrated also the need of well-considered methods for the preparation of a library catalog (Lubetzky 1953: 179). This was probably the first recorded urge felt for systematized library catalogue.

2.1. RULES FOR THE COMPILATION OF THE CATALOGUE (91 RULES) - PANIZZI

The British Museum rules formulated in 1841 has become a landmark in the history of modern cataloguing codes. They were formulated by a group of men authorized by the trustees of the British Museum with Anthoney Panizzi as the leader. Panizzi with the advice of the distinguished librarians of the United Kingdom drew up a body of rules known as the famous *'91 rules'*. It was Anthony Panizzi, who despite a stiff resistance from some of his colleagues and users of British Museum Library was able to fight the 'battle of the rules' and finally succeeded to publish his *Rules for the Compilation of the Catalogue* popularly known as *91 rules*. Beginning with the humble assignment to prepare a list of duplicates in the British Museum Library, he ended up unconventionally with a new code of ninety one cataloging rules which aroused a storm of criticism within and without the British Museum but which were later recognized as the 'Magna Charta of cataloging' (Garnett, Richard, 1899: 35).

Sir Anthony Panizzi (1797-1879), keeper of Printed Books at the British Museum in 1837, later Principal Librarian (1856), was the central figure in the 'battle of rules' controversy which raged around the deficiency and slowness of production of the British Museum Catalogues. With his associates (including J. Winter Jones and Edward Edwards) he formulated the first version of the famous 91 rules which were accepted in 1839 and published in 1841. Panizzi's code embodied many of the cataloguing principles upon which other subsequent codes were drawn up and it was widely acclaimed throughout the library world. (Hunter, 1974: 55) Although, the project of the printed catalog fell through after the issue of the first volume, it helped the cataloguing experts a lot to form the basis of present day catalogue.

Panizzi's concept of 'heading' was the most important bibliographical element in alphabetical catalogues. The other bibliographic data were brought under it in the catalogue. Panizzi emphasised the concept of uniformity in cataloguing. He was in favour of preparing entries based on the information found on the title-page so that other cataloguers also could use the same information for cataloguing. Ranganathan in his *Headings and Canons* (1955) described this concept as the 'Canon of Ascertainability'.

Panizzi was in favour of using 'form headings' as the main entry for certain types of publications. 'Form headings' which was almost similar to today's 'subject headings', was a means to bring together works of a common nature. Acts, memoirs, transactions, and minutes published by institutes, universities and learned societies were entered under the form heading 'academies'; whereas newspapers, magazines, and annuals were brought together under the heading 'periodical publications'.

So many concepts were there in *91 Rules* which became important in later cataloguing practice, like the use of slips of uniform size for catalogue entries (Rule I), the use of the vernacular in the authors' form of name (Rule X), the concept of corporate author (Rule IX) was first formulated in Panizzi's code. Some other important rules in it were rules for the preparation of main entry (Rule VIII) under author's name as given in the title page, with full description, provision for added entry etc.

It was Sir Anthony Panizzi who was successful to formulate the rules prescribing how the books of a library should be systematically catalogued. Despite vehement objections from some of the library staff and many of the users of the British Museum, who believed that catalogue was for the librarian not for the reader, Panizzi's cataloguing rules were widely applauded and welcomed by the library professionals in various countries.

2.2. ON THE CONSTRUCTION OF CATALOGUES OF LIBRARIES, AND OF A GENERAL CATALOGUE- JEWETT

Prof. Charles C. Jewett, Librarian of the Smithsonian Institute prepared a code of 39 rules in 1852. These rules were modeled after Panizzi's rules and issued under the title *On the Construction of Catalogues of Libraries, and of a General Catalogue; and their Publication by Means of Separate, Stereotyped Titles, with Rules and Examples.* These rules were again limited to the author entries, but included a model subject index. (Viswanathan, 1990: 21) Jewett, when Librarian of Brown University USA, published an author catalogue to which was appended an alphabetical 'topical index' in 1843. Later in 1852, he published a report *On the Construction of Catalogues of Libraries*, in which he set forth the first American rules for author entry and suggested an alphabetical list of subjects as supplementary to the general catalogue. Pette names Jewett, not Cutter, as the 'father of modern library methods'. (Hunter, 1974: 55)

At the beginning of his code (Jewett, 1852: 14) Jewett acknowledged his debt to Panizzi, and he departed in only a few instances from the precepts of the 91 Rules. These are instances in which can be seen the basis for some of the entry principles which have come to be entrenched in American usage. Jewett extended the principle of the corporate author further than Panizzi had and entered all corporate bodies directly under their names without the use of any intervening form headings. Academies, institutes, associations, universities, colleges, literary, scientific, economical, religious societies, national and municipal governments, boards, corporations, and other bodies of men were treated as the author of all works issued by them (Rule XXI). Jewett suggested that anonymous works should be entered under the first word of the title (Rule XXVIII), not under catchwords contained in the title as Panizzi did. Jewett did not use form headings for anonymous works like Panizzi also.

Jewett spelled out in detail his theory of what purpose a code should serve: "The rules for cataloging must be stringent, and should meet, as far as possible, all difficulties of detail. Nothing, as far as can be avoided, should be left to the individual taste or judgment of the cataloguer." In view of this theory, it is interesting to observe that Jewett's rule-book is a slim little pamphlet containing thirty-three regulations (Strout, 1956: 21). This view of Jewett is definitely in contrast to modern cataloguing concept which favours 'cataloguer's judgment' in several areas while practical cataloguing.

2.3. RULES FOR A DICTIONARY CATALOGUE- CUTTER

With the growth of libraries, production of more and more books continued. Obviously, new types of publications and novel problems of cataloging were encountered and fresh regulations had to be designed accordingly. Every successive edition of Cutter's Rules was more extensive than the preceding one. Cutter's *Rules for a Dictionary Catalogue* (RDC) presents the first conscious effort to set forth the rules in a systematic way. No such systematic code of cataloguing rules was produced before RDC. Cutter published his *Rules for a Dictionary Catalogue* in 1876 as a part of the *Special Report of the United States Bureau of Education on the history, condition, and management of public libraries in the United States of America*. In the first edition, there were 205 rules which were tested by applying them to the collection in the library of the Boston Athenaeum. The second edition in 1889, the third in 1891 and the fourth in 1904 were issued (Cutter died in September, 1903). In the fourth edition the number of rules increased to 369.

It was Cutter who first introduced the objectives of cataloguing so explicitly at the beginning of a cataloguing code. This certainly was very much helpful to the cataloguers to take independent decisions regarding the choice of details in a catalogue which is called 'cataloguer's judgment' today. Lots and lots of discussions have taken place during the last few years about freedom of the cataloguers or 'cataloguer's judgment' whenever revising AACR2 and formulating the rules in RDA. But if we go through RDC we can see that this provision was kept in RDC by this exceptionally talented cataloguing expert as early as 1876, almost at the dawn of modern cataloguing. Cutter's eight fold objectives of cataloguing under three main heads have become a classic and a land mark in the theory and practice of modern cataloguing. There have been lots of discussions on these objectives of cataloguing set by Cutter, but no other library scientist except S. R. Ranganathan could add any new dimension to them. Cutter's objectives of cataloguing are:

1. To enable a person to find a book of which either
   - (a) the author
   - (b) the title } is known
   - (c) the subject
2. To show what the library has
   - (a) by a given author
   - (b) on a given subject
   - (c) in a given kind of literature
3. To assist in the choice of a book
   - (a) as to its edition (bibliographically)
   - (b) as to its character (literary or topical)

Cutter not only mentioned the objectives of cataloguing in his code, but he had also shown the means to meet those objectives or achieve those goals while practical cataloguing. His proposed means are:

1. Author-entry with necessary references (for A and D)
2. Title-entry or title-reference (for B)
3. Subject-entry, cross-references and classed subject table (for C and E)
4. Form-entry and language entry (for F)
5. Giving edition and imprint, with notes when necessary (for G)
6. Notes (for H)

Cutter's is probably the most comprehensive code, apart from Vatican. Its overall arrangement is logical. It includes rules for the form and entry of personal authors, corporate authors, and titles; main entries, added entries, and references; description; subject and form; limited cataloguing and filling; definitions; and certain special materials; manuscripts, music, maps, and atlas, and even an acknowledgement of paintings, drawings, and status as bibliographic units. The rules are accompanied by a great deal of lively discussion, much of it still very relevant today (Horner, 1970: 64). In 1876, twenty-four years after Jewett's codification, Cutter issued the first edition of his Rules for a Printed Dictionary Catalogue. This he modestly calls a first attempt to set forth rules in a systematic way and to investigate what might be called the first principles of cataloguing (Pettee, 1936: 283).

Cutter extended the authorship principle to corporate bodies: "make the author entry under the name of the author, whether personal or corporate, or some substitute for it." He expanded this principle under the division 'corporate' in his rule: "bodies of men are to be considered authors of works published in their name or authority." He could see the difficulties that lie in the name of corporate bodies. Place name and corporate name demands equal importance. He weighs their importance and suggested formidable solutions and alternate plans.

The concept of literary unit, (idea that the literary unit

rather than the individual book should determine the entry word) started gaining importance among the cataloguers and the code makers gradually. Thomas Hyde accepted it for translations. It spread gradually in the British Museum rules which made special provisions for BIBLE and the IMITATIO CHRISTI. But Cutter used it to the whole group of anonymous classics. For a classic of unknown authorship he suggests the Latin form by which it was originally known; or, for a medieval legend, the name of the hero by which it is known, giving as examples, SEPTEM SAPIENTES and SIR GAWAIN. These entries are neither catch-title nor subject-word entries but entry under a fixed conventional name as substitute for author (Pette, 1936: 284).

Rules for a Dictionary Catalog was a comprehensive code that had provision for author, title, subject, form entry, description, and filing of entries. Cutter uses 'main entry', the full or 'principal entry'; that is usually the author entry for the fullest bibliographic record that consists of the author's name, title and the imprint and 'added entry' or the 'secondary entry' in abbreviated detail.

While comparing with some of the existing codes of his time Ranganathan vehemently appreciated the *Rules for a Dictionary Catalogue* in his book *Headings and Canons*: None of the above drafts (Panizzi's 91 Rules, Munich Code and Karl Dziatzko's code) set forth cataloguing rules in a systematic or exhaustive way. Nor was there much evidence of their roots streaming from some kind of first principles. Nor again was any of them a general code not particularly conditional by the practice of a single library. RDC was the first code to reach beyond these limitations. Its limitation was only in the linguistic context. The library profession has been fortunate in the author of this code. He was a genius. This is seen in the ring of certitude and the profoundness of penetration found in the rules and commentaries of RDC. They are the central epigrams of a sage. RDC is indeed a classic. It is immortal. Its influence has been over powering. It inhibits free re-thinking even today. It appears to have been the chief source of later codes in the English language (Ranganathan, 1955: 14).

2.4. JOINT CODE- ALA & BLA

The preface to the North American Text of AACR starts with, "In a very real sense the present work represents the result of thirty five years of activity in the codification of cataloguing rules for American and British libraries." In fact, as Escreet (1971: 17) rightly said, the history of Anglo-American Cataloguing co-operation in the preparation of cataloguing rules goes back to the *Cataloguing Rules: Author and Title Entries*, popularly known as *Joint Code*, compiled and published by the Committees of the American Library Association and the Library Association in 1908.

The necessity of such a co-operation was probably first felt during the last two decades of the previous century when the American Library Association and the [British] Library Association, established in 1876 and 1877 respectively and issued independently a set of cataloguing rules *Anglo-American Code* in 1878 and 1883. The American version was almost a condensation of Cutter's rules, while the British rules incorporated the features of British Museum rules and Bodleian rules. With a view of establishing greater co-operation and uniformity, the two associations combined together for the purpose of issuing a joint code in 1908 (Viswanathan, 1990: 24).

The two associations, ALA and LA came together with a common aim of issuing a joint code in 1908 to establish greater co-operation and uniformity. There were so many unsolved issues before the Joint Code initiative was taken. For instance, C. W Andrew's paper at a meeting of the Illinois Library Association in February 1901 dealt with issues raised by the emerging co-operative cataloguing system. He welcomed the economy, fullness, uniformity and legibility of printed cards. In a back to the future moment, Mr. Andrews opined "... the effect of this plan will not be to deprive cataloguers of their work, but to substitute the intellectual for the mechanical..." (Gorman, 2000: 3). The advisory committee on cataloguing formed by ALA publishing Board, met in Atlanta city in March 1901. Cutter and other luminaries attended the meeting. Issues dealt with in this meeting were cooperative cataloguing, topography of printed cards, content notes after the title, full names more important in heading, corporate entries etc. Here it was accepted as the statement "catalogue should be made for the user, not for the cataloguer." The committees of ALA and BLA finally published *Catalog Rules: author and title entries* in 1908.

The joint code was dominated by cases not conditions and principles and it was published without any explicit declaration of the objectives, reasons or principles which in long run led to demand for more and more specific rules to cope up with the increasing versatility of documents published. As Lubetzky reviews that the Catalog Rules of 1908, which superseded Cutter's fourth and last edition of the Rules, appeared without a declaration of objectives, and without explanation of reasons, except for a few prefatory remarks implying that the rules were designed to provide for the entry of books in the way readers were expected to look for them. It elucidated very little, and the rules were bound to drift. In the absence of general guiding principles there was a mounting need and demand for more and more rules and detailed specifications, to provide for variant cases not covered specifically by the compilation. The cumulative result was embodied in the preliminary American second edition of the A.L.A Catalog Rules, published in 1941 (Lubetzky, 1953: 181).

Gorman tries to give explanation why the 1908 code was dominated by cases not conditions and principles. In his views this arose because of the bilateral nature of its origins and construction. Nineteenth century codes were almost all product of single individuals (Panizzi, Cutter, Jewett, etc.). Despite the fact that Cutter was active on the American committee until his death, his was but one voice among many, often eminent others. Lacking a guiding hand

and a single set of unified principles, this, the first of the committee codes that have lumbered through the 20th century, was an assemblage of the best practices of Anglophone libraries. It was inevitable that such a code would be based on cases and ever more minute distinctions between cases. The later reached its reduction and absurdum in the full page devoted to the rule on exploring expeditions, with its two sub rules, the second of which has 6 sub-sub-rules. The 1908 code set in train a period of code making that was to lead, inevitably, to calls for reform from Andrew Osborn and others (Gorman, 2000: 4).

By the 1920's AA (Anglo American or Joint Code) was under criticism and the need for revision was repeatedly expressed. Some called for simplification, saying the rules were too fussy, others wanted more detail. Both were right: enumerative code always appear too fussy, yet are not capable of meeting all cases, as we have seen. Revision of principles was really needed- but this had to wait till Lubetzky in 1953. Those called for greater detail won. In 1930's Committees of the American Library Association (ALA) and Library Association (LA) began revision. The LA dropped out at the outbreak of war. The ALA continued alone, producing a draft code in 1941. The final version appeared in 1949 (Needham, 1971: 43).

2.5. CATALOGUING RULES FOR AUTHOR AND TITLE ENTRIES - ALA

The Anglo-American agreement, the first ever international co-operation in the field of cataloguing, reached in 1908, was abandoned when American Library Association decided to publish its own revision of the *Joint Code*. Although it is said that the outbreak of the Second World War halted further British participation, and it was until 1956 that the Catalogue Code Revision Committee was able to co-operate again with their American colleagues. (Tait & Anderson, 1971: 10). The deficiencies, inaccuracies, and complexities of this joint code have been the subject of discussion among librarians in conferences and in day to day work in libraries. The need to replace it by a more satisfactory code was unanimously felt. ALA appointed a subcommittee in 1930 to work on the revision of the cataloguing rules. It outlined the major problems as dissatisfaction on the grounds of omission; the basic rules were not in question. Nevertheless, expansion was required to meet the need of large scholarly libraries or specialized collection. "The preliminary edition, published in 1941, expanded the rules of 1908 to make more provision for special class of material: serial publications, government documents, publications of religious bodies, anonymous classics, music and maps, to amplify existing rules to cover scientific cases of frequent occurrence" (ALA, 1949: viii).

In 1949 the revised code *A.L.A. Cataloguing Rules for Author and Title Entries,* 2nd edition edited by Clara Beetle came out. That move certainly was not calculated to promote international agreement and co-operation which this country nevertheless desires and in which it should play a leading part. So revision in Great Britain take the form of rethinking the 1908 code, although the 1949 American changes are being taken into account (Osborn, 1956: 31).

The second edition of *ALA Cataloguing Rules for author and Title Entries* was an expansion and revision of the rules of 1908. We can get a clear picture of the revision from the J. H. Shera's review of the code. "Mr. Shera, like a cataloger, counted pages. The 40-some pages on entry in 1908 had blossomed into over 200 in 1949, an increase in bulk of some 500 percent, while the 15 or more pages on descriptive cataloging in 1908 were now over 100. Even with the inclusion of new material, such as microfilms and facsimiles, and even with simplification and liberalization in the L.C. rules, Mr. Shera was sure that these were too many pages. "To the cry for greater simplification," he proclaimed, "the answer of the profession has been to expand the code from a total of 88 pages in 1908 to a total of 406 pages in 1949." (Dunkin, 1956: 288) Thus the code faced serious criticism for over-elaboration. It can more truthfully be criticised for doing the wrong thing; supplementing and amending the 1908 code rather than defining principles (Needham, 1971: 44).

The *A.L.A. Cataloguing Rules for Author and Title Entries,* 2nd edition edited by Clara Beetle did not contain rules for description. The Library of Congress had been revising its own rules for the descriptive cataloguing, and in 1949 also published its *Rules for descriptive cataloguing; revised* edition. These were adopted by the American Library Association as their rules for description, so that the American cataloguer had, after 1949 two codes to consult-one for description, and one for determining the entry heading, and the form it should take. The *Library of Congress Rules for Descriptive Cataloguing* was generally accepted by the profession, but the same was not true of the ALA second edition (Tait & Anderson, 1971: 10).

While the ALA Rules 1949 tended to reflect a traditionalist enumerative complexity, the LC Rules moved towards the increasing demands of the cataloguers for more simplicity and brevity. Backwell has maintained that the two codes 'made strange bedfellows' and he considers the ALA Rules to be pedantic and more 'likely to result in a bio-bibliographical tool rather than an efficient location tool'. Horner points out that the LC Rules provide the 'raw material' for subsequent developments (Hunter, 1974: 73).

The ALA code faced serious criticism from all corners and Seymor Lubetzky, the consultant of Bibliographic and Cataloguing Policy of The Library of Congress, was assigned the task of reviewing and analyzing the rules of ALA Code. Lubetzky's seminal work *Cataloguing Rules and principles, a critique of the ALA Rules for Entry and a proposed Design for Revision,* was the result of his thorough investigation and logical analysis of each and every rule in the light of principle implied in it. He gazed in every parts of the code and asked "Is this rule necessary?" He justifies them if they are consistent with the principles and properly related with the other rules also.

2.6. CATALOGUING RULES AND PRINCIPLES: A CRITIQUE OF THE ALA RULES FOR ENTRY, AND A PROPOSED DESIGN FOR THEIR REVISION (1953) - SEYMOUR LUBETZKY

The dissatisfaction with the 1949 code resulted in Seymour Lubetzky, then Bibliographic Consultant to the Library of Congress, being asked by the Board of cataloguing Policy and Research of the American Library Association to make a detailed analysis of the second edition of 1949, and specially the rules for corporate authorship. His findings were published in the famous pamphlet entitled *Cataloguing Rules and Principles: a Critique of the ALA Rules for Entry, and a Proposed Design for their Revision, 1953.* The main theme of Lubetzky's work was that it was a mistake to attempt to provide specific guidance for every particular problem likely to face the cataloguer. Instead, we should look at the conditions that lie behind the problems. In this way, the multiplicity of rules can be reduced and the basic structure of the code made more apparent (Tait & Anderson, 1971: 11).

The international co-operation which ceased to work since the publication of *Joint Code* in 1908 once again renewed in 1951. In the words of P.K. Escreet, "Effective co-operation was resumed in 1951, when the Sub-committee was reconvened in response to overtures from A.L.A., which was seeking renewed collaboration with the Library Association with the object of arriving at a new Anglo-American code" (Escreet, 1971: 18). The Library Association reconvened its Cataloguing Sub-committee under the Chairmanship of Mr. J. D. Stewart in 1951, the American Library Association having expressed the desire, warmly reciprocated by the Library Association; the two Associations should together undertake a revision of the 1949 code. The British Sub-committee initially embarked on a critical examination of the 1949 code, and later studied in detail the successive draft rules formulated by Mr. Seymour Lubetzky, who in 1956 was appointed Editor of the proposed new code by the American Library Association (AACR British text, 1967: V).

In 1960 Lubetzky produced his *Code of Cataloguing Rules: Author and Title Entry; an Unfinished Draft* which provided a radical new shape to the rules and in which the author wished to demonstrate a departure from 'formalism' to 'functionalism' (Hunter, 1974: 74). According to Horner, "*CCR 1960, 'an unfinished draft'*, was for the most part an expansion of *'Design for a code'*. Its chief omissions were special rules for non-print materials, and of course rules for description" (Horner, 1970: 78).

Few seem to have been impressed at the time by Lubetzky's library-world-shaking pamphlet *Cataloging Rules and Principles* came out in 1953. (People are more interested in it now, and one cannot help wondering why the Library of Congress persists in not printing it.) (Horner, 1970: 77). Cutter did not felt the necessity to distinguish between 'book' and 'work' whenever formulating his eternal 'objectives of catalogue'; But Lubetzky contrasted the two ideas distinctively. In fact, Lubetzky brought back into play Panizzi's original emphasis on the relationship between a title and all of the different editions of that title that might exist.

Lubetzky's idea was that relationships among all the editions and variations of a given work and the author of that work, in all variations of the author's name, must be established and brought together, so that they can be found in one place. His was the idea that all the works of an author, in all their editions should be linked together and the objective of a catalogue should be not only to say yes or no to the users, but also to tell that the library holds so many editions and translations of the user's choice.

While examining the 1949 ALA rules, Lubetzky observed in his *Cataloguing Rules and Principles: a Critique of the ALA Rules for Entry and a Proposed Design for their Revision* that a complete reconstruction of our cataloguing will require, not a revision of any particular rules, but a complete reconstruction of our code in accordance with deliberately adopted objectives which should define the aim of our rules, and well considered principles which would outline the pattern and character of the code (Escreet, 1971: 18).

Lubetzky's name is most often uttered with the names of Panizzi and Cutter as one of the most significant influences in the field of cataloguing. Lubetzky's rationalized approach to catalog code design is even more relevant today as current cataloging principles are revisited and revised for a digital environment. Lubetzky's unfinished book, *Code of cataloging rules: author and title entry: an unfinished draft for a new edition cataloguing rules* (1960) was the basis for modern cataloging adopted by the first *International Conference on Cataloging Principles* (1961), called the *'Paris Principles'*. Lubetzky's thoughts of cataloguing were based on the fundamental concepts introduced by Panizzi in his *91 rules*. The ideas of giving preference to the user's choice in case of preparing entries that was the prime emphasis of Panizzi and Cutter got momentum in the safe hands of Lubetzky. He built upon and expanded the ideas of Panizzi and Cutter to create a version of a catalog that was truly user-friendly.

2.7. INTERNATIONAL CONFERENCE ON CATALOGUING PRINCIPLES (1961)- IFLA

International Conference on Cataloguing Principles (1961) held in Paris under the auspices of IFLA and attended by delegates from almost every country in the world was an attempt to reach agreement on the basic principles which should underlie any national cataloguing codes to be produced subsequently. The conference was considered a major triumph in reaching substantial agreement on almost all points (Tait & Anderson, 1971: 12). It was worth recalling again, that the principles worked out by Seymour Lubetzky virtually formed the basis for the discussion and evolution of the principles which emerged from the conference (Horner, 1970: 78).

The International Conference on cataloguing Principles (ICCP) was convened by the International Federation of Library Associations (IFLA) with the avowed intention of creating a set of principles upon which all countries or language groups would base their rules for entry and heading. The conference recognised the impracticability of a true international code of rules, and sought merely to establish a common basis from which international standardisation could proceed while preserving necessary local, national or linguistic individual practices (Gorman, 1977: 589). The main purpose of this conference was to make an attempt to meet the very urgent need for the acceptability and interchangeability of entries in catalogues and bibliographies made in different countries. There is also a related objective and that is to ensure speed and certainty in searches for information in catalogues produced in different countries. There is no need to emphasize the enormous value, both practical and psychological, which will accrue to all libraries from agreement on a set of principles achieved in an international meeting of this caliber. Such agreement would be invaluable not only as a guide for the revision of existing catalogue codes, but especially as a guide in the development of library and bibliographical activity in countries where such services are being newly built up (Francis, 1963: 19). Jolley says that with the growing size of the catalogues of libraries and still more with the growth of enormous union catalogues, it becomes everyday more essential to reduce the multitudinous labyrinth of references, and to lead the reader as directly as possible to the information he requires (Jolley, 1963: 159). The broad objective of the Paris Conference was to facilitate the international communication of knowledge by achieving the widest possible uniformity in library catalogues and other means of bibliographical communication (Petersen, 1963: 13).

The first General Session of the Conference was held on 9th October, where several questions were discussed mostly from the draft statement and from the working papers. Some of the most significant ones which were mentioned in the ICCP Report (ICCP, 1963: 22) may be discussed in brief here. The first question that was discussed was from Working Paper No 17: how far new developments in electronic apparatus for information and library work would affect the future of cataloguing.

Dr. Ranganathan thought it important first to reach agreement on normative principles, such as the canons of ascertainability, of prepotence, of sought heading, the principle of local variation and the law of parsimony. He suggested that the word 'book' throughout the text of the Draft Statement should be replaced by the term 'document' which would include conventional documents, 'neo-documents' such as micro-cards, and 'meta-documents' those in which physical and social phenomena were recorded automatically without the intervention of the human brain. M. Poindron saw a danger in replacing 'book' by 'document'; they might well find that the rules they were defining would not be valid for some categories of documents.

Mr. Chaplin pointed to the distinction made in the draft statement between the terms 'book' and 'work', the one being used of the physical object and the other reserved for the literary or verbal content, which might well be embodied in many forms. Dr. Shukla considered that the Draft Statement was more concerned with the detailed rules of cataloguing than with its basic principles; these which should be understood as permeating the whole text of a cataloguing code, were economy, permanence, the creation of a catalogue for present day use, and the consideration of the needs of the users.

Lubetzky feels that the catalogue will be a more efficient instrument if it is based on the consistent development of a few well defined principles (Jolley, 1960: 5). Lubetzky expressed his views in the Paris Conference in favour of using uniform headings for both author and title. But on the contrary, Verona was in favour of using uniform heading only for author. As Ball rightly says "Lubetzky advocated the use of a uniform heading for both author and title in order to bring together all works of an author and all editions of a work under the main entry. Verona advocated the use of uniform heading for author but the entry of each title under the form appearing in the work, relating them by added entries and references" (Ball, 1969: 191).

To follow certain principles in practical cataloguing there must have some guiding principles in the form of a code. The statement of principles commonly known as the '*Paris Principles*' was approved by the *International Conference on Cataloguing principles in 1961.* Its goal of serving as a basis for international standardization in cataloguing has certainly been achieved: most of the cataloguing codes that were developed world wide since that time followed the principles strictly, at least to a high degree.

2.8. ANGLO AMERICAN CATALOGUING RULES (AACR, 1967)-JSC

The Anglo American Cataloguing Rules (AACR1) which is based on the cataloguing principles adopted by the *International Conference on Cataloguing Principles* in Paris (ICCP 1961) is considered as the first cataloguing code with international scope and achievement. It is the only committee code till then which includes rules for both the access points (Title and Author entries) as well as the rules for descriptive cataloguing. Moreover, AACR is the only cataloguing code that includes specific rules to catalogue non-books materials for the first time. Thus AACR emerged as the most significant and fruitful outcome of the Anglo-American cataloguing initiatives, the earliest and sole international collaborative efforts which started by LA and ALA as early as 1908 with the publication of *Cataloguing Rules: Author and Title Entries*, popularly known as *Joint Code*.

As both Britain and America played important roles at Paris, it was inevitable that the new code would adhere closely to the *Paris Principles*. In fact, the editor in his introduction specially states that the rules are based on the *Paris principles*. Thus the new code is international not only because it is the joint production of Britain and America, but also because it is largely consistent with an internationally agreed set of principles for author and title entry (Tait & Anderson, 1971: 12). In 1967 the new code *Anglo-American Cataloguing Rules* was published in two texts British Text and the North American text. The American text contains some deviations from *Paris Principles* which were carefully listed. But the British Revision Committee did not agree with the Americans and therefore, the British text did not contain all those deviations.

AACR contains fifteen chapters arranged in three divisions. Part I 'Entry and Heading' contains five chapters: entry; headings for persons; headings for corporate bodies; uniform titles; references. Part II covers 'Description' in four chapters: monographs; serials; incunabula; photolithographic and other reproductions. Part III covers 'Entry and descriptions of non-book materials' in six chapters: manuscripts; maps; motion pictures; music; phonorecords; picture.

Anglo-American Cataloguing Rules (AACR) was a land mark in the history of cataloguing. It has the following merits according to C. D. Needham:

Although the code is designed primarily to meet the needs of research libraries other kinds of libraries have not been forgotten and in some cases alternative rules are provided.

Apart from rules for choice and style of author and the title headings, the code includes sections on descriptive cataloguing. And in addition to monographs, certain categories of special materials (maps films, music etc.) are given separate treatment, the rules for several of these types of materials, and for descriptive cataloguing, being based on Library of Congress practice.

Multiple entry through the use of unit cataloguing is accepted, but the need to distinguish between main and added entries and references is recognised throughout.

The most significant feature is the attention paid to matters of principle. The influence of Lubetzky and the *Paris Principles* has been profound. It can be seen in the general structure of the code and in the systematic arrangement of the rules (Needham, 1971: 45).

The 1941 and 1949 rules were sharply criticized for being too elaborate and often arbitrary. Emphasis had shifted from clearly defined principles to a collection of rules developed to fit specific cases, rather than conditions which the cases illustrated. Lubetzky commented that any logical approach to cataloguing problems was blocked by the maze of arbitrary and repetitious rules and exceptions of rules. The catalogue code revision committee who prepared 1967 *Anglo American Cataloguing Rules* realized that revision must be a complete reexamination of the principles and objectives of cataloguing, not merely a revision of specific rules. First, the objectives of the catalogue were agreed upon; further, it was decided that certain general principles should be the basis for rules of entry and heading. These general principles of the new code are based on the statement of principles approved by 53 countries at the *International Conference on Cataloguing Principles* in Paris, October 1961. This important step towards international bibliographic standardization, among other things, encourages continuation, and expansion of the shared cataloguing project between the United States and other countries (Wynar, 1967: 27).

The sad fact is that the code that resulted from this reactionary tide- the first AACR was not only a major fudge betraying Lubetzky's ideas in many instances but also could not even reconcile British and American Practice (the prophet Lubetzky was honoured far more in the UK than on his native heath). Also, and crucially, AACR failed to deal adequately with what we used to call 'non books'. The first AACR did have much strength and was a great improvement over its predecessors, but ultimately it represented a failure of nerve that has consequences to this very day (Gorman, 2000: 6).

The circumstances under which the 1967 AACR was a problem-solving innovation, no longer hold. A revised code will not only improve access to all forms of library materials, but also it will utilize in a positive way machine developments as an aid to the control of library collections (Edgar, 1975: 602). Many issues like the form subheadings of 'Laws, Status, etc" and 'Liturgy and Ritual', exclusion of motion pictures and filmstrips from general rules,, entry of maps under a geographic heading, headings of Government documents, introduction ISBD, etc., needed to be addressed in due course of time. Moreover, there were some faults which needed immediate attention like two texts British and North American, there were several amendments after its publication, the code still conceived as author-title code, and finally there were some areas of cataloguing like 'corporate authorship' which were not satisfactorily dealt with in AACR1.

The fast changes in the publication world, changes in the library services, availability of new automation techniques and the introduction of ISBD (1971) prepared the ground for another revision of the first cataloguing code which was built on the internationally accepted principles. The expectations from this revision were that the revised code would be more tightly organised, with considerably fewer special rules while at the same time covering many new media which were not provided in the first edition, especially audiovisual, special instructional and machine readable data files media.

2.9. INTERNATIONAL STANDARD BIBLIOGRAPHIC DESCRIPTION (ISBD)- IFLA

The increasing international cooperation in the field of information exchange aroused the necessity of a generally accepted common standard for the description of the bibliographic elements, so that the exchange of bibliographic data can be easier. As Hunter wrote for the international exchange of bibliographic information, whether written or machine readable form, it is obviously necessary to have a generally accepted standard which lists: i) the elements to be included in the descriptive part of an entry; ii) the order in which the elements are to be cited; and iii) the punctuation which is to be used to separate the elements. An International Working Party was set up by *International Meeting of Cataloguing Experts* in Copenhagen in 1969 to study the possibilities for an *International Standard Bibliographic Description (ISBD)* for monographs. Such a standard was subsequently drawn up and was officially adopted by the IFLA Committee on Cataloguing at its meeting in Liverpool in 1971 (Hunter, 1974: 95).

The main purpose of the ISBD was to provide a standard form of bibliographic description that could be used to exchange records internationally. This was aimed to support IFLA's program of universal bibliographic control. Many national and International cataloguing codes and national Bibliographies began following ISBD format. AACR1 revised its chapter- 6; Library of Congress implemented it in 1974. And our interest in including ISBD here in our study lies in the fact that ISBD had a major impact of the structure of AACR2, in fact, AACR2 was framed based on the ISBD structure and the punctuation.

After the publication of *General International Standard Bibliographic Description* ISBD (G), IFLA developed specialised ISBDs for specific types of materials. These were revised several times to respond to the requirements of automated systems with the latest in 2007. In 2007 a consolidated edition of the ISBD was published which was again revised in 2011, superseding earlier separate ISBDs for monographs, older monographic publications, cartographic materials, serials and other continuing resources, electronic resources, non-book materials, and printed music.

Although ISBD was designed to be followed by all the bibliographic and cataloguing agencies, specially, while displaying bibliographic records many of them are not following ISBD during the last few years. Even the new cataloguing code RDA is also free from any specific bibliographic format.

2.10. ANGLO-AMERICAN CATALOGUING RULES SECOND EDITION (AACR2, 1978)- ALA & LA

The experiences and observations of the performance of the 1967 edition in meeting the needs of a large number and kind of libraries across the world during a period of a decade had encouraged and influenced the preparation of AACR2. Considerable growth in libraries and extensions of cataloguing process, bibliographic services, and national library services throughout the world has been significant and called for a revised edition of AACR1, overcoming certain lapse, in order that AACR could meet the challenges posed by new developments in cataloguing, bibliography and information services. (Viswanathan, 1990: 31)

The sharp criticism of AACR(1) led the Anglo American countries to come to an agreement to revise AACR and produce a single unanimous cataloguing code. One representative representing both the library association and national library of the three Anglo-American countries – USA, Canada, and Britain reached an agreement in a tripartite meeting held in March 1974 where the objectives and policies of the new code were stated in the memorandum of agreement as follows:

i. to reconcile in a single text the North American and British text of 1967;

ii. to incorporate in the single text all amendments and changes already agreed and implemented under the previous mechanism;

iii. to consider for inclusion in AACR all proposals for amendments currently under discussion between the American Library Association, the Library Association, the Library of Congress, the Canadian Library Association; any new proposals put forward by these bodies and the British Library; and any proposals of national committees of other countries in which AACR is in use.

iv. to provide for international interest in AACR by facilitating its use in countries other than the United States, Canada, and the United Kingdom. This final objective was later intensified, as a condition of funding by the council on Library Resources, to one of making a contribution to the development of an international cataloguing code. (AACR2, 1978: vii)

2.10.1. Guidelines Followed by the JSC for the Revision of AACR1

i. Maintenance of general conformity with the Paris Principles of 1961, as manifested in the first edition

ii. Particular attention to developments in the machine processing of bibliographic records

iii. Continuance of conformity with the ISBD (M) as a basis for the bibliographic description of monographs, and commitment to the principle of standardization in the bibliographic description of all types of materials.

iv. Determination of the treatment of non-book materials primarily from a consideration of the published cataloguing rules of the Canadian Library Association, The library Association, and the Association for Educational Communications and Technology; and of the ALA revision of chapter 12 of the 1967 text (AACR2, 1978: vii).

The Joint Steering Committee (JSC) for Revision of AACR in a special meeting in Washington in April 1977 planned the concluding stages of drafting for the new code. In the final meeting in August in Washington, 1977 JSC considered all proposals and comments of reviewers, approved the whole text and authorize its presentation for publication. Finally, in 1978 the *Anglo-American Cataloguing Rules 2nd edition (AACR2)* appeared as a new and improved cataloguing code, the first of its kind, that was successful to involve maximum number of international cataloguing community in its developmental process.

2.10.2. Features of AACR2

Unlike the first AACR(1), in this edition (AACR2) the first part deals with descriptions of catalogue and the second part is access points / headings for them.

The descriptions of AACR2 are based on the *General International Bibliographic Description (ISBD (G))*. It follows the framework exactly in the order of elements and their prescribed punctuation.

Rules of AACR2 are designed for use in the construction of catalogues and other lists in general libraries of all sizes. They are not specifically intended for specialist and archival libraries.

AACR2 incorporates numerous agreements on the development of rules in the first edition and is based on a reconciliation of the British and North American texts of that edition.

In Part II of AACR2 rules are based on the proposition that one main entry is made for each item described, and that this is supplemented by added entries. The question of use of alternative heading entries was discussed but has not been embodied in the rules, largely because of the lack of time to explore the considerable implications of such a change.

Rule 1.0D of AACR2 contains a specification of three

levels of description. Each of these levels is considered as a minimum in that, when appropriate, further information is added to the required set of data. This standardization at three levels of description is to achieve uniformity of cataloguing.

AACR2 is an internationally recognised standard for descriptive cataloguing that contains rules for describing all types of library materials. In the nearly thirty years since its publication it has been revised and updated several times. It is this constant updating in response to changes in the realities of the cataloguing world that have kept AACR2 a relevant standard for so many years. AACR2 may serve as an example of a cataloguing standard that was developed and expanded to accommodate new formats. (Intner, 2006: 75)

AACR2 was welcomed by the cataloguing communities initially with great applause, where very few issues of that time remained unattended. But with the progress of more and more implementation of AACR2 in different types of libraries, short comings of the code began to be detected gradually by the cataloguers. Soon the deficiencies, inconsistencies, and complexities of this code had been the subject of discussion among librarians in conferences and day-to-day work in libraries. The Joint Steering Committee for Revision of AACR (JSC) took initiatives for regular revisions of AACR2 also.

Areas of the code where the rules have been revised or reorganized relate to the treatment of computer files, cartographic materials, uniform titles for music, and materials for visually impaired. More specific rule changes cover the selection of source for series titles, choice of main entry for revised text, provision for subordinate entry for those subordinate corporate names that do not convey the idea of a corporate body; deletion of articles from uniform titles and headings for corporate bodies (Viswanathan, 1990: 35).

The Joint Steering Committee for Revision of AACR issued three sets of revisions in the year 1982, 1983 and 1985 to intimate the changes. The 1985 edition of the code included all the revisions since 1978. In 1986 revision effort was made to rationalize the rules based on the principles of AACR2 and to fulfill the deficiencies traced during the period. The final revised version of AACR2 was published in 1988 as AACR2R.

2.11. FUNCTIONAL REQUIREMENTS FOR BIBLIOGRAPHIC RECORDS (FRBR)- IFLA

FRBR (Functional Requirements for Bibliographic Records) is an entity relationship concept for the description of bibliographic data. FRBR is a conceptual entity relationship model designed by *IFLA Study Group on Functional Requirements for Bibliographic Records* (FRBR), for the bibliographic universe, intended to be independent of any cataloguing code. FRBR deals with entity relationship concept that identifies the relationship among entities of a bibliographic record, i.e., relationship between the works, their creators and their subjects to assemble and organize literary units. The book in hand here is considered not as a single item but as a representative of a literary unit. The much talked about latest cataloguing code *RDA* (*Resource Description and Access*) is designed on this FRBR concept.

2.12. THE INTERNATIONAL CATALOGUING PRINCIPLES, ICP (2009)- IFLA

The *Statement of International Cataloguing Principles* (ICP) was published in February 2009. Exactly forty years after the publication of the statement of principles adopted by the *International Conference on Cataloguing Principles* held in Paris in 1961, in 2001 the IFLA Cataloguing Section, proposed the convening of an international conference to discuss the principles of cataloguing in the light of the significant changes which had taken place in the cataloguing environment. According to IFLA, "over forty years later, having a common set of international cataloguing principles has become even more desirable as cataloguers and their clients use OPACs (Online Public Access Catalogues) around the world. Now, at the beginning of the 21st century, an effort has been made by IFLA to produce a new statement of principles that are applicable to online library catalogues and beyond. The first principle is to serve the convenience of catalogue users".

A series of meetings took place between 2003 and 2007 to formulate a set of principles to facilitate the international exchange of bibliographic data and to promote standards for bibliographic records. The Statement of International Cataloguing Principles got its final shape in December 2008. It was published online in February 2009 and presented at the 75th IFLA Congress in Milan.

This statement replaces and broadens the scope of the Paris Principles from just textual works to all types of materials and from just the choice and form of entry to all aspects of bibliographic and authority data used in library catalogues. It includes not only principles and objectives (i.e., functions of the catalogue), but also guiding rules that should be included in cataloguing codes internationally, as well as guidance on search and retrieval capabilities (IFLA, 2009: 1).

This statement was built on the great cataloguing traditions of the world, and also on the FRBR data model aiming that this statement will increase the international sharing of bibliographic and authority data and guide cataloguing rule makers in their efforts to develop an international cataloguing code.

2.12.1. General Principles

International Cataloguing Principles were designed giving highest preference to the convenience of the user.

2.12.1.1. Convenience of the User : Decisions taken in the making of descriptions and controlled forms of names for access should be made with the user in mind.

2.12.1.2. Common Usage : Vocabulary used in descriptions and access should be in accord with that of the majority of users.

2.12.1.3. Representation : Descriptions and controlled forms of names should be based on the way an entity describes itself.

2.12.1.4. Accuracy : The entity described should be faithfully portrayed.

2.12.1.5. Sufficiency and Necessity : Only those data elements in descriptions and controlled forms of names for access that are required to fulfil user tasks and are essential to uniquely identify an entity should be included.

2.12.1.6. Significance : Data elements should be bibliographically significant.

2.12.1.7. Economy : When alternative ways exist to achieve a goal, preference should be given to the way that best furthers overall economy (i.e., the least cost or the simplest approach).

2.12.1.8. Consistency and Standardization : Descriptions and construction of access points should be standardized as far as possible. This enables greater consistency, which in turn increases the ability to share bibliographic and authority data.

2.12.1.9. Integration : The descriptions for all types of materials and controlled forms of names of all types of entities should be based on a common set of rules, insofar as it is relevant.

The rules in a cataloguing code should be *defensible* and *not arbitrary*. It is recognized that these principles may contradict each other in specific situations and a defensible, practical solution should be taken.

2.12.2. Differences with Paris Principles

There is a line of continuity between the Paris Principles and the 2009 Statement of International Cataloguing Principles – this is testified by some passages which have remained substantially identical. However, there are also significant differences between the two texts. The ICP are designed for electronic and online catalogues. They aim to apply to any type of bibliographic resource, to any kind of library (not just research libraries, as was the case for the Paris Principles) and even to other information communities. The Paris Principles and their theoretical bases (Charles A. Cutter, Seymour Lubetzky, Eva Verona) remain an important reference for the ICP, but they are complemented by new references: the IFLA's conceptual models Functional Requirements for Bibliographic Records (FRBR) and Functional Requirements for Authority Data (FRAD), the work of Elaine Svenonius and the ISBD. The ICP extend the Paris Principles, which only concerned the choice and form of the heading, to every aspect of descriptive cataloging. They include directions for authority records and express their intention to apply to subject indexing. The ICP extend the finding (to find a book of which either the author, title or subject is known) and collocation (to find all books by a particular author, on a particular subject or kind of literature) functions of the Paris Principles with the functions of FRBR (Find, Identify, Select and Obtain a bibliographic resource), in a perspective that emphasizes the centrality of the user. The ICP combine guiding rules for cataloguing codes, already present in the Paris Principles, with some directions for OPAC search capabilities. Finally, the ICP update the terminology: they drop the term 'heading' in favour of 'access point'. Wherever possible, they prefer the term 'bibliographic data' to 'bibliographic records', in line with the trend of current catalogs, that focus on individual data rather than on bibliographic records. (Genetasio, 2008: 4)

In conclusion, it may be said that there are some aspects of the ICP 2009 which are not entirely satisfactory. But the IFLA announced its intention to continue revision of the 2009 Statement and further development. The IME ICC 2008 resolution stated its intention to continue to revise the ICP. IFLA Cataloguing Section Strategic Plan 2009/2011 confirmed the need to revise the ICP on a five-year basis. Strategic plan 2011/2013 also confirmed this, which states its intention to form a working group to assess the expediency of clearly separating the specific cataloguing rules from the principles and of expanding "the statement further towards becoming" a complete cataloguing code.

2.13. AACR3: RESOURCE DESCRIPTION AND ACCESS- JSC

After the publication of AACR2R (1988) JSC continued to revise the code regularly to fulfill the growing needs. It brought out two more revised versions of AACR2 one in 1998 with major changes in 'cartographic materials' and another in 2002 for 'Serials'. Lots of updates also took place in 2001 (for 'Computer files/ Electronic Resources'), 2004 and in 2005. But despite its frequent revisions, AACR2 seemed unable to satisfy the needs of the cataloguing community. The Joint Steering Committee for Revision of AACR in 1997 drew together an international group of invited experts to discuss the issue. Obviously, demand for a new code emerged to cope up with the situation. *International Conference on the Principles and Future Development of AACR* held in Toronto in 1997 advocated strongly in favour of a new cataloguing code.

Depending on the outcome of that conference, JSC decided to continue revision of AACR2 till 2005. The Joint Steering Committee (JSC) for Revision of AACR2, continued revising and updating AACR2 till 2005. But there was a growing recognition that a new code was needed. JSC began working on the new set of rules according to the strategic plan developed in 2002. In 2004 an editor (Tom Delsey) was engaged for the designing of a new code *AACR3: Resource Description and Access.*

In December 2004, the first draft of 'AACR3' was released. Based on the comments from the constituency review the JSC decided that a completely new approach, different from that of AACR2 was needed and work began in that direction. In April 2005 meeting, the AACR portion of the title was dropped, and the working title was changed to *RDA: Resource Description and Access*. Finally the new code *RDA* was published in June 2010 and after a lot of controversy and hesitation, the implementation process started in April 2013 from the Library of Congress. Till now some renowned libraries of USA and UK have implemented it with very little progress in the other countries.

2.14. CONCLUSION

AACR2 which had a legacy of Anglo American cataloguing tradition starting from Panizzi, has gone through lots of ups and downs in its more than three decades journey which apparently ended with the publication of RDA. Although the AACR part is dropped from the name of the new code, it has clearly mentioned in its introduction that RDA is developed on the foundation of the cataloguing traditions of the world and of AACR. Therefore, while discussing the origin, growth and development of AACR2 all these codes as well as the important international events on bibliographic descriptions like ICCP, Paris 1961 and IME ICC, 2001 (that developed ICP, 2009) also were discussed here in great details. Without them the study would remain incomplete and getting a clear picture of the same was quite impossible because these are all interlinked with one another.

REFERENCES

American Library Association. (1949). *Cataloguing Rules for Author and Title Entries*. 2nd ed. edited by Clara Beetle. Chicago: ALA.

Anglo-American Cataloging Rules. (1967). Prepared by the American Library Association the Library of Congress, the Library Association, and the Canadian Library Association. British Text.

General editor C. Sumner Spalding. London: The Library Association.

Anglo-American Cataloguing Rules. (1978). Prepared by the American Library Association, the British Library, the Canadian Committee on Cataloguing, the Library Association and the Library of Congress; edited by Michael Gorman and Paul W. Winkler. 2nd. ed. Chicago: American Library Association.

Ball, Katharine L. (1969). The Paris Conference. In Rowland, Arthur Ray (ed.). *The catalogue and Cataloguing* (pp. 190- 195). London: Crosby Lockwood & Sons.

Edgar, N.L (1975). What Every Librarian should Know about Proposed Changes in Cataloguing Rules: a Brief Over view. *American Libraries, 6* (10), 602-607.

Escreet, P.K.(1971). *Introduction to Anglo-American Cataloguing Rules*. London: Andre Deutsch.

Francis, Frank. (1963). Addresses. In A. H. Chaplin (ed.) *International Conference on Cataloguing Principles: report, Paris, 9th – 18th October, 1961* (pp.13-15). London: Organizing Committee of the ICCP.

Garnett, Richard. (1899). *Essays in Librarianship and Bibliography*. New York: F. P. Harper.

Genetasio, Giuliano. (2012).*The Statement of* International Cataloguing Principles *and* their Future. Retrieved September 7, 2012 from http://leo.cilea.it/index.php/jlis/issue/view/326.

Gorman, Michael. (1977).Changes in Cataloguing Codes: Rules for Entry and Heading. *Library Trends, 25* (3), 587-601.

Gorman, Michael. (2000). *From Card Catalogues to Webpacs: Celebrating Cataloguing in the 20th Century*. Retrieved August 9, 2011 from http://lcweb.loc.gov/catdir/bibcontrol/gorman_paper.html.

Horner, John. (1970). *Cataloguing*. London: Association of Assistant Librarians.

Hunter, Eric J. (1974). *Cataloguing: a guide book*. London: Clive Bingley.

ICCP. (1963). *Report: International Conference on Cataloguing Principles Paris, 9th – 18th October, 19961*. London: Organizing Committee of the ICCP.

IFLA (1997). *Functional Requirements for Bibliographic Records: final report*. Retrieved September 7, 2011 from www.ifla.org.

IFLA. (2009). *The Statement of International Cataloguing Principles.* Retrieved September 7, 2012 from www.ifla.org.

Intner, Sheila S., Lazinger, Susan S. and Weihs, Jean. (2006). *Metadata and its Impact on Libraries.* Westport: Libraries Unlimited.

Jewett, Charles C. (1852). *Smithsonian Report on the Construction of Catalogues of Libraries, and of a General Catalogue; and their Publication by Means of Separate, Stereotyped Titles, with Rules and Examples.* Washington: Smithsonian Institution.

Jolley. L. (1960). *The Principles of Cataloguing.* London: Crosby Lockwood & Sons.

Jolley, L. J. (1963). Function of the Main Entry in the Alphabetical Catalogue: a Study of the Views put Forward by Lubetzky and Verona. In A. H. Chaplin (ed.) *International Conference on Cataloguing Principles: report, Paris, 9th – 18th October, 1961* (pp.159-163). London: Organizing Committee of the ICCP.

Lubetzky, S. (1953). Development of cataloging rules. Retrieved August 9, 2011 from https://www.ideals.illinois.edu/bitstream/handle/2142/5511/librarytrendsv2i2c_opt.pdf?

Needham, C. D. (1971). *Organizing Knowledge in Libraries: an introduction to information retrieval.* London: Andre Deutsch

Osborn, Andrew D. (1956). Cataloguing and Cataloguing Codes in other countries today. In *Toward a Better Cataloguing Code: Papers presented before the Twenty-first Annual Conference of Graduate Library School of the University of Chicago June 13-15, 1956.*(pp.26-35). Chicago: The University of Chicago Graduate Library School.

Petersen, E. N. (1963). Addresses. In A. H. Chaplin (ed.) *International Conference on Cataloguing Principles: report, Paris, 9th – 18th October, 1961* (pp.13-15). London: Organizing Committee of the ICCP.

Pettee, Julia. (1936). The Development of authorship entry and the formulation of authorship rules as found in the Anglo-American Code. *Library Quarterly, 6*(3), 270-90.

Ranganathan, S. R. (1955). *Heading and canons: comparative study of five catalogue codes.* Madras (India): S. Viswanathan.

Strout, Ruth Frence (1956). Development of the Catalog and Cataloguing Codes. *Library Quarterly, 26*(4), 254-275.

Tait, James A. and Anderson, Douglas (1971). *Descriptive Cataloguing: a students' introduction to the Anglo-American cataloguing rules.* 2nd. revd. & enl. ed. London: Clive Bingley.

Tillett, Barbara. (2004). *What is FRBR? A conceptual model for the bibliographic universe.* Retrieved on December 2, 2007, from http://www.ifla.org/VII/s13/frbr/frbr.pdf

Viswanathan, C.G. (1990). *Cataloguing theory and practice.* 6th ed. New Delhi: Ess Ess Publications.

Wynar, Bohdan S. (1967). *Introduction to Cataloguing and Classification.* Colorado: Libraries Unlimited.

3

Dynamism in Descriptive Cataloguing

3.0. INTRODUCTION

The world of knowledge is ever expanding, so are the publications. The expansion is taking place not only in quantum but in varieties also. With the introduction of multiple new disciplines and several new subjects in science and technology, the types and nature of documents have not been confined among the traditional physical documents of previous centuries. Several new manifestations of works have added new dimensions in the publication industry as well as to the information storage and retrieval process of the same. Library have now become Library and Information/ Resource Centre. Obviously, changes came in the storage, retrieval and day-to-day operations of the libraries. Accordingly, the tools of a library have been changing as and when need arises. Cataloguing code is the most important tool in the process and retrieval of documents in a library which is ever changing with every bit of changes in the nature of the documents, in the changes of information storage and retrieval process, and most significantly with the changes in the information seeking behavoiur of the users of today's libraries. Therefore, a descriptive cataloguing code cannot be static; it must be dynamic enough to get revised with the changing needs.

The aim of this chapter is to assess the role and importance of dynamism in descriptive cataloguing. A thorough search is made to see how far dynamism is followed throughout the cataloguing codes of Anglo-American origin, especially in AACR2. How far dynamic is AACR2 as a descriptive cataloguing code has been discussed with special attention. The shortcomings of AACR2 and its consequences are discussed in brief. For better understanding of the same, some basics like what actually the descriptive cataloguing is and the objective and purpose of descriptive cataloguing has also been discussed in details here. The emergence of RDA form the revision of AACR2 has also been discussed.

3.1. ROLE OF DYNAMISM IN DESCRIPTIVE CATALOGUING

Dynamism is the life-blood of descriptive cataloguing. It keeps descriptive cataloguing alive. With the fast and easy access of the common people to the Information Communication Technology (ICT), the job of the library cataloguers has become too much challenging. The world of information is changing very fast. The nature of the documents, the medium, and the information seeking behavoiur of the users has been changing rapidly. To cope up with the situation, cataloguing rules must be changed accordingly. This can easily be substantiated with the development that took place during the last ten years of revisions of AACR2. Almost every year updates containing changes in the rules and examples of AACR2 were released to adapt with the fast changing information world and fulfill the needs of the cataloguing communities to deal with the changing environment. During this period three major chapters- Cartographic Materials, Serials/ Continuing Resources, Computer files/ Electronic Resources were thoroughly revised along with major changes in the General Rules for the description chapter.

This is not a new phenomenon, it has been happening

slower or faster since the inception of Descriptive Cataloguing Codes. It was seen in case of *Rules for Dictionary Catalogue (RDC)* also. RDC is the most comprehensive code that includes rules for the personal authors, corporate authors, titles, main entry, added entry, references, description, subject and form, limited cataloguing, special materials, manuscripts, music, maps and atlases, and even for filing also. In the first edition of RDC, there were 205 rules which were tested by applying them to the collection in the library of the Boston Athenaeum. The second edition in 1889, the third in 1891 and the fourth in 1904 were issued. In the fourth edition the number of rules increased to 369. Thus, it is obvious that dynamism prevailed through the first systematic code of cataloguing in the modern period.

In the preface to the 4th edition of RDC Cutter himself recognised the increase in the number of rules. According to him, the increase in the number of rules is due chiefly not to making new rules, but to taking out from the long notes many recommendations that were in effect rules, and are more especially referred to and found in their present place. The changes are largely for the sake of greater clearness and of better classification. (Cutter, 1904: 6)

Descriptive cataloguing deals with recording of bibliographic descriptions of documents holding in libraries. As the bibliographical features of documents are ever changing descriptive cataloguing also needs to be change frequently.

3.1.1. Issues Related to the Revision of Joint Code (1908)

The Anglo-American or Joint Code (1908) is a result of the combined effort of Committees of Great Britain and America with a view to establish unity of practice throughout the English-speaking race.

AA (1908) Code deals with choice and form of personal and corporate author and title, main entry headings, added entries, references, and description, including some Library of Congress supplementary rules. It incorporates a list of definitions, although there are some noteworthy omissions, e.g., societies and institutions as categories of corporate authorship; also it has a list of abbreviations stating where they may be used, and several transliteration alphabets (Horner, 1970: 67).

The Anglo-American or Joint Code (1908) had the following limitations which led its revisions in due course of time:

1. Despite the arrangement, analysis into conditions and cases is by no means complete; there is frequent enumeration of types of document and types of organization. Therefore, there are:
   (a) Inconsistencies- e. g. Thematic catalogues under composer but concordance under compiler.
   (b) Too many rules- thus many of the first twenty-two rules are simply examples of dependent works.
   (c) Many omissions- enumeration if attempted must be as complete as possible, yet there are no rules in the section on government publication for reports by committees, royal commissions, etc., or for government institutions such as the Science museum. Again there is no rule for change of name in corporate authors.
2. Inadequate definitions- Examples over lapping and confusion where the examples add to the difficulties
3. The examples are one of the weakest elements of the code. Many are in German or in Latin.
4. Tendency to ignore author's identity as found in document. Thus Initials are never to be used as headings and pseudonyms must not be used if the real name can be found, even though the author may never have written under his real name.
5. Whether the catalogue is to be basically direct, or collocative is not finally settled. There is no introductory statement of principles. Many rules favour collocation, but there are inconsistencies-

especially in the American rules.

6. Non-author headings sometimes suggested.
7. Corporate authors:
   (a) Primary divisions
   (b) Division into societies and institutions is not relevant to the cataloguing problems underlying this division. (Needham, 1971: 42)

Thus the deficiencies, inconsistencies, and complexities finally led American Library Association to issue the preliminary second edition in two parts, a) Entry and Heading and b) Description. In 1949 American Library Association published the final second edition *ALA Cataloguing Rules for Author and Title Entries.* It was found that a huge number of increases in the number of rules had taken place. The 40 some pages on entry in 1908 increased into 200 in 1949, while 15 pages of descriptive cataloguing in 1908 were increased over 100 pages. Thus the total 88 pages in 1908 had increased to 406 in 1949. (Shera, 1950: 150)

3.1.2. Issues Related to the Revision of Anglo American Cataloguing Rules (AACR, 1967)

The Anglo American Cataloguing Rules which was based on the Paris Principles adopted by the *International Conference on Cataloguing Principles* in 1961 is considered international in its scope and achievement. It's a successful example of international cooperation.

Since AACR has been long awaited as the first 'conditions' code, it is disappointing to find that there are special rules for many 'case'. In the 'condition' versus 'case' argument, the code is about two thirds conditions and one-third cases. Even so, many rules seem to be superfluous as they fit into the overall conditions structure of the code. (Horner, 1970: 82). There were several other issues:

1. Despite a worldwide consensus and large measure of

agreement, still there were two texts- the British text and the North American text.

2. Several amendments took place during the post publication years, still there were the difference in the thinking of the two texts
   a. The major point of difference occur as a result of the inclusion in the American text of Chapter-3 'Corporate Bodies' of two rules for 'Exceptions for Entry and Place' whereby 'Local Churches' and 'Certain Other Corporate Bodies' were entered under place rather than directly under name.
   b. Among the differences in descriptive rules- British text rule 136 'Statement of Editor, Compiler, Translator, Illustrator, etc.' Differences in specifications for insertion of reprint date (American text rule 141, British text rule 142)
3. The code was still conceived as an author and title code for cataloguing of books, with emphasis on the choice of main entry. The cataloguing of non book material being treated as modification of that for books.
4. There were still areas of traditional author and title cataloguing which were unsatisfactory, mainly the corporate authorship.
5. Gorman had pointed out two general weakness
   a. A lack of adequate definition of the nature of authorship and responsibility, both personal and corporate.
   b. An occasional failure of nerve: an unwillingness to accept the consequences of its decisions on principles.

There is no denying that both texts are rooted in existing practices, rather than in assumptions about the requirements and possibilities of computerized catalogues of the future. (Escreet, 1971: 23)

With the emergence of new media of communication the libraries face more difficulties to cope up with them with the existing rules of cataloguing. Therefore, more clarifications sought every now and then. Here is a good instance of this kind. Jolley (1967: 349) says that the whole intellectual structure of our cataloguing process will be radically changed, as computer stored catalogues become firmly established, but this change had not taken place by 1967, and it is perhaps as well that the makers of the code concentrated on an attempt not always successful to devise the best rules for today's catalogue, rather than dissipating their forces in an attempt to foresee the needs and capabilities of the future. The sharp criticism of the code finally led to produce the unanimous second edition of AACR, i.e., AACR2 in 1978.

3.1.3. Issues Related to the Revision of Anglo American Cataloguing Rules (AACR2, 1978)

Since the inception of AACR2, cataloguers became vocal against some issues which needed immediate attention. Some of those most discussed issues were 'main entry', 'content verses carrier', 'rule of three', 'unpublished items' 'problems with serials', and 'electronic resources' etc. These issues appeared as major difficulties to catalogue properly with AACR2.

Despite so many revisions of the rules of AACR2, it is found that very few fundamental changes had taken place during the revisions. Most of the revisions were cosmetic in nature, which could not fulfill the expectations of the cataloguing communities.

3.2. LACK OF DYNAMISM IN AACR2 AND ITS CONSEQUENCES

AACR2 has been updated almost every year, with a number of thorough revisions; but in most cases the revisions remains confined within the cosmetic changes. The language, syntax, arrangements of rules, sequences or preferences of rules and examples, all have been modified frequently. Segregation or merger of more than one rule also has taken place in a lot of cases. But the burning issues containing the basic concepts mentioned below have hardly been addressed in time.

3.2.1. Issues of Controversy in AACR2

Some of the most controversial issues like 'main entry', 'content verses carrier', 'rule of three', 'unpublished items' etc. are much discussed almost since the introduction of AACR2 in 1978. In due course of time, problems like dealing with serials and electronic documents appeared as major difficulties to catalogue properly following AACR2.

3.2.1.1. Main Entry

The first and foremost point among the unresolved issues of AACR2 is the issue of main entry. What is most unfortunate is that this issue has been haunting the JSC not only from AACR2 but since the birth of first edition of AACR (AACR1) in 1967. The following words of Michael Gorman, the first Editor of AACR2, substantiate it: "The first edition of AACR was based firmly on the concept of main entry. The prime task of the descriptive cataloguer was to determine the main entry heading based on the idea of authorship; all other decisions stemmed from this initial and basic choice. Since AACR1 was published, many people– particularly those with a thorough knowledge of the implications of computerization- have disagreed either with the entire concept of main entry or at least with the primary emphasis placed on it." (Gorman, 1977: 596) There is hardly any change in present age also as Read says, "The main entry is a useful concept if you are creating a card index, but largely irrelevant in computer catalogues." (Read, 2003:72)

Some other views can also be mentioned here as Bierbaum says, "I have an exceedingly modest proposal for MARC records, which I offer before the integrated machine-readable cataloguing format is cast forever in electronic bronze. In the immortal words of the Red Queen, 'off with its head!' In computer-speak: 'Delete main entry.' (Bierbaum, 1994: 81)

The above concepts is contradicted by Fattahi, "Like its predecessors, AACR2 distinguishes between main entry and added entries. However, with the advent of computerized catalogues, the value of the main entry concept, which developed in the context of book and card catalogues, has been questioned, but no satisfactory and practical solution has emerged as to how its functions can be otherwise fulfilled. As stated, a major justification for the concept often lies in its collocating function, in bringing together both different editions of a work and the works of an author. As a collocating device, the concept of main entry has been retained not only in multiple entry-card catalogues but also with the same justification in automated catalogues." (Fattahi, 1998:25)

Gorman takes moderate stand and says that too much time is wasted arguing about the merits of one main entry over those of another; Cutter himself recognised that some choices are too difficult, and recommended double entry as a solution. Perhaps what is needed is not to abolish main entries, but to ensure that all entries are main entries. (Gorman, 1977: 596)

3.2.1.2. Content versus Carrier

Rule 0.24 of the AACR2 says, " It is a cardinal principle of the use of part I that the description of a physical item should be based in the first instance of the chapter dealing with the class of materials to which that item belongs... In short, the starting point for the description is the physical form of the item in hand, not the original or any previous form in which the work has been published " (AACR2, 1978: 8). Obviously, cataloguing done following AACR2 is based on the carrier rather than the intellectual or the artistic content of the work.

The division of the code (AACR2) into two parts is linked directly to the two stage sequence of the cataloguing process, the first part dealing with the description of the object being catalogued, the second dealing with the determination and establishment of headings under which the description will be presented in the catalogue. The rules in part-1 are centered primarily on the 'item'; those in part-2 focus on 'work'... Given the complexity of the relationships that exist between the physical nature of object being catalogued and the intellectual nature of the content, and interweaving of aspects of both elements across the two parts of the code, it is perhaps not surprising that there has been continuing debate around the "content versus carrier" issue. (Delsey, 1998: 3)

In other words, descriptions made in the catalogs following AACR2 completely depend on 'item' rather than 'work'. This is the point where the issue of content versus carrier has arisen. In today's fast changing information world, the nature of documents changing very fast. Besides the conventional form, electronic documents have occupied an important place everywhere. Along with various tangible electronic documents like Audio Video Cassettes, Micro films, CD/ DVD ROMs, a huge collection of resources are in the World Wide Web (www), accessible via Internet. Howarth rightly asks the question here, "Can we appropriately apply the provisions of the rule 0.24 to a 'carrier' where physicality is an intangible, and not readily definable?" (Howarth, 1998: 150)

3.2.1.3. Rule of Three

In case of multiple authors, AACR2 has limited them within three. If more than three authors are responsible for a work, title is given priority as entry heading and only the first author is mentioned in description area. This rule has been criticized times and again for doing injustice to the others authors.

Rule1.1F5. of AACR2 says, if a single statement of responsibility names more than three persons or corporate bodies performing the same function, or with the same degree of responsibility, omit all but the first of each group of each persons or bodies. Indicate the omission by the mark of omission (...) and add [et al.] (or its equivalent in a non roman script) in square brackets (AACR2, 1988: 25).

Regarding the 'rule of three' Jane M. Read says "...it is obvious why this rule was invented in the days of card catalogues, and it does cut down on the amount of work necessary to catalogue documents with multiple authors. However, for the user of the library, it is frustrating to be unable to find all an author's works from the catalogue" (Read, 2003: 74).

3.2.1.4. Problems with Seriality

AACR2 is called a complete code for it is the only cataloguing code that dealt for the first time with books, book like materials and non-book materials in the library with equal importance. The makers of AACR2 wanted to make consistent records for every type of library materials. But the problem arises when they wanted to treat serials in the same manner as the monographs. To be specific, the problem starts again with the cardinal principle, rule 0.24 of the AACR2, that says, "It is a cardinal principle of the use of part I that the description of a physical item should be based in the first instance of the chapter dealing with the class of materials to which that item belongs... In short, the starting point for the description is the physical form of the item in hand, not the original or any previous form in which the work has been published" (AACR2, 1988: 8). This rule has the following short comings:

i. emphasis on the description of a single issue
ii. Do not recognise the necessities of describing items not held by the library
iii. can't deal with the electronic media with no tangible forms

AACR2 is structured so that the cataloguer uses the general chapter 1 and one or more specific chapters when creating cataloguing records. For printed serials, chapters 1 and 12 are used; for non-print serials, the appropriate non-print chapter is also consulted. Thus, for computer files, rules in chapter 1, 12, and 9 are used. While the idea of universally applicable rules is a noble one, the current code does not achieve its full potential. This is because chapter 1 is too specially based on books and chapter 12 is too specifically written for printed serials. And although the definition acknowledges that a serial can be published in any medium, this principle is not carried through in the rules for non print media. Furthermore, chapter 12 doesn't go far enough in addressing the needs of traditional printed serials. The rules almost always presuppose that one has the first issue, and there is little guidance on how to handle changes that appear on later issue. For example, there is no mention in rule 12.7B6 (notes relating to statement of responsibility) of when and how to record changes in the issuing body. Nor is there clear instruction on what to do about the publication date when the first issue is not in hand. (Hirons & Graham, 1998: 185)

3.2.1.5. Absence of Principle and Objectives

Another serious lapse which caused much harm to the cataloguing during last few decades of AACR2 is the absence of explicate presence of principles and reasons. The cataloguers hardly have any other alternative, but to blindly follow the rules without knowing why they are doing that. The single mans' codes like Cutter and Ranganathan, bore clearly stated principles of cataloguing which not only helped in practical cataloguing, but also encouraged the cataloguer to apply his knowledge and intelligence in cataloging following those principles, so that the document can reach to the maximum number of readers in the least time.

Despite frequent revisions, AACR2 could not fulfill the expectations of the cataloguers. The general and specific rule structure and the provision of alternatives have made it more complex day by day. The principles, on which AACR2 was developed was not clearly stated in the code, even after so many revisions. Therefore, there were limited alternatives that would enable cataloguers to build their own judgment using their expertise.

What Andrew D. Osborn wrote in 1941in his world famous article *The Crisis in Cataloging* almost 70 years ago seems very much contemporary till today. In his words, "Actually there are a number of theories of cataloging more or less vaguely in application today. The principal ones might be characterized as the legalistic, the perfectionistic, the bibliographic, and the pragmatic. The dominant one is probably the legalistic. According to it, there must be rules and definitions to govern every point that arises".

Cataloging, according to Osborn is an art that needs only a few basic rules. But the legalist insists to have a rule for every point that comes up during cataloguing. He pointed out many short comings of this 'legalistic approach' where he tried to establish that inclination towards fixed rules is detrimental to cataloguing. With too much dependence on codified rules, approach to cataloguing has become "less and less a matter of comprehending principles and more and more a matter of mere learning of arbitrary rules and definitions." (Osborn, 1941: 395)

3.2.2. Consequences

By 1997 AACR2 was beginning to show its age and it was realized that a plan was needed for its future development. In particular, there was a need to examine the underlying principles of AACR2 and evaluate the need for fundamental changes to the rules to resolve some underlying issues. (Kiogaard, 2006: 2) The approach of AACR2 was dynamic. It may be said that the effort of JSC was also very dynamic but not in the true sense of dynamism. Despite many revisions, the fundamental approach of AACR2 remains unchanged from its original edition. In light of the many changes that libraries have encountered in their collections, access services and patron behavoiur, the library community is preparing to adopt a new set of rules in 2008. (Knowlton, 2006: 1)

3.3. CONCLUSION

AACR2 despite its frequent revisions seems unable to satisfy the needs of the cataloguers. The Joint Steering Committee for Revision of AACR in 1997 drew together an international group of invited experts to discuss the issue. Obviously, demand for a new code emerged to cope up with the situation. *International Conference on the Principles and Future Development of AACR* held in Toronto in 1997 advocated strongly in favour of a new cataloguing code.

Depending on the outcome of that conference, JSC decided to continue revision of AACR2 till 2005. The Joint Steering Committee (JSC) for Revision of AACR2, continued revising and updating AACR2. Major revisions took place in 1998 and 2002, with lots of updates in 2004 and 2005. But there was a growing recognition that a new code was needed. JSC began working on the new set of rules according to the strategic plan developed in 2002. In 2004 an editor (Tom Delsey) was engaged for the designing of a new code *AACR3: Resource Description and Access.*

In December 2004, the first draft of 'AACR3' was released. Based on the comments from the constituency review the JSC decided that a completely new approach was needed and work began in that direction. In April 2005 meeting, the working title was changed to *RDA: Resource Description and Access.* Finally the new code *RDA* was published in June 2010 and although slow, the implementation process is in progress in some of the renowned libraries of USA and UK.

REFERENCES

American Library Association. (1949). *Cataloguing Rules for Author and Title Entries.* 2nd ed. edited by Clara Beetle. Chicago: ALA.

Anglo-American Cataloging Rules. (1967). Prepared by the American

Library Association the Library of Congress, the Library Association, and the Canadian Library Association. British Text. General editor C. Sumner Spalding. London: The Library Association.

Anglo-American Cataloguing Rules. (1978). Prepared by the American Library Association, the British Library, the Canadian Committee on Cataloguing, the Library Association and the Library of Congress; edited by Michael Gorman and Paul W. Winkler. 2nd. ed. Chicago: American Library Association.

Anglo-American Cataloguing Rules. (1988). Prepared under the direction of the Joint Steering Committee for the Revision of AACR; edited by Michael Gorman and Paul W. Winkler. 2nd. ed. 1988 revision. Chicago: American Library Association.

Bierbaum, E.G. (1994). A modest proposal: no more main entry. *American Libraries, 25*(1), January. 81-84.

Cutter, C. A. (1904). *Rules for a dictionary catalogue*. 4th ed. Washington: Government Printing Office.

Delsey, Tom. (1998). Modeling the Logic of AACR. In Jean Weihs (ed.) *the principles and Future of AACR: proceedings of the International Conference on the Principles and Future Development of AACR, Toronto, Ontario, Canada, October 23-25, 1997* (pp.1-16). Ottawa: Canadian Library Association.

Escreet, P.K.(1971). *Introduction to Anglo-American Cataloguing Rules*. London: Andre Deutsch.

Fattahi, Rahmatollah (1998). AACR2 and Catalogue Production Technology: Relevance of Cataloguing Principles to the Online Environment. In Jean Weihs (ed.) *the principles and Future of AACR: proceedings of the International Conference on the Principles and Future Development of AACR, Toronto, Ontario, Canada, October 23-25, 1997* (pp.17-43). Ottawa: Canadian Library Association.

Gorman, Michael. (1977).Changes in Cataloguing Codes: Rules for Entry and Heading. *Library Trends, 25* (3), 587-601.

Henderson, K.L. (1976).Treated with a degree of uniformity and common sense: descriptive cataloging in the United States 1876-1975. Library Trends, *25*(1), 227-71.

Hirons, Jean and Graham Crystal. (1998). Issues related to Seriality. In Jean Weihs (ed.) *the principles and Future of AACR: proceedings of the International Conference on the Principles and Future Development of AACR, Toronto, Ontario, Canada, October*

23-25, 1997 (pp.180-212). Ottawa: Canadian Library Association.

Horner, John. (1970). *Cataloguing.* London: Association of Assistant Librarians.

Howarth, Lynne. (1998).Content versus Carrier. In Jean Weihs (ed.) *the principles and Future of AACR: proceedings of the International Conference on the Principles and Future Development of AACR, Toronto, Ontario, Canada, October 23-25, 1997* (pp.148-156). Ottawa: Canadian Library Association.

ICCP. (1963). *Report: International Conference on Cataloguing Principles Paris, 9th – 18th October, 19961.* London: Organizing Committee of the ICCP.

Jolley, L. (1967) [Review of] Anglo-American Cataloguing Rules, North American Text. *Journal of Documentation, 23* (4), 349.

Kiorgaard, Deirdre. (2006). *A Rose by any other Name? from AACR2 to Resource Description and Access.* Retrieved December 19, 20010 from www.valaconf.org.au/vala2006/papers2006/83_Kartus_Final.pdf

Knowlton, Steven A. (2006). A Preview of the New Cataloging Code. *MLA Forum, 5(1).* Retrieved October 01, 2012 from http://www.mlaforum.org/volumeV/issue1/article2.htm

Library of Congress. (1946). *Studies of Descriptive Cataloging.* Library of Congress: Washington D.C.

Needham, C. D. (1971). *Organizing Knowledge in Libraries: an introduction to information retrieval.* London: Andre Deutsch.

Piggot, Mary. (1963).*Uniformity in descriptive cataloguing.* Libri, 13(1), 45-54.

Read, Jane M. (2003). *Cataloguing Without Tears: Managing Knowledge in the Information Society.* Oxford: Chandos.

Shera, J.H. (1950). Review of 1949 code. *Library Quarterly, 20,*147-150.

Strout, Ruth Frence (1956). Development of the Catalog and Cataloguing Codes. *Library Quarterly, 26*(4), 254-275.

Tait, James A. and Anderson, Douglas (1971). *Descriptive Cataloguing: a students' introduction to the Anglo-American cataloguing rules.* 2nd. revd. & enl. ed. London: Clive Bingley.

Thompson, Elizabeth H.(comp.). (1943). *A.L.A. Glossary* of *Library Terms.* Chicago, ALA, 1943, p. 45.

Viswanathan, C.G. (1990). *Cataloguing theory and practice.* 6th ed. New Delhi: Ess Ess Publications.

4

FRBR: Now and Then

4.0. INTRODUCTION

IFLA Study Group on Functional Requirements for Bibliographic Records (FRBR), from 1992 to 1995 developed an entity relationship model (FRBR) for the bibliographic universe. FRBR is an entity relationship concept for the description of bibliographic data that identifies the relationship among entities of a bibliographic record to assemble and organize literary units. The book in hand here is considered not as a single item but as a representative of a literary unit. The most important part of this chapter is the journey back to the root of the literary unit concept on which the FRBR (Functional Requirements for Bibliographic Records) had been devised. It has been found that FRBR which IFLA devised in 1997 has its root in the late 16th Century and from then on it had reminded its presence in almost all the renowned cataloguing codes of modern period.

The first formulation of the idea of assembling literary units under a single heading can be seen in 1595. It was Andrew Maunsell, who in his code *Catalogue of English Printed Books* in 1595 used the uniform heading 'Bible' to assemble its various versions and translations together. Although not much instance of its acceptance to the cataloguing community can be traced till 1674. Thomas Hyde, the Librarian of the Bodleian from 1665 to 1701 assembled the literary units of a given author (except pseudonymous works) under a uniform heading where the titles were arranged in a chronological order. According to Julia Pettee, Thomas Hyde formulates the first principles of modern cataloguing- that the cataloguer should recognise and assemble literary units under a single caption (Pette, 1936: 278). Panizzi in the mid nineteenth century bore the legacy of the Bodleian in his famous '*91 Rules*' where he wanted to include all the information regarding the peculiarities of different editions of a work in the library catalogues. Again, the echo of this concept can be heard in Cutter. The idea of literary unit rather than individual books gained prominence in Cutter which is more evident in his treatment of the anonymous classics. Even, it was thoroughly discussed in the *International Conference on Cataloguing Principles, Paris (ICCP, 1961)* also as Lubetzky spoke in favour of using the concept while designing new cataloguing codes.

4.1. FUNCTIONAL REQUIREMENTS FOR BIBLIOGRAPHIC RECORDS

FRBR is an entity relationship concept for description of bibliographic data. FRBR is a conceptual entity relationship model designed by *IFLA Study Group on Functional Requirements for Bibliographic Records* (FRBR), for the bibliographic universe, intended to be independent of any cataloguing code. FRBR deals with entity relationship concept that identifies the relationship among entities of a bibliographic record, i.e., relationship between the works, their creators and their subjects to assemble and organize literary units. The book in hand here is considered not as a single item but as a representative of a literary unit. The duty of the cataloguer is to assemble these literary units issued in various forms, under a single caption. Although IFLA has designed it very recently for the versatile bibliographic universe of 21st century, the root of FRBR can be traced far back in the cataloguing of the 16th century.

The 1990 Stockholm Seminar on Bibliographic Records, sponsored by the *IFLA Universal Bibliographic Control and International MARC (UBCIM) Programme and the IFLA Division of Bibliographic Control* recognized the economic realities faced by libraries and the need to reduce the cost of cataloguing. They also acknowledged the importance of meeting user needs and addressing more effectively the broad range of needs associated with various types of material and the various contexts within which bibliographic records are used.

It was recognized that continuing pressure to do "minimal level" cataloguing required a careful re-examination of the relationship between individual data elements in the record and the needs of the user. It was also recognized that in this context the viability of shared cataloguing programs, both nationally and internationally, required an agreed standard for a "basic" or "core" level record.

Among nine resolutions adopted at the Stockholm Seminar, one resolution called for the commissioning of a study to define the functional requirements for bibliographic records.

The purpose of this study was to delineate in clearly defined terms the functions performed by the bibliographic record with respect to various media, various applications, and various user needs. The study aimed to cover the full range of functions for the bibliographic record in its widest sense- i.e., a record that encompasses not only descriptive elements, but access points (name, title, subject, etc.), other "organizing" elements (classification, etc.), and annotations. According to Barbara Tillett, FRBR offers us a fresh perspective on the structure and relationship of bibliographic and authority records, and also a more precise vocabulary to help future cataloguing rule makers and system designers in meeting users needs (Tillett, 2004: 1).

The study group completed its lengthy deliberations

for its draft report in the fall of 1995. After a thorough discussions and revisions the final report was presented at the *63rd (1997) General Conference of the International Federation of Library Associations and Institutions* held in Copenhagen, Denmark. The Standing Committee approved the study group's final report at its meeting on September 5, 1997 (IFLA, 1997: 2).

4.2. WHAT IS FRBR?

FRBR is a framework that identifies and clearly defines the entities of interest to users of bibliographic records, the attributes of each entity, and the types of relationships that operate between entities. It was designed to produce a conceptual model that would serve as the basis for relating specific attributes and relationships to the various tasks that users perform when consulting bibliographic records.

According to IFLA "the aim of that study was to produce a framework that would provide a clear, precisely stated, and commonly shared understanding of what it is that the bibliographic record aims to provide information about, and what it is that we expect the record to achieve in terms of answering user needs."

4.2.1. FRBR Entities

The entities are at the centre of interest of the users. They are divided into three groups here. The first group includes 'work', 'expression', 'manifestation', and 'item'. The second group comprises 'person' and 'corporate body' and in the third group an additional set of entities have served as the subjects of the works. This includes 'concept', 'object', 'event', and 'place'. The entities as depicted in the IFLA FRBR Final report are discussed in details leter.

4.2.1.1. Group 1 Entities: Work, Expression, Manifestation, Item

The entities in the first group represent the different aspects of user interests in the products of intellectual or artistic endeavour. The entities defined as work (a distinct intellectual or artistic creation) and expression (the intellectual or artistic realization of a work) reflect intellectual or artistic content. The entities defined as manifestation (the physical embodiment of an expression of a work) and item (a single exemplar of a manifestation), on the other hand, reflect physical form.

4.2.1.2. Group 2 Entities: Person, Corporate Body

The entities in the second group represent those responsible for the intellectual or artistic content, the physical production and dissemination, or the custodianship of the entities in the first group. The entities in the second group include person (an individual) and corporate body (an organization or group of individuals and/or organizations).

4.2.1.3. Group 3 Entities: Concept, Object, Event, Place

The entities in the third group represent an additional set of entities that serve as the subjects of works. The group includes concept (an abstract notion or idea), object (a material thing), event (an action or occurrence), and place (a location).

From the discussions above it is obvious that FRBR was devised on the long standing fundamental principles and objectives of cataloguing. Instead of listing only the current item in hand it gives the details of work, expression, manifestation and item. It also includes the creators and subjects associated with these entities. Although seems ideal conceptually, implementing FRBR in practice would be difficult due to its abstract ideas like expression.

4.3. PRESENCE OF FRBR IN LIBRARY CATALOGUING SINCE 16TH CENTURY

The principle of *Functional Requirements for Bibliographic Records (FRBR)* on which the new code *RDA (Resource Description and Access)* is designed was published in the report of the IFLA Study Group in 1998. The report mainly covers the user-oriented functions that bibliographic records should fulfill, and the data elements necessary to fulfill those functions, which is nothing but going back to the basics described by Pannizzi and Cutter. But the term *FRBR* is usually used in reference to the entity-relationship model described in the report, which defines the characteristics of works, expressions, manifestations, and items and this concept too has been delineated from the earlier catalogues of 16th and 17th century which used 'literary unit' concept, to assemble the works of an author together.

4.4. USE OF LITERARY UNIT CONCEPT IN CATALOGUING

RDA (Resource Description and Access) is a content standard, a set of guidelines for describing a resource. RDA is based on FRBR model- a conceptual entity relationship model designed by *IFLA Study Group on Functional Requirements for Bibliographic Records (FRBR),* for the bibliographic universe, intended to be independent of any cataloguing code. FRBR deals with entity relationship concept that identifies the relationship among entities of a bibliographic record, i.e., relationship between the works, their creators and their subjects to assemble and organize literary units. The book in hand here is considered not as a single item but as a representative of a literary unit. The first and foremost aim of a cataloguer is to put together these literary units issued in various forms, under a single heading. The IFLA Study Group has given it a new look keeping parity with the modern diversified bibliographic universe. But the root of FRBR can be traced far back in the cataloguing of the 16th century.

The idea of bringing together literary units under a single heading can be first seen in use in 1595. Andrew Maunsell in his code *Catalogue of English Printed Books* used the uniform heading 'Bible' first to assemble its various versions and translations together. This is the first instance of its kind. The then Librarian of the Bodleian, Thomas Hyde, from 1665 to 1701 assembled the literary units of a given author under a uniform heading, in which the titles were arranged in a chronological order. According to Julia Pettee, Thomas Hyde formulates the first principles of modern cataloguing- that the cataloguer should recognise and assemble literary units under a single caption. (Pettee, 1936: 278)

Panizzi in his famous *XIC Rules* wanted to include all the information regarding the peculiarities of different editions of a work in the library catalogues. After Panizzi, Jewett and Cutter also used the literary unit concept in their cataloguing code. Lubetzky in the *International Conference on Cataloguing Principles (ICCP, 1961)* spoke in favour of using the literary unit concept while designing cataloguing code. It was thoroughly discussed in the Conference (Biswas & Rath, 2014: 8), but neither was it adapted by IFLA nor was it implemented in AACR1 (1967) or AACR2 (1978) which were based mainly on *Paris Principles*.

4.4.1. Catalogue of English Printed Books

The sixteenth century library catalogues were unable to serve the stalwarts like Scaliger, Galileo, Grotius, Descartes, Bacon and Kepler. The library catalogues, more specifically, the then cataloguers could not keep pace with the enthusiasm for the scholarship and intellectual activities of the period. Sometimes the scholars themselves and the book sellers pointed out to the libraries the potentialities of library catalogue. It was Andrew Maunsell, who first tried to assemble and organise literary units in cataloguing as early as in 1595. Maunsell, who was an English bookseller, compiled *Catalogue of English Printed Books* and in the preface stated his rules for entry. He was the first to set up the principle of uniform heading, where he used the heading 'Bible' to assemble its various versions and translations (Strout, 1956: 264; Viswanathan, 1990: 22). Among many other rules, he advocated for the entry of personal names under surnames rather than Christian names.

Maunsell's code was neither immediately, nor universally adopted by librarians and bibliographers. As

Strout mentioned, "even after the way had been pointed out, it was by no means followed by the majority of cataloguers. The great and seemingly obvious improvements in cataloguing which appear in Maunsell's code were neither immediately nor universally adopted by librarians and bibliographers." (Strout, 1956: 264). Only an extended use of this 'literary unit' concept can be found in the Bodleian Catalogues compiled by Thomas Hyde and published in 1674 which was further enhanced by Cutter in his *Rules for a Dictionary Catalogue* (RDC).

4.4.2. Bodleian Catalogues

In the history of modern cataloguing, the Bodleian Catalogues of 1674 and 1738 played a significant role that had a far reaching impact upon the cataloguing practice of that period and subsequently. Bodleian catalogues of 1674 and 1738 bears the signature of the craftsmanship of the then cataloguers who provided ample provision in their catalogues to disseminate right document to the right people within the least possible time and with minimum effort. Which is most interesting is that this century old catalogues have a lot of characteristic features which are similar, or as good as that of the IFLA's latest introduced cataloguing concept FRBR, i. e., recognition of literary unit concept, where a book is treated as representative of a literary unit (work). "The preface to the 1674 catalog and the structure of both catalogs show an awareness of an important question now being raised in modern cataloguing theory: the distinction between 'book' and 'work'." (Frost, 1976: 248)

Thomas Hyde, Librarian of the Bodleian Library should be regarded as the father of the entity relationship concept in library science. Although Maunsell in 1595 had used the heading 'Bible' to assemble its different versions and translations, he kept his use limited within the entry of Bible only. It was Hyde who extensively used the concept whenever assembling the different versions, translations and forms of the works belong to a certain author.

Thomas Hyde, the Librarian of the Bodleian from 1665 to 1701 assembled the literary units of works of a given author (except pseudonymous works) under a uniform heading where the titles were arranged in a chronological order under that heading. According to Pettee, Thomas Hyde formulates the first principles of modern cataloguing- that the cataloguer should recognise and assemble literary units under a single caption (Pettee, 1936: 278). Verona differs with Pettee and opines that, Hyde did not provide for a real identification of literary units but only for the assembling of the works by a given author (with the exception of works published under pseudonym) under a uniform heading. Under such a heading titles were as a rule arranged in a chronological sequence (Verona, 1959: 82).

Frost (1976: 259) contradicts Verona, "It is true that we do not find in Hyde's preface any formulation of a rule for assembling literary units under a single heading. However, he does express a concern for the problem which occurs when different editions of a work appear under different titles and, accordingly, he attempted to place together all the editions in different forms so that there is the least possibility of error on the part of the reader:

> . . . *omnes illas Editiones diversisformis enuntiata, Lectoris ob oculus simulposui...*"

He illustrates this point with an example of a work which is entitled in one edition *Paratitlorum libri tres*, but which in subsequent editions is called more correctly *Collectionem Constitutionum Ecclesiasticarum*. In the catalog, this appears as:

Theodorus BALSAMON ...

> Collectio Constitutionum Ecclesiasticarum, Gr. Lat. e Cod. Dig. & Novellis Justiniani, (a Leunclavio olim edita sub nomine Paratitlorum,) cum Notis Leunclavii & Fabroti . . .

Another example which Hyde mentions is the dissertations of Maximus Tyrius which are sometimes called

Sermones and sometimes *Disputationes*. Frost after studying examples from the catalogs rightly observed that, "Although there is no uniform heading to identify the different versions of a work, the concept of a literary unit is still recognizable in the arrangement of the titles." He was absolutely right when he opined that "Chronological order is apparently not the prime determinant as Verona suggested" (Frost, 1976: 259). Chronology was not always followed strictly whenever arranging the entries in the catalogues. It can be substantiate with examples from 1674 catalogue:

Rob. BELLARMINUS...
Doctrina Christina...1613.
Et Grace...1637.
Same in English, out of Italian by R. Hadock...
Same with Pictures...1614

Further study proves that the Bodleian catalogues was not far behind of today's FRBR centered catalogues that speaks of 'work' 'expression' 'manifestation' and 'item'. Although these exact terms were not very much in use then, the Bodleian catalogues provided the readers means to select their desired item from among the different versions, editions and translations of the same work which it used to group together in its author and title catalogue. Let us see how the sixteen versions of Ovid's Metamorphoses are grouped together there:

Publius OVIDUS ...

Metamorphoses: ex recognitione Jo. An. Episcopi Alerien in Cyrno ... 1471 ...

Les Metamorphoses en Latin & Francois: avec de nouvelles Explications Historiques &c. sur toutes les Fables; de la Traduction de Mr Pierre du Ryer ... 1677 ...

Le Metamorfosi ridotte da Gio Andr. dall Anguillara; con l'Annota- tioni di M. Gioseppe Horologgi ... 1589 ...

Las Transformaciones en Lengua Espanola, con las

Allegorias al fin dellos, y sus figuras, &c.... 1595 ...
The fyrst fower Bookes of the Metamorphosis oute of Latin into English Meter by Ar. Golding Gent .. . 1565 ...
Metamorphosis Englished, Mythologiz'd, and Represented in Figures by G. Sandys . . . 1632 ...
Same Translation (without the Figures and Notes) ... 1669 . . .

Different versions, translations and editions, of a work grouped together in the catalogue and recorded under the author as a heading, shows nothing but the literary unit concept here. The above example proves doubtlessly the presence of 'literary unit' concept (the essence of today's FRBR) very much in the Bodleian catalogues, although it was not well termed and expressed explicitly then like that of today.

Hyde's rules for main entry also show that the aim of the cataloguer was to bring together all the literary units under a single heading. He brought authors named in several names under single form of a name. Translations were entered under the author of the original work and the actual authors of the pseudonym used were searched thoroughly and used cross-reference entries from them. Hyde's rules for the main entry as depicted in Pettee's description (1936: 278) may be summarized like this:

Personal authors

If author is given in book, enter under surname, choosing one form if he is known under several names. For the sake of uniformity, even if author is always known by his given name, use surname, although it may inconvenience the reader. If author's name is not given, enter under assumed name or initials, but always ferret out name of author and make cross-reference. Enter translations under original author.

Anonymi (Compilations)

Enter under such words as LEXICA,

CONCORDANTIA, JUS, CONCILIA, those books which are likely to be thumbed to pieces by use, but enter others (not in demand) under place or editor.

Other anonymous books are to be entered under person referred to or under a subject word.

He assembled the author's works in one place under a uniform heading to show which works of a given author the library has. Works published anonymously but with known authors appear under the author's name. Authors writing under pseudonym were entered under real names. For theses authorship might have been ascribed from different sources other than the title page of the document. All these were done to keep the works of an author together. The following example is taken from the catalogue of 1738:

Tho. TRYON.

The Way to Health, long Life, and Happiness, or a Disc. of Temperance, &c. to which is added a Treatise of most sorts of English Herbs. [Anonym.] Lond. 1683 ...

Moonthly Observations for the preserving of Health, &c. [by Philotheus Physiologus.] Lond. 1688 ...

A new Art of brewing Beer, Ale, and other Sorts of Liquors, also the Art of making Mault, &c. Lond. 1691 ...

The good House-Wife made a Doctor, or Health's choice and sure Friend, &c. Lond. 1692 .

Aminadab BLOWER, a devout Bellowse-mender of PIMLICO. Some Small and Simple Reasons delivered in a Hollow-Tree, in Waltham Forrest, in a Lecture on the 33 of March last (1648;) shewing the Causes in general and particular, wher-efore they doe, might, would, or ought, except against, and quite Refuse the Liturgy, or Booke of Common-Prayer. Printed, Anno Millimo, Quillimo, Trillimo...

The above discussion shows doubtlessly that the concept of assembling literary units together for the convenience of the users is nothing new. It has been a practice almost since the introduction of modern cataloguing practice. The effort for easy retrieval of information using literary unit concept was very much there in the cataloguing practice of the bygone days. Only the terminologies like 'expression' and 'manifestation' might have been introduced in FRBR recently. In Pettee's words, "The identification of the literary unit and the attribution of authorship in establishing the form of entry is so thoroughly ingrained in our catalogers, it may be a surprise to many to be told that these principles, in the long history of cataloging, are something very new and that they have not yet attained universal acceptance." (Pettee, 1936: 271)

4.4.3. Panizzi's XCI Rules

It won't be an exaggeration to say that the use of literary unit concept began to be dropped from modern catalogue since the introduction of the famous XCI Rules of Panizzi in 1841. Panizzi asserted that catalogues should bear information about all the peculiarities of different editions of a work: "a reader may know the work he requires; he cannot be expected to know all the peculiarities of different editions; and this information he has a right to expect from the catalogues." The frequent reorganizations of literary unit concept of the Bodleian Catalogue had been dropped. Nowhere did Panizzi try to bring together the different editions, versions or translation of works, as his predecessors in the Bodleian, except in one case. The identification of literary units was fully recognized only for various editions of the Bible which were all brought together under one heading ("The Old and New Testament and their parts, to be catalogued under the general head 'Bible', and arranged in the following order..."- rule LXXIX). Julia Pettee observed that in the famous *XCI Rules* the idea of treating literary units under a single caption is extended to the word BIBLE to collect editions of that classic, and in large measure Rule IX and Rule LXXX assemble works of corporate bodies. (Julia Pettee, 1936: 281)

The identification of literary units is fully recognized only for various editions of the Bible. In sub-arrangement under authors, or under other headings, Panizzi tends towards the recognition and assembling of literary units (rules LXXV, LXXVI, LXXVIII); but since the same author appears in certain cases under different headings, such assembling is obviously possible only in a restricted measure. No provision is made for the various editions and translations of anonymous works in general; they are apparently treated as single items. (Verona, 1959: 83)

4.4.4. Jewett's Code

Panizzi's rules were taken over and modified by Jewett. Compared with the original rules, Jewett's modification published in 1852, goes considerably further in the recognition of the following two objectives: (i) the provision of information concerning all editions, translations, etc. of a given work as far as they exists in the library (ii) and the provision of information concerning all works of by a given author as far as they exist in the library. Thus anonymous and pseudonymous works are entered under the identified author if any edition, continuation or supplement has been published under his name (rules XXVIII, XXIX); all translations (including translations of anonymous works) are entered under the heading of the original text irrespective of the fact whether the original text exists in the library or not (rule XXIII) (Verona, 1959: 84).

4.4.5. Rules for a Dictionary Catalogue

Cutter was the first to observe that the object of catalogue is not just to provide the information regarding a particular book by a given author, or merely helping the reader in making available a book kept in the library by a given author, but to provide information regarding all the books by a given author. In other words, the basic elements of a catalogue should be so that instead of pointing to an individual publication, it should organise the literary works or literary units of a given author. Here, particular books should not be considered as single items but as representatives of a whole group of similar items, all belong to the same literary unit. The object is not merely to facilitate the finding of a given book by an author's name, but to provide for the finding of all the books of a given author- and this can most conveniently be done if they are all collected in one place. (Cutter, 1904: 31)

The most important contribution to American cataloguing theory was C. A. Cutter's rules published first in 1876. These rules introduce a fundamental innovation: along with the assembling of all works by a given author under one heading, the recognition of literary units is for the first time accepted almost completely, and extended to personal and title entries as well. Thus all works by a given author whether issued under his name, under a pseudonym or anonymously, are brought together under a single heading (rules 1, 2, 7); revisions, translations, excerpts of any given work are entered under the author or under the title of the original text, respectively, and filed immediately after it (rules 17-19, 123, 124, 131, 132) (Verona, 1959: 84).

Before *Rules for a Dictionary Catalogue* all the available codes provided rules for author and title entries. It was Cutter who strengthened the concept that catalogues not only should point the way to an individual publication but should also assemble and organize literary units (Strout, 1956: 272). The procedure of cataloguing should be preceded by the identification of the literary unit, to which the book belongs, i.e. by the identification of the title and author of the literary unit. A catalogue compiled in this way will be primarily a finding list for literary units. It will be of great help to users who approach the catalogue in order to look for a literary work in whatever edition, translation or excerpt it may exist in the library (Verona, 1959: 80).

The idea of literary unit rather than individual books gained prominence in Cutter which is more evident in his treatment of the anonymous classics. Here he tried to bring together all the different texts under the heading of the original work to show its consistency to the idea that catalogue should assemble and organise literary units, rather than individual publications. As Pettee rightly observed thus, in dealing with anonymous classics Cutter makes an original and vital contribution to the authorship principle. He regards this species of literature as a class by itself. He sees that it is the function of the catalog to assemble these classics and consider as a unit of literature, under a single heading, all texts derived from the same source, however the individual titles may read. The entry form should go back to the original source. (Pettee, 1936: 284)

Pettee even goes further to extract the modern cataloguing principles from the rules devised by Cutter in his RDC as follows:

We find in Cutter, fixed for all time, I believe, the two fundamental principles of the modern author catalog:

i. the author catalog is more than a finding list of separate and particular books. It deals with literary units and its function is to assemble under a convenient heading all issues or forms of the same literary unit.

ii. the most satisfactory method of doing this is through the attribution of authorship, using as heading the name of the person, or corporate body responsible for the work, or using as a substitute for author heading, a conventional name not derived from the title-page but from the literary source of the book or document. The cataloger must identify the literary unit and provide the unit, not the single book, with an entry name; and this name goes back to the source of its authorship.

While this was not an entirely new principle, since Maunsell in 1595 had used the heading 'Bible' to assemble its various versions and translations, Panizzi in 1841 had strengthened it as a concept by introducing corporate and government entries, and Jewett had had given it still further support by his use of real names rather than pseudonyms, yet it was Cutter who actually stated it as a formal principle (Strout, 1956: 272).

4.4.6. A.L.A. Rules

A.L.A. Cataloguing Rules for Author and Title Entries, declares its principle explicitly in favour of the literary unit concept. In the introduction to the code it clearly mentions about the extended function of catalogue that locates a single book as well as the literary units. "The principle on which the cataloguing is planned is the use as main entry of the author, personal or corporate, considered to be chiefly responsible for the creation of the intellectual content of the work. Thus the finding list function of the catalogue is extended beyond what is required for location of a single book to the location of literary units about which the seeker has less precise information... Added entries serve also to complete the assembling of related material as a part of a literary unit. (A.L.A., 1949: xx)

Works of a single author including various editions, translations, versions etc. are brought together under a single form of his name, whether or not this form appears in the book itself (rules 2, 20-22, 32, 36). Anonymous classics are treated as literary units and entered under uniform headings (rule 33-35).

The basic principles of the L.C. Studies are the foundation on which were built the L.C. *Rules for Descriptive Cataloging* published in 1949 and accepted by the ALA as a substitute for Part II of the ALA Catalog Rules, whose preliminary edition in 1941 had provoked Mr. Osborn's Crisis. In 1949 also appeared the ALA' s own revised version of Part I on author and title entries. It confessed that it was only an "expansion and revision of the rules of ...1908," and in its Introduction some three basic principles were implied, although not specifically stated as such:

i. The rules were "intended to represent the best or the most general practice."

ii. "The finding list function of the catalog is extended beyond what is required for location of a single book" to include also location under one heading of all issues and forms of the same 'literary unit.'

iii. "Exceptions or qualifications are made when too strict an application of a general rule would result in a heading not giving the most direct approach."

The second principle on 'single book' and 'literary unit' derives from Miss Pettee's analysis of the historical development of Cutter's rules. (Dunkin, 1956: 288)

4.4.7. Seymour Lubetzky

International Conference on Cataloguing Principles organised by International Federation of Library Associations and Institutions (IFLA) held at Unesco headquarters, Paris in 1961 was the first ever successful international agreement of the century on cataloguing. Representatives of fifty four countries and twelve international organizations worked rigorously for 10 days and through a friendly discussion worked out a statement of principles for catalogues to be followed throughout the world.

Almost after forty years IFLA initiated a fundamental re-examination of cataloguing theory and practice on an international level and *IFLA Study Group on the Functional Requirements for Bibliographic Records* in 1997 devised a new 'structured framework' (FRBR) for relating the data that are recorded in bibliographic records. This new framework, which it calls the entity-relationship concept, is fundamentally based on literary unit concept- the book in hand is considered not as a single item but as a representative of literary unit.

The literary unit concept which distinguishes clearly between a book and a work is hardly a new idea to the cataloguing community. What is most interesting is that it was thoroughly discussed and debated in the *International Conference on Cataloguing Principles* of 1961 held in Paris, but no where it is found to be incorporated or implemented in AACR (1967) or AACR2 (1978) which were based on the principles adapted in that conference (Paris Principles).

Lubetzky clearly stated in his paper presented at the Conference on Cataloguing Principles, 1961 that the function of the main entry presupposes recognition of the facts:

i. that the materials of a library- books, manuscripts, phono-records, etc. are representations of the works of authors, not the works themselves;
ii. that a given work may be represented in a library in different forms or editions, under different names of the author or under different titles; and
iii. that the catalogues of a library must be designed not only
   a. to show whether or not that library has a particular item or publication, issued under a certain name of the author or under a certain title, but also
   b. to identify the author and the work represented by the item or publication and to relate the various works of author and the various editions and translations of the work.

Although this second objective is the source of most difficulties in cataloguing, it has always been recognized as essential to the basic purposes of the catalogue – to enable a user of the catalogue to determine with certainty whether or not the library has a particular work, under whatever name or title, and to select the edition or translation which will best serve his purpose." (Lubetzky, 1963: 139)

4.4.8. AACR1 and AACR2

There are evidences that this literary unit concept was also used in AACR1 and AACR2 to assemble different manifestations of a work through the use of Uniform titles. Both the codes used the same means to bring different manifestations of a work together. The use of literary unit concept is quite evident from the following description of

AACR1 (British Text):

Uniform titles : The following rules for uniform titles provided the means for bringing together catalogue entries for all editions of a given work when its editions, translations, etc., have appeared under various titles, and for properly identifying a work when its title is obscured by the wording on the title page. The need to apply the rules will vary from library to library and will depend on such factors as the general renown of the work, the number of editions, translations, etc., involved;

Rule no 100 (Basic rules)

A. When the editions, translations, etc., of a work appear under various titles, select one title as uniform title under which all will be catalogued.

B. In case of works entered under title, treat the uniform title as heading. Make references from variants of the title but prefer an added entry for any title that applies to a particular edition rather than to the work itself. (AACR1, 1967: 123)

The same idea was reintroduced in AACR2, 1978 and continued till 2005 without any changes in the basic concept and purposes of its use. The following description of uniform titles clearly proves it:

Use of uniform titles : Uniform titles provide the means for bringing together all catalogue entries for a work when various manifestations (e.g., editions, translations) of it have appeared under various titles. They also provide identification for a work when the title by which it is known differs from the title proper of the item being catalogued. The need to use uniform titles varies from one catalogue to another and varies within one catalogue... Although the rules in this chapter are stated as instructions, apply them according to the policy of the cataloguing agency (AACR2, 1978: 441).

Thus it can be said that the same literary unit concept

that is the book in hand is a single representation of the intellectual or artistic creation 'work', has been very much in use throughout the *Anglo American Cataloguing Rules* also.

4.5. CONCLUSION

From the discussions above, it can be said unhesitatingly that the presence of the concept of FRBR was very much there in our catalogues since long past. Only the naming (FRBR) is a new phenomenon. Practically, the concept FRBR (as we call it today) was created much earlier than the formation of ISBD and even before the creation of AACR1, in 16th and 17th Century. Then it was percolated among the code makers like Panizzi, Jewett and Cutter. Even if we look back at the very recent past of the cataloguing history, we can find that it was a topic for discussion which got ample importance in the international forum like ICCP, Paris in 1961 also. It was in this Paris Conference Seymour Lubetzky presented the paper *Function of the main entry in the alphabetical catalogue: one approach* where he vividly described this concept. Let's see once again in brief what he said there:

(i) the materials of a library- books, manuscripts, phono-records, etc. - are representations of the works of author, not the work themselves;

(ii) the catalogues of a library must be designed to identify the author and the work represented by the item or publication and to relate the various works of the author and the various editions and translations of the work.

There was everything of today's 'entity relationship' concept. Let us see what others said in response to Lubetzky's paper:

Verona said that it has repeatedly been pointed out that books (publications) are only physical representations of work and that accordingly the object of the reader's essential interest is not the publication, but the work represented by it (ICCP, 1963: 147).

Jolley in the *Function of the main entry in the alphabetical catalogue: a study of the views put forward by Lubetzky and Verona* observed that both Verona and Lubetzky agreed in stressing the distinction between works and publications. It is quite obvious that the reader is normally interested primarily in a work, rather than in a specific publication, but care must be used in processing this distinction. (ICCP, 1963: 160)

The terms 'book' and 'work' were consciously used in different meanings to indicate 'work' and its various manifestations in the Statement of Cataloguing Principles, 1961. In the ICCP, whenever discussing the draft statement Mr. Chaplin pointed to the distinction made in the draft statement between the terms 'book' and 'work', one being used for the physical object and the other reserved for the literary or verbal content, which might well be embodied in many forms" (ICCP, 1963: 23). Thus, the concept of principles of 'literary unit' and today's 'entity relationship' concept was very much there and the claim of introducing a completely new concept 'FRBR' by IFLA can hardly be substantiated. Rather, it's the inefficiency of IFLA and JSC who failed to utilize the knowledge represented by Lubetzky half a century ago. If they could use the concept in Paris Principles and in AACR2, and design the code accordingly, the cataloguing history of last 50 years would have been written in different ways.

The claim that IFLA has devised a new framework through FRBR cannot be supported. The same is true in case of ISBD also. ISBD is the bibliographic standard developed under the resolution at the *International Meeting of Cataloguing Experts* held in Copenhagen in 1969 to establish international standards for form and content of bibliographic descriptions. The first standard developed under this resolution was ISBD (M). Here also nothing new was introduced; only the prevalent ideas of that time were reproduced with a new name. Hunter (1974: 96) has given a sample comparing two entries of descriptive cataloguing by AACR, 1967 and ISBD like this.

> Partley, Gerald
>
> The cinema of Otto Preminger, by Gerald partley. London: Zwemmer, 1971.
>
> 192p; illus., ports. 16cm. (The international film guide series)

Entry by AACR (British Text)

And now look at the entry made by ISBD:

> Partley, Gerald
>
> The cinema of Otto Preminger/ by Gerald partley._ London: Zwemmer, 1971.
>
> 192p.: ill., ports.; 16cm._ (The international film guide series)
>
> ISBN 0 302 02152 3 Pbk.: £0.90

Nothing new was introduced in ISBD, except the order and punctuation which are also not beyond controversy. The cataloging community is well aware about the turmoil that took place during the implementation of the new format next few years after the production of ISBD and their after effects. Probably, the same is going to happen in case of FRBR also which is formed almost the same way like that of ISBD. The effort of implementation of this concept through RDA has already raised several questions. Majority of the cataloguers voiced against its implementation (studies made by U.S. *RDA Test Coordinating Committee* and others show this; please refer to chapter-8 for more details) questioning the feasibility of its necessities in conventional libraries. But to those who have engaged themselves to design and develop it, have left no stone unturned to get their views established by any means. It seems that it's a kind of whim of some of the apex bodies in the bibliographic world who rediscover certain ideas from time to time and impose them on others to follow and act accordingly. They love to do experiments with the existing systems at the cost of services to the users.

But history shows that these apex bodies are always lagging behind time. That's why such frequent shifts in the concept and design of cataloguing take place hampering the stability of the age old means of document search and retrieval. Thus, ISBD centered -MARC-UNIMARC-MARC21 came and died, or about to die, and now comes the FRBR & FRAD (on which RDA is designed). But if we analyse the objectives and functions of catalogues we can find that nothing new, even not a single new dimension is added with the classical views of it. Then it must admit here that if our cataloguing standards were based on sound cataloguing principles it would never be shifted from one concept to another so frequently.

REFERENCES

American Library Association. (1949). *Cataloguing Rules for Author and Title Entries*. 2nd ed. edited by Clara Beetle. Chicago: ALA.

American Library Association. (1949). *Cataloguing Rules for Author and Title Entries*. 2nd ed. edited by Clara Beetle. Chicago: ALA.

Anglo-American Cataloging Rules. (1967). Prepared by the American Library Association the Library of Congress, the Library Association, and the Canadian Library Association. British Text. General editor C. Sumner Spalding. London: The Library Association.

Anglo-American Cataloguing Rules. (1978). Prepared by the American Library Association, the British Library, the Canadian Committee on Cataloguing, the Library Association and the Library of Congress; edited by Michael Gorman and Paul W. Winkler. 2nd. ed. Chicago: American Library Association.

Anglo-American Cataloguing Rules. (1988). Prepared under the direction of the Joint Steering Committee for the Revision of AACR; edited by Michael Gorman and Paul W. Winkler. 2nd. ed. 1988 revision. Chicago: American Library Association.

Biswas, Subhankar and Rath Durga Sankar. (2014) From Maunsell to Lubetzky: a journey back in search of the root of FRBR among the cataloguing codes of Anglo American origin. Annals of Library and Information Studies, 61(1), March 2014, 7-14.

Cutter, C. A. (1904). *Rules for a dictionary catalogue.* 4th ed. Washington: Government Printing Office.

Dunkin, Paul S. (1956). Criticisms of current cataloging practice. *The Library Quarterly, 26* (4), 286-302.

Frost, Carolyn O. (1976). The Bodleian Catalogs of 1674 and 1738: an Examination in the Light of Modern Cataloguing Theory. *The Library Quarterly, 46*(3), 248-270.

Hunter, Eric J. (1974). *Cataloguing: a guide book.* London: Clive Bingley.

ICCP. (1963). Report: International Conference on Cataloguing Principles Paris, 9th – 18th October, 19961. London: Organizing Committee of the ICCP.

IFLA (1997). *Functional Requirements for Bibliographic Records: final report* .Retrieved September 7, 2011 from www.ifla.org.

Lubetzky, Seymour. (1963). The Function of the main entry in the alphabetical catalogue: one approach. In A. H. Chaplin (ed.) *International Conference on Cataloguing Principles: report, Paris, 9th – 18th October, 1961* (pp.139-143). London: Organizing Committee of the ICCP.

Pettee, Julia. (1936). The Development of authorship entry and the formulation of authorship rules as found in the Anglo-American Code. Library Quarterly, 6(3), 270-90.

Strout, Ruth Frence (1956). Development of the Catalog and Cataloguing Codes. *Library Quarterly, 26*(4), 254-275.

Tillett, Barbara B. (2004). What is FRBR? *A conceptual model for the bibliographic universe.* Retrieved on December 2, 2007, from http://www.ifla.org/VII/s13/frbr/frbr.pdf

Verona, Eva. (1959). Literary unit versus bibliographical unit. *Libri. 9*(2), 79-104.

Viswanathan, C.G. (1990). *Cataloguing theory and practice.* 6th ed. New Delhi: Ess Ess Publications.

5

Development of Cataloguing Theory and Canons of Ranganathan

5.0. INTRODUCTION

By the word cataloguing what we mean today, is of a modern origin. It has got very little from ancient or medieval cataloguing as legacy. The gradual development of practical cataloguing since Panizzi, leads to ensure a strong theoretical base of cataloguing behind the curtain. With the improvement of practical cataloguing, a simultaneous growth has taken place in the field of theory of cataloguing also. The first physical appearance of which was observed in the *Rules for Dictionary Catalogue* of C. A. Cutter and it reached its zenith in the *Classified Catalogue Code* of Dr. S. R. Ranganathan.

In this chapter I have tried to capture this development of the recent past to record those milestones that contributed profusely to build up a sound theoretical base of cataloguing as a vital part in the discipline of library science.

S. R. Ranganathan made a significant contribution with his introduction of the scientific principles of cataloguing. His normative principles of cataloguing, commonly known as principles and canons are well accepted throughout the global cataloguing community today. These canons and principles are discussed here in details along with their latest developments. A thorough search has also been made to trace how far Ranganathan's canons and principles are followed in AACR2 and RDA.

Efforts are also made to find out the presence of canons and principles of cataloguing in the cataloguing codes which were devised before Ranganathan formulated his normative principles (here two major codes of that period, Panizzi and Cutter's code have been chosen), to see how far they comply with the principles and canons of cataloguing. Although the theory of cataloguing developed much later, definitely some principles were followed through the cataloguing rules since Panizzi. Therefore, this study would help to portray how Dr. Ranganathan delineated the normative principles of cataloguing from his forerunners.

5.1. RANGANATHAN'S PRINCIPLES AND CANONS FOR CATALOGUING

Normative principles were introduced by S. R. Ranganathan in his *Classified Catalogue Code* (1934) and *Theory of Library Catalogue* (1938) and developed over a period of time. He further made elaborate descriptions of these Normative Principles in his *Headings and Canons* (1955). The *Classified Catalogue Code* (CCC) is based on the normative principles consisting of general normative principles, laws of library science, canons of cataloguing and principles of cataloguing. Ranganathan recognized three levels of normative principles here, namely- general normative principles, specific normative principles for library science and specific normative principles for cataloguing. Each level of normative principles has its own sphere of application.

5.1.1. General Normative Principles

Four general laws, namely Laws of Interpretation, Law of Impartiality, Law of Symmetry, Law of Parsimony are applicable to any situation. General laws are those laws which are applicable to the discipline of library science as a whole and must be satisfied by all the branches of library science. These laws are applicable to cataloguing as well as other branches of library science. The rules of a catalogue code should be framed keeping in view all these laws. Ranganathan formulated two more principles- Principles of Local Variation and Principles of Osmosis as a part of these General Normative Principles.

5.1.1.1. Law of Parsimony

Perhaps the most elementary general principle governing cataloguing or any other scientific practice is the Law of Parsimony. Its watchword is economy- in materials, space, time and energy. Its function is like that of the Finance Secretariat in a modern Government; it would oppose anything that involves expenditure. But on their side the Laws of Library Science have a right to insist that economy be interpreted as actual saving of expense in money or time not only in the library budget but also for the public as a whole (Ranganathan, 1938: 54).

According to Law of Parsimony, between two or more possible alternative rules bearing on a particular phenomenon, the one leading to overall economy of man power, materials, money, and time considered together with proper weightage, is to be preferred (Ranganathan, 1988: 63).

5.1.1.2. Law of Impartiality

Law of Impartiality prescribes that whenever making a choice between two or more claimants for heading, the information to be rendered in the heading should be determined based on some specific principles, not arbitrarily. Between two or more claimants, say for use as heading, the preference of any one should be made only on sufficient grounds, and not arbitrarily. For example, in case of joint authorship, the Law of Impartiality would recommend equal right to the names of all the authors for choice as heading. (Ranganathan, 1955: 56)

5.1.1.3. Law of Symmetry

According to the Law of Symmetry, between two entities or situations which are symmetrical counterparts of each other, weightage should be given to both of them. Like in case of joint authorship author index entries should be prepared under the both authors. In Ranganathan's words, "The principle that of two entities or situations which admit of being regarded as symmetrical counterparts of each other, if one of them is given weight in any particular context, the other too should be given a corresponding weight." (Ranganathan, 1976: 126)

5.1.1.4. Laws of Interpretation

A catalogue code is like a legal document. Any rule in it should be interpreted like a legal text. For example there may be conflict between one rule and another. In actual application, the conflict should be resolved with the aid of the Laws of Interpretation. Periodically, the rules should be amended in the light of experience, so as to remove conflicts or at least to reduce them to a minimum, if they could not be totally removed. (Ranganathan, 1955: 56)

A new cataloguing problem created by a document may have to be met by a proper interpretation of the rules in the catalogue code. There is often conflict between the Law of Parsimony, the Laws of Library Science, and the Canons of Cataloguing. The conflict has to be removed quite often with the aid of Laws of Interpretation. (Ranganathan, 1988: 59)

5.1.1.5. Principles of Local Variation

That in any discipline and technique there should be provision for the users of them to secure, for strictly local use, results, alternating to those for general use.

This law assumes four levels of codes in the context of cataloguing:

i. International cataloguing code
ii. National cataloguing code
iii. Linguistic cataloguing code, and
iv. Local cataloguing code

The principle states that:

a. The International Cataloguing Code should mark out the factors to be left to the care of each National Cataloguing Code.
b. A National Catalogue Code should mark out the factors to be left to the care of each Linguistic Catalogue Code in a multilingual country such as India
c. A National Cataloguing Code or a Linguistic Cataloguing Code, as the case may be should mark out the factors, to be left to the care of the Local Catalogue Code of each individual Library
d. The Catalogue Codes in each hierarchical line should be consistent with one another without any mutual contradiction; and

Each lower link in each hierarchical line should be a supplement to all the upper links taken together.

5.1.1.6. Principles of Osmosis

The principle that, when a change in the catalogue code or in the scheme for classification becomes necessary in deference to the canon of context, on and after a chosen date

i. All the new accessions be catalogued and classified according to the new catalogue code and the new scheme for classification
ii. Just those of the old collection as are known to be in much use be re-catalogued and re-classified, with an additional temporary staff, if necessary, during the first few months

iii. The new accessions and the re-catalogued and re-classified books be kept in a new collection and similarly their catalogue cards to be kept in a new collection

iv. The rest of the old collection be kept as old collection and similarly their catalogue cards to be kept as old collection

v. Readers' attention be invited by the reference Librarian to the existence of the two collections; and

vi. If any book is taken out by a reader from the old collection on its return by him it be re-catalogued and re-classified and absorbed in the new collection and similarly with its catalogue cards according to the principle of parallel movement. (Ranganathan, 1976: 136)

5.1.2. Specific Normative Principles for Library Science

Five laws of library science are specific normative principles. These are the fundamental laws of library science. These laws are applicable to and must be satisfied by all the branches of the discipline of library science. A code of cataloguing must satisfy the demands of these fundamental laws, namely the Five Laws of Library Science. These laws can be applied to any problem faced in library service and practice:

5.1.2.1 Books are for use

5.1.2.2 Every reader his book

5.1.2.3 Every book its reader

5.1.2.4 Save the time of the reader

5.1.2.5 Library is a growing organism

The specific normative principles applicable to any problem arising in library science, library service, and library practice. These are the fundamental laws of library science. These form the normative principles containing in a latent form all the library practices current at any time and to be evolved at a later time. (Ranganathan, 1976: 115)

In these laws, 'Book' should be interpreted to include any macro and micro document. 'Time' should be interpreted to include objective time and subjective time. 'Growth' should be interpreted to include child-growth by addition and adult-growth by replacement. (Ranganathan, 1955: 57)

5.1.3. Specific Normative Principles for Cataloguing

Canons of Cataloguing are the specific normative principles applicable to cataloguing only. They are all implications of the laws of library science specific to the field of cataloguing. In case of a conflict between canons, an appeal is made to the laws of library science. These serve as a court of appeal. If there is a conflict between the canons of cataloguing and general normative principles, then a compromise can be achieved with the aid of laws of library science. Ranganathan has enunciated nine canons of cataloguing.

5.1.3.1. Canon of Ascertainability

Canon of Ascertainability says that the information for the heading and description of catalogues should be taken mainly from the title pages and the overflow pages of a document, so that the information used can easily be ascertainable. The choice and rendering of main entry and specific added entry, and the heading and every other element in either entry should be determined by the information found in the title-page of the document and its overflow pages; in extreme cases the information may be taken from other pages of prel; but it is not desirable to go beyond the prel. A safer course is to base catalogue rules on what is ascertainable about the cataloguing elements of a document within the document itself. (Ranganathan, 1955: 58)

This canon requires that no entry shall include any information that is not definitely ascertainable. One might think it unnecessary to enunciate this as a principle but many difficulties in cataloguing in fact arise from overlooking this obvious rule. In cataloguing practice the term 'ascertainable' is taken in the restricted sense of ascertainable from the words found on or at the back of the title page of the book. As a rule only the subject entry takes the cataloguer beyond the title-page and even then it is simply to seek the appropriate word for the heading. (Ranganathan, 1938: 62)

5.1.3.2. Canon of Prepotence

This canon ensures the assemblage of the most important information at the leading section of a catalogue. The potency to decide the position of an entry among the various entries in a catalogue should, if possible be concentrated totally in the leading section; and even there, it should be concentrated, as much as possible, in the entry element. If total concentration in the leading section is not possible, the minimum possible potency should be allowed to flow beyond it, to later sections; and even this should be distributed in the later sections in decreasing order of intensity. (Ranganathan, 1955: 60)

The Canon of Prepotence yields an important deduced principle applicable to the choice of entry element in a multi-worded-heading- that is, in the rendering of a multi-worded term chosen for use as heading. The principle is a statistical one. "The entry element should be chosen from among that group of the words, occurring in the multi-worded term chosen for use as heading that is more numerous than the groups of the other words occurring in it."(Ranganathan, 1988: 36)

5.1.3.3. Canon of Sought-Heading or Canon of Relevance

This canon prescribes that the decision relating to the choice and rendering of heading in an entry should be such that the users or the library staff search that document under the heading used. As Ranganathan says, another principle that should be borne in mind both in framing and applying cataloguing rules may be called the Canon of Relevance. It demands that the items included in an entry should be relevant to its purpose. (Ranganathan, 1938: 61)

The decision whether an entry

a. with a particular type of heading, or

b. with a particular choice for that heading, or

c. with a particular rendering of that choice, or

d. with a particular added entry arising out of it,

should be based on the answer to the question; "Is reader or library staff likely to look for a book under the particular type or choice or rendering of heading?"

The answer to this question is a matter of flair. The flair should be based on experience in reference service- that is, in eliciting from readers their requirements and finding the appropriate documents for them. Induction should be applied to the words usually brought up by readers in looking into the catalogue to choose their documents. The flair should also be based on experience in book selection. Induction should be applied to the types of heading found necessary to help either in filling up gaps in the library collection or in avoiding unintended duplication. (Ranganathan, 1988: 44)

5.1.3.4. Canon of Context

Canon of Context prescribes that the rules and provisions in a cataloguing code should be formulated in the context of mode of book production and nature of organisation of library services. In other words, they should be dynamic enough in the changing context. The rule in a catalogue code should be formulated in the context of: the nature of cataloguing features of a book, prevalent in the mode of book production; the nature of the organization of libraries prevalent in regard to mode and quality of library service; and the coming into experience of published bibliographies and particularly bibliographical periodicals. The rules should also be changed from time to time to keep steps with changes in context. (Ranganathan, 1955: 70)

The world of book is not static. Context is ever changing. Nature of book changes. Make up of title-page changes. Nature of readers changes. Out-look of library service changes. Extent of national and international co-operation changes. The Canon of Context demands that cataloguing practice should also change. For this purpose, it demands that catalogue code too should change in consonance with the change in the other factors. (Ranganathan, 1988: 50)

5.1.3.5. Canon of Permanence

According to the Canon of Permanence the entry elements, particularly the headings, should be permanent. They should never be changed unless the rules of the cataloguing code themselves are changed obeying the canon of context. In Ranganathan's words, "No element in an entry, and the heading in particular, should be subjected to change by the rules of a catalogue code, except when the rules themselves are changed, in response to the Canon of Context. The Canon of Permanence is backed by the Canon of Ascertainability." (Ranganathan, 1955: 335)

According to this canon the item chosen to occupy the leading section of an entry should represent something permanent. The ideal is, however, seldom realized in practice. (Ranganathan, 1938: 67)

5.1.3.6. Canon of Currency

The name chosen for the heading of an entry should be the current one. The term used to denote a subject in a subject heading of dictionary catalogue and of a class index entry of classified catalogue should be one in current usage. Name of a subject keeps changing with time. Unless the current name is used in the heading readers can not benefit by it. To satisfy this canon the headings of subject entries and class index entries should be changed as and when a new name stabilizes itself. This leads inevitably to a violation of the Canon of Permanence. This conflict between two canons is resolved by a partition of the field of sway. Canon of Currency has sway only over subject heading in dictionary catalogue and class index heading in classified catalogue.

The Canon of Permanence has sway only over name-heading other than subject heading. It has sway only in heading made of name of person, geographical entity or corporate body. (Ranganathan, 1955: 76)

At the time of preparing entries for subjects only currently used names of the subjects should be used in headings. Again, between the term used by specialists and common men for a subject, the term current or in use with the common men should be preferred because it is known by both.

5.1.3.7. Canon of Consistence

Canon of Consistence prescribes that the catalogue code must maintain consistency whenever formulating rules and provisions. In practical cataloguing too, all the added entries should be consistence with the main entries. Whenever preparing main entries (in case of choice rendering and style of writing etc.) consistency among all documents should be maintained.

The rules of a catalogue code should provide for all the added entries of a document to be consistent with its main entry. Also the main entries of all documents should be consistent with one another in certain essentials such as choice, rendering and style of writing the heading and the other sections. (Ranganathan, 1988: 54)

At lower level this canon stands for strict consistency with the code adopted. At a higher level the canon of consistency will impose it on the code itself that similar situations shall be similarly dealt with. The Canon of Consistency must be paramount in a code of rules for cataloguing. Any departure from consistence practice will eventually cause trouble and its cumulative effect will be far greater in proportion to the apparent importance of the original lapse than can be foreseen. The truth of this statement is difficult to demonstrate but it must be accepted as the result of experience and the principle it contains must be adopted in the framing of any cataloguing code. (Ranganathan, 1938: 60)

5.1.3.8. Canon of Individualisation

This canon says that the headings used in a catalogue should be presented in such a way that indicates only a single entity. Individualising elements should be added as and when required. This is to avoid confusion among similar headings that may mislead the readers. The principle that the name of any entity- be it of a person, a geographical entity, a corporate body, a series, a document, a subject, or a language- used as the heading of a catalogue entry should be made to denote one and only one entity, by adding to it the necessary and sufficient number of individualising elements. (Ranganathan, 1988: 40)

Thus the name used for heading should indicate one and only one entity; otherwise the readers will be confused. There are so many authors whose surnames and fore names are common. In these cases date of birth (and also of death if not alive) of the author is incorporated in the heading to individualise the author so that the name indicates to a particular author. In case of corporate body, place may be added for individualisation.

5.1.3.9. Canon of Recall Value

According to this canon, in case of selecting the name of a person, corporate body, title of a document, series etc. as entry element those words should be treated as entry element which have highest recall value, i. e., probability of being recalled in the memory easily.

The concept of the canon of recall value was conceived by Dr. Ranganathan in his Theory of Library Catalogue in the year 1938. But it was finally propounded and published in 1969. Although there are differences of opinions regarding how far it is always possible to decide which word has more recall value. There is every possibility of choosing different words as entry element by different cataloguers.

5.2. HOW FAR THE PRE-RANGANATHAN CATALOGUING CODES SATISFY THE PRINCIPLES AND CANONS OF CATALOGUING?

The unique contributions of S. R. Ranganathan in almost every spheres of library science have been recognised throughout the world. Ranganathan had written on almost all aspects of library science. He had written 50 books and over 1000 articles. Ranganathan had contributed several original ideas in cataloguing. His most important contribution in the field of cataloguing is his introduction of 'principles and canons' which is not only important for practical cataloguing but for the formulation of the rules of a catalogue code.

In his *Theory of Library Catalogue* (1938), he explained the normative principles of cataloguing, popularly known as canons of cataloguing. In his *Headings and Canons* (1955) he had further discussed and explained these canons. Ranganathan did not stop just propounding these principles and canons theoretically. He had shown his genius by his applications of the principles and canons in his remarkable achievement *Classified Catalogue Code* (CCC, 1934). CCC is completely based on the principles and canons formulated by Ranganathan himself. Although Ranganathan devised his normative principles in early twentieth century, it has been observed that most of the principles were followed in the catalogue codes of Panizzi and Cutter long before him. Ranganathan delineated his normative principles by means of his rigorous research with practical cataloguing taking cues from the cataloguing codes of these stalwarts.

5.2.1. Rules for the Compilation of the Catalogue (91 Rules) - Panizzi

5.2.1.1. Canon of Sought Heading in 91 Rules

Rule II of 91 Rules reads, "Title to be arranged alphabetically, according to the English alphabet only (whatever be the order of the alphabet in which a foreign name might have to be entered in its original language) under the surname of the author, whenever it appears printed in the title, or any other part of the book." This rule is in great compliance with the Canon of Sought Heading for its choice of the heading, rendering and arrangement which is made keeping in mind the need, convenience and information seeking behaviour of the library users.

Rule XLI says "In case of pseudonymous publications, the book to be catalogued under the author's feigned name and his real name, if discovered, to be inserted in brackets, immediately after the feigned name, preceded by the letters i.e." This rule also is in compliance with the Canon of Sought Headings. Author heading and subject heading are the most popular among sought headings. Here by choosing the feigned name, Panizzi had given importance to the name most sought by the readers.

5.2.1.2. Canon of Recall Value in 91 Rules

Rule VIII complies with the Canon of Recall Value and Canon of Sought Heading. It instructs to take the Christian name as heading. When an author uses a Christian or first name only (either real or assumed) such name to be taken as heading.

The rule certainly chose the right words as entry element which had highest recall value as well as heading those words which would be most sought by the library users.

5.2.1.3. Canon of Permanence in 91 Rules

Rule XI says "works of authors who change their name or added to it a second , after having begun to publish under the first, to be entered under the first name, noticing any alteration which may have subsequently taken place." This rule is in great compliance with the Canon of Permanence that says that no element in an entry, the heading in particular, should be subject to change by the rule of a catalogue code.

The Canon of Permanence is backed by the Canon of Ascertainability. If the latest name was entered as heading, the library had to change all the entries under earlier names. Such a change automatically violates the Canon of Ascertainability in regard to the earlier documents.

5.2.1.4. Law of Impartiality in 91 Rules

Rule III, VIII, XXXVII instructs to take first person as leading name in case of multiple authors. It fails to satisfy the Law of Impartiality which says that between two or more claimants, say for use as heading, the performance of any one should be made only on sufficient grounds, and not arbitrarily.

Rule XXXVII says if two names occur seeming to have an equal claim, the first to be chosen. This violates the Law of Impartiality. In case of joint authorship the Law of Impartiality would recommend equal right to the names of all the authors for choice as heading.

5.2.2. Rules for the Dictionary Catalogue- Cutter

5.2.2.1. Canon of Ascertainability in RDC

Rule 2 & Rule 7- Rule 2 says that anonymous books are to be entered under the name of the author whenever it is known. This goes against the Canon of Ascertainability.

Again Rule 7 says "enter pseudonymous works generally under the author's real name, when it is known..."

Canon of Ascertainability asserts that the choice and rendering of main entry and specific added entry, and the heading should be determined by the information found in the title page of the document and its overflow pages.

In the words of Ranganathan, "Many of the internal inconsistencies of existing catalogue codes are traceable to their stepping out of the title page and prel and going into the market place so to speak, in search of data for choice and rendering of headings of entries. RDC itself started this practice".

5.2.2.2. Canon of Currency in RDC

Rule 44 says use the modern name of a city and refer to it from the ancient, provided its existence has been continuous and there is no doubt as to the identity. This rule satisfies the Canon of Currency as the instruction is given here to use the modern name of a city in the headings instead of the ancient name.

5.2.2.3. Canon of Context in RDC

Cutter divided the then cataloguing as full cataloguing, medium cataloguing and short cataloguing (General Remarks). He called the catalogue that contains the detailed description of size, collection, and even peculiarities of individual leaves of the manuscripts as 'full' catalogue. He recommended the 'short' catalogue for service libraries which was readily accepted because of the great increase in the annual output of printed book. Moreover, increase in the annual accession in library become too costly to practice 'full' cataloguing.

This change in context is given weightage by the Canon of Context. Canon of Context says that rules of a catalogue code should be formulated in the context of the nature of the cataloguing features of the book, prevalent in the mode of book production. While adopting the 'short' cataloguing, it supported the Law of Parsimony also.

5.2.2.4. Law of Parsimony in RDC

Rule 230- Abbreviate certain common words always, and less common words in a long title which cannot be shortened in any other way. This rule complies with the Law of Parsimony that suggests utmost economy of manpower, money, materials and time. The provisions made in RDC (General Remarks) for 'full' 'medium' and 'short' styles in cataloguing are also contributions towards the Law of Parsimony.

5.2.2.5. Law of Impartiality in RDC

Rule 11 & Rule 8: The rule says "Enter musical works doubly, under the author of the words and under the composer of the music". Here Cutter has given equal importance to them that complies with the law of impartiality. The same is also true to Rule 8 where the author and the illustrator are given equal rights whenever preparing headings.

Rule 218 instructs that the heading for a joint author entry should be the name of the first author only. Law of Impartiality is violated here.

5.3. RANGANATHAN'S PRINCIPLES AND CANONS IN CONTEMPORARY CATALOGUING CODES

5.3.1. Principles and Canons of Cataloguing in AACR2

Dr. Ranganathan is the first person to formulate principles for the contribution of an international code. He enunciated, propounded discussed, and analyzed the normative principles of cataloguing to introduce a scientific method in cataloguing. In his book *Theory of Library Catalogue* (1938), Ranganathan published the principles under the heading 'Guiding Principles'. Later in his *Heading and Canons* (1955) he termed the 'Guiding Principles' as 'Normative Principles'.

Ranganathan did not stop just framing and publishing the principles in his books. He was active enough to present them in the international forum like *International Conference of Cataloguing Principles* (ICCP, 1961). ICCP general sessions summery of discussion says, "Dr. Ranganathan thought it important first to reach agreement on Normative Principles, such as canons of Ascertainability, of prepotence, of permanence, of sought heading, the principles of local variation and the law of parsimony." We will try to find out how AACR2 started to follow these canons from it very first edition (1978).

5.3.1.1. Canon of Ascertainability in AACR2

The canon prescribes that the choice and rendering of main entry and specific added entry, and the headings and every other element in either entry should be determined by the information found in the title page of the document and its overflow pages; in extreme cases the information may be taken from the other preliminary pages. But it is not desirable to go beyond the preliminary pages.

A clear reflection of this canon can be seen in rule 2.0B1 (Chief Source of Information) of AACR2. The rule states "The chief source of information for printed monographs is the title page, or if there is no title page, the source from within the publication that is used as substitute for it". It also prescribed the specific sources of information for each area of description. The same also suggested for other forms of publications.

Ranganathan always advocated for the principles of least range of search to solve problems. In order to enable the cataloguer to depend on title page he advocated for the standardization of title page in collaboration with the publishing and printing treads. It would have been ideal if ICCP would have first agreed on normative principles such as canon of Ascertainability, canon of prepotence, canon of permanence, canon of sought heading and other important principles propounded by Ranganathan (Guha & Prashad , 1986: 358).

5.3.1.2. Canon of Individualisation in AACR2

The name of any entity – be it a person, a geographical entity, a corporate body, a series, a document, a subject, or a language used as the heading of a catalogue entry should be made to denote one and only one entry, by adding it to the necessary and sufficient number of individualising elements.

There are so many authors who have same surnames. They are individualized by their forenames. So many cases are there where the surname and the forename both are common. Date of birth (and of death if not alive) of the authors are incorporated to distinguish among these authors so that the heading indicate one individual author only. Thus, this canon is very much important to eliminate confusion of the readers about similar named authors and save their valuable time as well as the time of the users.

If we go through the AACR2 we can find out an enormous numbers of applications of this canon throughout the code. Some of them are referred below along with their section numbers in the code:

22.15A : ... make additions to the surnames alone only when they are needed to distinguish two or more persons with the same name.

22.15C : Do not add other titles or terms associated with names entered under surname unless they are required to distinguish between two or more persons with the same name and neither dates nor fuller forms of name are available.

22.17A : Add a person's dates (birth, death etc.) in the form given below as the last element of a heading if the heading is otherwise identical to another.

22.19 B1 : If neither a fuller form of name nor dates are available to distinguish between identical headings of which the entry element is a given name, etc., devise a suitable brief term and add it in parenthesis.

23.1 : The names of geographic entities are used to distinguish between corporate bodies with the same name as additions to other corporate names and commonly, as headings for governments.

23.4B : If necessary, to distinguish between two or more places of the same name, add to each name the name of a larger place.

23.4J : If the addition of a larger place is insufficient to distinguish between two or more places with the same name, include a word or phrase commonly used to distinguish them.

Frankfurt-am-Main (Germany)
Frankfurt-an-Oder (Germany)

24.4C1 : If two or more bodies have the same name, or names so similar that they may be confused, add a word or phrase to each name as instructed in 24.4C2- 24.4C10.

24.4C2 : If a body has a character that is national, state, provincial, etc., add the name of the country, state, province, etc., in which it is located.

Republican Party (Ill.)
Republican Party (Mo.)

24.4C3 : In case of all others bodies, add the name of the local place in which the body is located or that is commonly associated with its name, unless the name of an institution, the date(s) of the body, or other designation provides better identification.

24.4C4 : In case of bodies located outside the British Isles (the United Kingdom and the Republic of Ireland), add the name of the smallest or most specific local political jurisdiction in which the body is located or that is commonly associated with its name.

24.6A : If governments with the same name are not differentiated by 23.4, make a further addition as instructed in 24.6B- 24.6D.

24.6B : Add the type of jurisdiction in English if other than a city or a town. If there is no English equivalent for the vernacular term, use the vernacular term.

Cork (Cork, Ireland)
Cork (Ireland: County)

24.6C : It the type of jurisdiction does not provide a satisfactory distinction, add an appropriate word or phrase.

Germany (Democratic Republic)
Germany (Federal Republic)

24.6D : If two or more governments lay claim to jurisdiction over the same area, add a suitable designation, to one or each of the governments, followed by inclusive years of existence.

France

France (Territory under German Occupation, 1940-44)

24.19 : Direct or Indirect Subheading: Enter an agency belonging to one or more of the types listed in 24.18 as direct subheading of the heading for the government unless the name of the agency has been, or is likely to be , used by another agency entered under the name of the same government. In that case, add between the name of the government and the name of the agency, the name of the lowest element in the hierarchy that will distinguish between the agencies.

5.3.1.3. Canon of Sought Heading in AACR2

Canon of sought heading prescribes that the choice and rendering of heading in a catalogue entry should be such that the readers and the library staff search the document under the heading used.

Rule 22.1A Suggests, choose as the basis of the heading for a person, the name by which he or she is commonly known. This may be the person's real name, pseudonym, title of nobility, nickname, or other appellation.

Caedmon

William Shakespeare

Jimmy Carter

Not James Earl Carter

22.1B Determine the name by which a person is commonly known from the chief sources of information of works by that person issued in his or her language. If the person works in a nonverbal context (e.g., a painter, a sculptor) or is not known primarily as an author, determine the name by which he or she is commonly known from reference sources issued in his or her language or country of residence or activity.

Rule 22.2A Says if a person is known by more than one name, choose the name by which the person is clearly, most commonly known.

24.1 Enter a corporate body directly under the name by which it is predominantly identified, except when the rules that follow provide for entering it under the name of a higher or related body (see 24.13) or under the name of a government.

All these are instances where Canon of Sought Heading is clearly followed in AACR2.

5.3.1.4. Canon of Consistence in AACR2

The rules of a catalogue code should provide for all the added entries of a document to be consistence with its main entry and the main entries of all documents should be consistence with one another in certain essentials, such as choice of heading. This canon ensures a great deal of uniformity in cataloguing and saves the time of the reader making him familiar easily with the consistent form of catalogue.

AACR2 is indebted to IFLA to observe this canon of cataloguing. Part-I of AACR2, description, is based on the ISBD (M) format developed by IFLA in 1974 & ISBD (G) in 1977. ISBD has prescribed the order of elements in a record, standard set of data elements and standard punctuation to be used whenever preparing a description in a catalogue.

The second part of AACR2 deals with the heading or access point of a catalogue was prepared based on the principles adapted in the ICCP 1961.

21.0B Determine the access points for the item being catalogued from the chief source of information for that item or any part of the item that is being used as substitute. Take other statements prominently stated in the item into account. Use information appearing only in the content of an item or appearing outside the item only when the statements appearing in the chief source of information are ambiguous or insufficient.

21.0C The examples, in general follow ISBD conventions (including ISBD punctuation). However, in some cases, a transcription of the data is given without those conventions and punctuation. Thus AACR2 has been following the canon of consistency since its first appearance.

5.3.1.5. Canon of Context in AACR2

Dr. Ranganathan in this canon has said that the rules and provision in a code of catalogue should also be changed from time to time to keep steps with changes in context. These contexts include:

(i) the nature of the cataloguing features of a book, prevalent in the mode of book production

(ii) the nature of the organization of libraries prevalent in regard to mode and quality of library service.

(iii) The coming into existence of published bibliographies, and particularly bibliographical periodicals.

The most interesting thing is that AACR2 has included an entire chapter (Chapter 13 Analysis) to deal with the situation mentioned in the context.

The tremendous turbulence in the universe of knowledge of today throws a heavy burden on the library profession engaged in literature search. The search has to be expeditious. To discharge this new function, the library profession has to throw a new burden on the library catalogue. Subject analytics have to be multiplied to highlight micro thought embodied in articles in periodicals and portions of books. To cope successfully with this increasing demand, AA2 (AACR2) devotes an entire chapter, chapter-13: 'analysis' to detail the various ways of creating bibliographical records that describes a part or parts of a larger item (Subhramanium, 1994: 138)

The canon of context is bound to have effect on AACR2 for obvious reasons like the change in the book production and the form of documents. In this electronic age we are making use of non-conventional types of documents. The documents in electronic forms are available. If this trend continues, the rule of AACRII have to be modified as the demand of the canon of context, with the printing of bibliographies and bibliographical data available online, the AACRII rules will need re-examination. Already in view of mechanized cataloguing AACRII has incorporated ISBD rules. Ranganathan's normative principles to have the potentiality to act as yardstick and guide in the framing of rules in the future. The AACRII has to be alert in visualizing the change in context. (Guha & Prashad, 1986: 359)

Canon of context prescribes changes in rules and provision in the cataloguing code in the changing context. In other words, it suggests revision of the code from time to time. This principle has been religiously followed by AACR2. This code has been revised in frequent intervals. Since 1978, AACR2 has been thoroughly revised at least three times with regular minor updates almost every year to meet the needs in the changing context and to adapt the changing nature of the information seeking behaviour of the users.

Major Revisions of AACR2 made since 1978 to 2005:

i. 1988

ii. 1998

iii. 2002

Besides this, almost every year after 1978 regular updates were published and AACR2 was last updated in the year 2005 to keep its relevance intact in the changing context.

Ranganathan believed that a catalogue code should not be a static document. He was of the view that the rules should be revised from time to time, keeping step with the changing context. Thus, a code should be revised to adapt to the changes in the context. This is the massage of the canon of context, expounded by him. This goes to show that he was a futurist. (Kumar, 1986: 392)

5.3.1.6. Canon of Recall Value in AACR2

Canon of Recall Value prescribes that in case of

selecting the name of a person, corporate body, series, or title of a document as entry element, words which have highest recall value should be chosen as entry element. The headings of catalogue entry should be such that the users can easily remember them. There are instances that can be cited where the application of canon of recall value can clearly be seen.

22.1A In general, choose, as the basis of the heading for as person, the name by which he or she is commonly known. This may be the person's real name, pseudonym, title of nobility, nickname, initials, or other appellation.

24.3c (chapter-24, Headings for Corporate Body) states that if a body is frequently identified by a conventional form of name in reference sources in its own language, use the conventional name.

Westminster Abbey

not Collegiate Church of St. Peter in Westminster.

24.3E states, use the conventional name of a government, unless the official name is in common use;

France

not Republique francaise.

The Canon of Recall Value has been evolved to serve as a guideline to assign such names to headings which users are likely to look for on the basis of their recall value. This canon helps the cataloguer in rendering of multi worded name of person, of an organ of government, of an institution, and of a conference and the title of a document in the heading of a catalogue entry. (Guha & Prashad, 1986: 360)

5.3.1.7. Principle of Local Variation in AACR2

AACR2 has ample provision to catalogue according to the Principle of Local Variation. It has given so many optional rules to follow according to the need and capacity of the concerned library, choice and requirements of the cataloguing agency and the users' need of the concerned library. It has even provided option about the details of description to be recorded in the catalogue. Among three prescribed levels of description, any one suitable for the cataloguing agency/ library may be chosen.

The necessity for judgment and interpretation by the cataloguer is recognised in these rules. Such judgment and interpretation may be based on the requirements of a particular catalogue or upon the use of the item being catalogued. The need for judgment is indicated in these rules by words and phrases; if appropriate, if necessary, if considered important by the cataloguing agency, and optionally. These indicate recognition of the fact that uniform legislation for all types and sizes of catalogues is neither possible nor desirable and encourages the application of individual judgment based upon specific local knowledge. (Subhramaniyan, 1994: 139)

1.0D offers a choice of three levels of description, minimum, standard and a full to match the varying types of libraries or usages of library materials of sizes of collections.

0.29 says that Rule 1.0D contains a specification of three levels of description. Each of these levels is to be considered as a minimum in that, when appropriate, further information may be added to the required set of data...

1.4G4 Optional addition. Give the place, name of manufacturer, and/ or date of manufacture if they differ from the place, name of publisher, distributor, etc., and date of publication, distribution, etc., and are found in the item and are considered important by the cataloguing agency.

1.8D. Optional addition. Terms of availability.

2.1C. Optional addition. General Material Designation.

2.4E. Optional addition. Statement of function of distributor

2.4G1. Optional addition. Give the place, name of printer, and/ or date of printing if they differ from the place, name of publisher, etc., and date of publication, etc., and are found in the item and are considered important by the cataloguing agency.

There are so many optional rules like the above one throughout the code AACR2 which are meant for application according to the nature, size of collection, and the users' need and the requirements of the cataloguing agency. This complies with the Principle of Local Variation propounded by Ranganathan.

5.3.2. Ranganathan's Principles and Canons in RDA

Application of Principles and Canons of Cataloguing was found in almost every vital part of AACR2, though nowhere it was acknowledged. The same is true to RDA also (Biswas, 2015: 963). There are so many sections where the rules are constructed following the principles and canons propounded by Dr. S. R. Ranganathan and as usual nowhere any acknowledgement can be traced.

5.3.2.1. Canon of Individualisation in RDA

Canon of Individualisation is followed throughout RDA. The preferred access points in RDA carry individualising elements like the year of birth and year of death, place of birth etc.

Rule 0.6.3 says if the preferred title for a work is the same as or similar to a title for a different work, or to a name for a person, family, or corporate body, record as many of the additional identifying elements listed below as necessary to differentiate them. Record the elements either as additions to the access point representing the work, as separate elements, or as both.

Form of work
Date of work
Place of origin of the work
Other distinguishing characteristic of the work
Medium of performance (for music)
Numeric designation (for music)
Key (for music)
Signatory to a treaty, etc.

e. Rule 0.6.3 and 10.10.1.3 says to add a date or dates associated with the family, if necessary, to distinguish one access point from another. Nguyon (Dynasty: 1558-1775)

f. Nguyon (Dynasty: 1802-1945)

10.10.1.4 Instructs to add the name of a place associated with the family, if necessary, to distinguish one access point from another

Yan (Family: Philippines)
Yan (Family: China)

10.10.1.5 says to add the name of a prominent member of the family, if necessary, to distinguish one access point from another.

Peale (Family: Peale, Charles Willson, 1741–1827)

Peale (Family: Peale, Norman Vincent, 1898–1993)

5.3.2.2. Canon of Recall Value in RDA

9.2.2.5 (Different Forms of the Same Name) : This rule says if a person is known by more than one form of the same name, choose the Preferred name for the person depending upon the fullness and language of the most commonly used names.

9.2.2.5.1 (Fullness) : If the forms of a person's name vary in fullness, choose the form most commonly found as the preferred name.

Juan Valera

Most common form: Juan Valera.

Occasional form: Juan Valera y Alcalá Galiano

9.2.2.5.2 (Language) : If a person's name has appeared in different language forms in resources associated with the person, choose the form corresponding to the language of most of the resources as the preferred name.

George Mikes
not György Mikes
Philippe Garigue
not Philip Garigue

Sixt Birck
not Xystus Betulius
Hugo Grotius
not Hugo de Groot
Philipp Melanchthon
not Philipp Schwarzerd
Friedrich Wilhelm Ritschl
not Fridericus Ritschelius

People who use terms such as 'jr.' identify themselves this way and users may look for them with the term included. In RDA, terms indicating relationship, such as 'jr.' are treated as part of the name. This complies with the Canon of Recall Value and Canon of Sought Heading.

5.3.2.3. Canon of Permanence in RDA

9.2.2.5.4 Spelling : If variant spellings of a person's name are found, and these variations are not the result of different transliterations, choose the form found in the first resource received.

This rule says to choose the form of the name found in the first resource received. This is quite at per with the rule XI of Panizzi's *91 Rules* that instruct to enter under the first name in this case.

It complies with the Canon of Permanence. AACR2 says to choose the officially changed spelling. This satisfies the Canon of Currency as well as Canon of Recall Value, where as it violates the canon of Ascertainability in regard to the earlier documents.

5.3.2.4. Canon of Context in RDA

According to this canon the nature of book changes, makeup of the title page changes, nature of readers changes, outlook of library service changes- accordingly the cataloguing practice should also change and for this purpose catalogue code too should also change in consequence with the change in the other factors. The fast changing nature of books and publications and the changes in the information seeking behavoiur of users has led the JSC to go for RDA.

RDA according to JSC is a web based cataloguing tool mainly designed for the digital world which is the need of the hour. Due to the revolution of ICT electronics documents like ebook, ejournals etc. has flooded in the libraries and information centres. These needed to be included in the metadata of the libraries. Moreover the information seeking behabviour of the users also got changed during recent times. Accordingly the catalogue of the libraries should also be changed. This according to JSC was not possible with the previous code AACR2. RDA is possibly capable to take care of all these factors now and complies with the Canon of Context.

5.3.2.5. Canon of Ascertainability in RDA

AACR2 1.1D1 says that parallel titles are to be transcribed from the chief source of information (Canon of Ascertainability).

According to RDA (2.3.3.2.) parallel titles proper may be taken from any source within the resource. This is a clear cut violation of the Canon of Ascertainability in respect to the printed documents, but may have some merit in support of the electronic documents like ebook, ejournal and web pages.

2.2.4- AACR2 1.1 A2 says to record statement of responsibility within squire brackets which is not on the chief source of information.

RDA instructs to put those records within squire brackets which are taken from outside the resource only. It is a clear violation of the Canon of Ascertainability.

5.3.2.6. Law of Impartiality in RDA

According to AACR2 21.7C1 when a compilation lacks a collective title, it is entered under the heading for the first work in the compilation.

In RDA 6.27.1.4 separate access points will be constructed for each work in the compilation, with an alternative to construct an authorized access point for the compilation using a devised title. It complies with the Law of Impartiality which recommends equal rights for each other of the claimants.

19.3.2- AACR2 21.36C6 & 21.36C7 limit added entries to the "first named party on each side" which is a clear cut violation of the Law of Impartiality.

RDA 19.3.2. does not have this limitation. Giving equal importance to each heading it has compiled with the Law of Impartiality.

In case where there is both a collective title and titles of individual works, AACR2 1.1B10 specifies that the titles of individual works should be given in a contents note. This does not go with the law of impartiality for it does not give equal importance to all the titles as headings, but in RDA, Rule 2.3.2.6 there is an optional addition to record the titles of the individual contents as titles of related works. This optional additional addition satisfies the Law of Impartiality by giving them equal importance.

AACR2 1.1F5 limits the number of people or corporate bodies which can be recorded in a single statement of responsibility (Rule of Three). RDA does not have this artificial limitation. By giving equal rights to all the authors, RDA satisfies the Law of Impartiality, which advocates for equal rights, and if any preference is made, it should be made only on sufficient grounds, not arbitrarily.

Law of Impartiality is violated by AACR2 by the process of omission of names of the authors, other than the first author in case where the responsibility is shared by more than three authors. (Rule of Three) The same has been rectified in RDA by giving equal importance to all the author or collaborators in case where the numbers of authors or collaborators are more than three.

5.3.2.7. Law of Parsimony in RDA

Law of Parsimony that prefers overall economy of man

power, money, materials and time is grossly violated in RDA. In case of use of abbreviation, RDA refuses to use even the globally accepted abbreviations like i. e. Instead, it prefers the full form. This goes against the Law of Parsimony. Besides, most of the common abbreviations like cm. for centimeter, v. for volume, p. for pages ed. for edition, ill. for illustrations etc. are used in its full form which goes against the Law of Parsimony.

RDA gives the publication date as well copy right date-this is hardly required in case of printed documents. In case of electronic documents, this may bear some merit, but otherwise it is redundant and goes against the Law of Parsimony.

5.3.2.8. Laws of Interpretation in RDA

It suggests, the rule should be amended in the light of experiences, so as to move conflicts or at least reduce them to a minimum, if they could not be totally removed. AACR2 has followed this rule since beginning as well as RDA also doing the same, the RDA final drafts has been amended several times till its publication. And after its publication several minor amendments are being made to keep it always up to date.

5.3.2.9. Principle of Local Variation in RDA

Presence of Principle of Local Variation in RDA can be seen in the following rule numbers under their headings:

0.6 Core elements. 0.6.1 General. Specific elements in RDA are identified as core elements. As a minimum, a record describing a resource should include all of the core elements that are applicable to that resource. The description should also include any additional elements that are required in a particular case to differentiate the resource from one or more other resources bearing similar identifying information.

A record describing an entity associated with a resource should include all core elements that are applicable to that entity. The record should also include any additional elements that are required in a particular case to differentiate the entity from one or more other entities with same name or title.

The inclusion of other specific elements is discretionary. The agency responsible for creating the data may establish policies and guidelines on levels of description and authority control to be applied either generally or to specific categories of resources and other entries, or it may leave decisions on the level of detail to the discretion of the individual creating the data.

0.8 Alternatives and options. RDA includes a number of guidelines and instructions that are designated either as alternatives or as options.

Alternative guidelines and instructions provide an alternative to what is specified in the immediately preceding guideline or instruction... The agency responsible for creating the data may establish policies and guidelines on the application of alternatives and options or it may leave the use of alternatives and options to the discretion of the individual creating the data.

0.10.2 Language and script. Specified elements are transcribed in the language and script in which they appear on the source of information from which the data are taken. However, allowance is made for recording the data in a transliterated form if they cannot be recorded in the script used on the source from which they are taken, or recording the data in a transliterated form in addition to the form in the original script. Other elements are generally recorded in the language and script preferred by the agency creating the data.

There are however, a number of instructions that specify the use of an English-language term (e.g., publisher not identified) or provide a controlled list of terms in English (e.g., the terms used to designate media type, carrier type, based material, etc.). Agencies creating data for use in a different language or script context may modify such instructions to reflect their own language or script preferences and replace the English-language terms specified in RDA with terms appropriate for use in their context. Authorized translations of RDA will do likewise.

0.10.4 Dates. Dates recorded in specified elements are transcribed in the form in which they appear on the source of information from which the data are taken. However, allowance is made for recording the data in the form preferred by the agency creating the data, either as a substitute for in addition to the data in the original form.

Dates appearing in certain other specified elements are also generally recorded in the form in which they appear on the source of information from which the data are taken. However, allowance is made for substituting equivalent numerals in the script preferred by the agency creating the data. Allowance is also made for adding dates in the Georgian or Julian calendar if the data on the source of information are not in that form.

0.10.5 Units of Measurement. Units of measurement recorded in specified elements are transcribed in the form in which they appear on the source of information from which the data are taken. Dimensions of carriers and containers are recorded using metric units of measurement. However, allowance is made for recording dimensions in the system of measure preferred by the agency creating the data. Playing speeds are generally recorded either in metric units (e.g., meters per second) or in terms of revolutions per minute, frames per second, etc. Playing speeds for analog tapes, however, are recorded in inches per second.

0.11 Encoding RDA Data. RDA has been designed for use with a variety of encoding schemes typically used in library applications. Appendices D and E provide mappings of RDA elements to the MARC 21 formats for bibliographic and authority data and to the Dublin Core metadata scheme.

For certain elements, the RDA instructions reference external vocabulary encoding schemes (e.g., the instructions on recording the original language of a work and those on recording the language of an expression reference the list of languages specified in ISO 639-2).

For other elements, the RDA instructions include a vocabulary encoding scheme that is internal to RDA (i.e., a controlled list of terms defined specifically for use with RDA). For those elements, data may be encoded using a substitute vocabulary encoding scheme, provided the encoding scheme is identified.

RDA thus followed Principle of Local Variation almost throughout the code for resource description and access. It has given enormous liberty to the cataloguer's judgment. Options are open to describe a resource according to the need of the cataloguing agency who decides their requirements depending upon their local knowledge.

5.4. CONCLUSION

Dr. S. R Ranganathan, who provided cataloguing theory a solid foundation by his introduction of the principles and canons of cataloguing is the first library scientist after Cutter who contributed so profusely for the development of cataloguing. Study made here shows that he delineated the principles by his tireless research from the principles followed in the famous catalogues of modern times, like that of Panizzi and Cutter. A thorough study has shown that numerous rules in Panizzi's *91 Rules* and Cutter's *RDC* comply with the normative principles designed by Ranganathan.

After the publication of the principles and canons of cataloguing, the code which followed them the maximum is AACR2. Dozens and dozens of rules have been quoted in the study here to show to what extent the principles and canons of cataloguing of Ranganathan have been followed by the Anglo-American code makers. But if they were used more effectively as the basic guidelines for the cataloguing rules, it could offer better stability to the code. Same is true to RDA also. Huge number of rules quoted and analysed here proves doubtlessly the influence of Ranganathan's principles of cataloguing on the new code developed by the Joint Steering Committee for the Development of RDA. The most significant aspect it proves that although designed and developed for the cataloguing of paper based or physical documents, the principles have passed the test of time and proved equally relevant in the digital era also. That's why RDA which is said to be designed for the online environment follows these principles to such an extent.

REFERENCES

Anglo-American Cataloguing Rules. (1988). Prepared under the direction of the Joint Steering Committee for the Revision of AACR; edited by Michael Gorman and Paul W. Winkler. 2nd. ed. 1988 revision. Chicago: American Library Association.

Anglo-American Cataloguing Rules. (2002). Prepared under the direction of the Joint Steering Committee for the Revision of AACR .- 2nd. ed., 2002 revision, 2004 update. Chicago: American Library Association.

Biswas, Subhankar. (2015). Reflections of Ranganathan's Normative Principles of Cataloging in RDA. Cataloging & Classification Quarterly. 53(8), 948-963.

Clark, John Wills. (1909). *The Care of Books*. Cambridge: Cambridge University Press.

Guha, B. & Prashad, H. N. (1986). Ranganathan's normative principles and AACR-II. In T. S. Rajagopalan (Ed.) *Ranganathan's philosophy: assessment, impact, and relivance.* (pp. 352-362) New Delhi: Vikas Publishing House.

Horner, John. (1970). *Cataloguing*. London: Association of Assistant Librarians.

Joint Steering Committee for Development of RDA (2013). RDA : Resource Description and Access. Chicago : American Library Association.

Kumar, Krishan (1986). Ranganathan's Canons of Cataloguing and Scientific Method. In T. S. Rajagopalan (Ed.) *Ranganathan's Philosophy: Assessment, Impact, and Relivance*. (pp. 383-394). New Delhi: Vikas Publishing House.

Ranganathan, S. R. (1938). *Theory of library catalogue*. Madras (India): Madras Library Association.

- (1955). *Heading and canons: comparative study of five catalogue codes.* Madras (India): S. Viswanathan.

- (1976). *Prolegomena to library classification.* 3rd ed. Bombay: Asia Publishing House.

- (1988). *Classified catalogue code: with additional rules for dictionary catalogue code.5th ed.* Bangalore: Sarada Ranganathan Endowment for Library Science.

Shera, J. H & Egan M. E. (1956) *The Classified Catalogue.* Chicago: American Library Association.

Strout, Ruth Frence (1956). Development of the Catalog and Cataloguing Codes. *Library Quarterly, 26*(4), 254-275.

Subhramanium, V.K. (1994). Dr. S.R. Ranganathan in Anglo-American Cataloguing Rules, 2nd Edition: a Survey and Observations. *Library Science, 31*(3), 135-151.

Thompson, James Westfall. (1957). *The Medieval Library.* New York: Hafner Club.

Viswanathan, C.G. (1990). *Cataloguing theory and practice.* 6th ed. New Delhi: Ess Ess Publications.

6

Comparative Study of the Revisions of AACR2 Since 1978

6.0. INTRODUCTION

The Joint Steering Committee for Revisions of AACR2 (JSC) has updated the code almost every year with a number of major revisions of the same. Here, in this study a very detailed comparison, almost line by line comparison of the rules were made among different revisions of AACR2 from 1978 to 2004 and presented in a tabular form. The aim of this study is to get a clear picture of the actual changes that have taken place in the code due to the revisions.

Almost every chapter of AACR2 witnessed some changes during the revisions more or less. Among them, three important chapters witnessed most comprehensive changes in the revisions that took place between 2001 and 2004. They were Chapter-3, (Cartographic Materials), Chapter- 9 (Machine Readable Data Files/ Computer Files/ Electronic Resources) and Chapter -12 (Serials/ Continuing Resources). My study covers all these three chapters vividly along with chapter- 1 (General Rules for Description).

Revisions of AACR2, with every minute detail of the changes in rules, in examples, in language and syntax of rules that took place during the last three decades of the revisions are compared and contrasted here and presented in a tabular form. These were analysed to find out the quantum of changes that took place along with the reasons if any, behind the changes. This was done to determine how far the changes were basic or fundamental changes and how far they were cosmetic.

Numerous revisions of AACR2 have taken place since its first publication in the year 1978. Revisions were made to accommodate the new rules or the new aspects of cataloguing among the existing rules of the code and to address the issues which were not properly attended in the previous revisions. Despite frequent revisions, JSC could not find amicable solutions to the unresolved issues of AACR2 which were much discussed as shortcomings of the code since its inception.

AACR2 could not meet up the expectations of the cataloguers to move forward with the changing needs of cataloguing. Study shows that although revisions and updating was a continuous and regular process of JSC, very few basic changes had taken place during those revisions. Changes that were made during so many revisions of the code were mostly cosmetic in nature. This made it very difficult for AACR2 to adapt with the fast changing cataloguing world. For the ease of data representation abbreviation N.P. is used for Not Present.

6.1. COMPARISON OF RULES OF CHAPTER-1 (GENERAL RULES FOR DESCRIPTION) OF AACR2

6.1.1. Table of Comparison

Year	*Rule No.*	*Headings*	*Details*
1978	1.1B1	Title Proper	Transcribe the title proper exactly as to wording, order, and spelling, but not necessarily as to punctuation and

			capitalization. Give accentuation and other diacritical marks that are present in the chief source of information.
1988	Do	Do	Do
1998	Do	Do	Do
2004	Do	Do	Transcribe the title proper exactly as to wording, order, and spelling, but not necessarily as to punctuation and capitalization. Give accentuation and other diacritical marks that are present in the chief source of information. For inaccuracies in the title proper of a serial or an integrating resource in any area except the series area, see 12.B1, (12.B1 says- Base the description of a serial on the first issue or part, lacking this on the earliest available issue or part.) **Observations:** Inadequacy of provisions in AACR2 regarding serials was addressed in 2004.
1978	N.P.	N.P.	N.P.
1988	N.P.	N.P.	Do
1998	N.P.	N.P.	Do
2004	1.1B1	Title Proper	Do not transcribe words that service as an introduction and are not intended to be part of the title. Give the title including those words in a note. **Observations:** This change did not bear much significance because the glossary of AACR2 defines title proper as "the chief name of an item..." No sensible cataloguer can treat introduction as title.
1978	N.P	N.P	N.P.
1988	1.1B1	Title Proper	If the title proper not taken from the chief source of information, give the source of the title in a note.
1998	Do	Do	Do
2004	Do	Do	Do
1978	N.P.	N.P.	N.P.
1988	1.1B10	Title Proper	If the chief source of information bears both a collective title and the title of individual works, give the collective title as the title proper and give the titles of individual in contents note.

			Observations: It's a significant development for the documents having both the collective title as well as titles for individual works
1978-2004	1.1D	Parallel Titles	No significant changes observed up to 2004. Only some changes noticed in language and syntax.
1978-2004	1.1E	Other Title Information	No changes in rule found till 2004, only some rearrangements found in case of examples.
1978	1.1F10	SOR	If an item has parallel titles but a statement or statements of responsibility in only one language or script, give the statement of responsibility after all the parallel titles or other title information.
1988	Do	Do	If an item has parallel titles but a ... other title information. If an item has parallel titles and a statement or statements of responsibility in more than one language or script, transcribe each statement after the title proper, parallel title, or other title information to which it relates. If it is not practicable to give the statements of responsibility after the titles to which they relate, transcribe the statement of responsibility in the language or script of the title proper and omit the others.
1998	Do	Do	Do
2004	Do	Do	Do
			Observations: In 1988, two section numbers, 1.1F10 & 1.1F11 merged. No significant changes observed except minor modifications in language. This merger was done to accommodate a new rule in between rule no 1.1F10 & 1.1F12.
1978	1.1F11	SOR	If an item has parallel titles and a statement or statements of responsibility in more than one language or script, give each statement after the title proper, parallel title, or other title information to which it relates. If it is not practicable to give the statements of responsibility after the titles to which they relate, give the

			statement of responsibility in the language or script of the title proper and omit the others
1988	Do	Do	If there are no parallel titles and a statement of responsibility appears in more than one language or script, transcribe the statement in the language or script of the title proper. If this criterion does not apply, transcribe the statement that appears first. Optionally, transcribe the parallel statements, each preceded by an equal sign.
1998	Do		Do
2004	Do		Do
			Observations: Rules of 1978 was shifted to earlier number in 1988 revision. And a new rule was added.
1978	1.1F14	SOR	Transcribe a statement of responsibility even if no person or body is named in that statement.
1988	Do	Do	Transcribe a statement of responsibility even if no person or body is named in that statement. A statement of responsibility may include words or phrases that are neither names, nor linking words.
1998	Do	Do	Do
2004	Do	Do	Do
			Observations: Minor addition with the existing rule was made. Actually, this was part of the next rule (1.1F15) in the 1978 edition. New arrangement is more logical than the previous one.
1978	1.1F15	SOR	Omit statements found in the chief source of information that neither constitutes other title information, nor form part of the statements of responsibility. A phrase such as "with spoken commentary by the artist" is a statement of responsibility. Statement of responsibility may include words or phrases which are neither names nor linking words.
1998	Do	Do	Omit statements found in the chief

			source of information that neither constitutes other title information nor form part of statement of responsibility.
1988	Do	Do	Do
1998	Do	Do	Do
2004	Do	Do	Do
			Observations: Later part of the rule of 1978 was shifted and added to the earlier rule (1.1F14) in 1988 revision, which is more logical.
1978	1.1G1	Items without a collective title	If in an item lacking a collective title, one work is the predominant part of the item, treat the title of that part as the title proper and name the other parts in a note.
1988	Do	Do	If in an item lacking a collective title, one work is the predominant part, treat the title of that work as the title proper and name the other work in a contents note.
1998	Do	Do	Do
2004	Do	Do	Do
			Observations: The minor parts in a work were earlier treated as general note. But 1988 revision onwards, it has been treated as contents note.
1978	1.1G2	Items without a collective title	If, in an item, lacking a collective title, no one predominates, record the title information, and statement of responsibility and a full stop followed by two sources of information, or in the order in which they appear in the item if there is no single chief source of information. Separate the titles of the parts by semicolons if the parts are all by the same person(s) or body (Bodies), even if the titles are linked by a connecting word or phrase. If the individual parts are by different persons or bodies, or in case of doubt, follow the title of each part by its parallel titles, other titles of the individually titled parts in the order in which they are named in the chief spaces.
1988	Do	Do	If in an item, lacking a collective title, no one work predominates, either

			describe the item as a unit or, optionally, in the case of cartographic materials (3.1G), sound recordings (7.1G1), computer files (9.1G1), and microforms (11.G1), make a separate description for each separately titled work, linking the separate descriptions with notes (1.7B21).
1998	Do	Do	If in an item lacking a collective title, no one work predominates, either describe the item as a unit (1.1G3) or make a separate description for each separately titled work, linking the separate descriptions with notes (1.7B21).
2004	Do	Do	Do
			Observations : The rule in 1978 was made a chaotic one with lots of unnecessary details. The same was a bit refined, but not completely done. It took 26 years to get it finally streamed lined! But there have not been many changes in the rules; mainly the language of the rule has been changed from time to time.
1978	1.1G3	Items without a collective title	Make the relationship between statements of responsibility and titles clear by additions, as instructed in 1.1F8
1988	1.1G3	Do	If describing the item as a unit, transcribe the titles of the individually titled works in the order in which they appear in the chief source of information, or if there is no single chief source of information, in the order in which they appear in the item, treating multiple sources of information as if they were one source. Separate the titles of the works by semicolons if the works are all by the same person(s) or emanate from the same body (bodies), even if the titles are linked by a connecting word or phrase. Follow the title of each work by its parallel title(s) and other title information. If the individual works by different persons or emanate from different bodies, or in case of doubt, follow the title of each work by its parallel title(s), other

			title information, and statement(s) of responsibility. Separate the groups of data with a full stop followed by two spaces.
1998	Do	Do	Do
2004	Do	Do	Do
			Observations: The rule of 1.1G2 & 1.1G3 of 1978 are recognised and rewrote in 1988 and followed in 1998 & 2004.
1978	1.2B5	Edition statement	If an edition statement appears in more than one language or script, record the statement that is in the language or script of the title proper. If this criterion does not apply, record the statement that appears first.
1988	Do	Do	If an edition statement appears in more than one language or script, record the statement that is in the language or script of the title proper. If this criterion does not apply, record the statement that appears first. Optionally, transcribe the parallel statement(s) each preceded by an equals sign.
1998	Do	Do	Do
2004	1.2B5	Do	Do
			Observations: The 1988 revision was followed till 2004.
1978	1.2C2	SOR relating to edition	In case of doubt about whether a statement of responsibility applies to editions or only to some, or if there is no edition statement, give such a statement in the title and statement of responsibility area.
1988	Do	Do	In case of doubt about whether a statement of responsibility applies to editions or only to some, or if there is no edition statement, give such a statement in the title and statement of responsibility area. When describing the first edition, give all statements of responsibility in the title and responsibility area.
1998	Do	Do	Do

2004	Do	Do	Do **Observations:** The 1988 addition to the old instructions seems superfluous because the first edition of a book is never treated from the edition point of view.
1978	N.P.	N.P.	Not Present
1988	1.2C3	SOR relating to edition	If an item has parallel edition statements that have been recorded and a statement of responsibility relating to the edition in only one language or script, give the statement of responsibility after all the parallel edition statements.
1998	Do	Do	Do
2004	Do	Do	Do **Observations:** Lapses of 1978 recovered in 1988.
1978	N.P.	N.P.	Not Present
1988	1.2C5	Do	If an item has an edition statement in only one language or script and a statement of responsibility relating to the edition in more than one language or script, give the statement of responsibility in the language or script of the title proper. If this criterion does not apply, give the statement that appears first. Optionally, transcribe the parallel statements of responsibility after the edition statement, each preceded by equals sign.
1998	Do	Do	Do
2004	Do	Do	Do **Observations**: Lapses of 1978 made up in 1988.
1978	1.2D1	Subsequent edition statement	If an item is designated as a reissue containing changes from a particular edition, give that statement following the edition statement and its statement of responsibility.
1988	Do	Statement relating to a named revision of an edition.	If an item is a revision of an edition (a named reissue of a particular edition containing changes from that edition), transcribe the statement relating to that

			revision following the edition statement and its statement of responsibility.
1988	Do	Do	Do
2004	Do	Do	Do
			Observations: Heading changed, but the rule was rewrote with additional clause- 'named revision'.
1978	N.P.	N.P.	Not Present
1988	1.2D2	Do	If the statement relating to the revision appears in more than one language or script, follow the instructions in 1.2B5
1998	Do	Do	Do
2004	Do	Do	Do
1978	N.P.	N.P.	Not Present
1988	1.2D3	Do	Do not record statements relating to a reissue of an edition that contains no changes unless the item is considered to be of particular importance to the cataloguing agency.
1998	Do	Do	Do
2004	Do	Do	Do
			Observations: Changes of 1988 hardly bears any significance.
1978	1.20E+01	SOR relating to subsequent edition statement	Record a statement of responsibility relating to one or more designated subsequent editions (but not to all subsequent edition) of a particular edition following the subsequent edition statement.
1988	Do	SOR relating to a named revision of an edition	Transcribe a statement of responsibility relating to one or more named revisions of an edition (but not to all such revisions) following the statement relating to the revision(s).
1998	Do	Do	Do
2004	Do	Do	Do
			Observations: Heading changed from 'designated subsequent editions' to 'named revision' and the terms were replaced in the rules also.
1978	N.P.	N.P.	Not Present
1988	1.20E+02	SOR relating to a named revision	If an item has parallel statements relating to revision of an edition that

		of an edition	have been recorded and a statement of responsibility relating to that revision in only one language or script, give the statement of responsibility following all the parallel statements relating to the revision.
1998	Do	Do	Do
2004	Do	Do	Do
			Observations : Addition made in 1988 for parallel statements of responsibility and followed till 2004.
1978	N.P.	N.P.	Not Present
1988	1.20E+03	Do	Optional addition: If the statement of responsibility referred to in 1.2E1 appears in more than one language or script, give each statement as instructed in 1.2c4 & 1.2c5
1998	Do	Do	Do
2004	Do	Do	Do
1978	1.4B1	Pub. dist. etc. (General rule)	This area is used to record all information about the place, name, and date of all types of publishing, distributing, releasing and issuing activities. This area, record information about the place, name and date of all types of publishing, distributing, releasing, and issuing activities.
1988	Do	Do	Do
1998	Do	Do	Do
			Observations: Nothing was said about unpublished materials.
1978	1.4B4	Do	Give names of places, persons, or bodies as they appear, omitting accompanying prepositions unless case endings would be affected.
1988	1.4B4	Do	Give names of places, persons or bodies as they appear, omitting accompanying prepositions unless case endings would be affected. Use abbreviations as instructed in Appendix-B.
1998	Do	Do	Do
2004	Do	Do	Do

			Observations: Important instruction regarding abbreviations added in 1988.
1978	1.4B5	General rules	If the publication, distribution, etc., details appear in more than one language or script, record the details that are in the language or script of the title proper. If this criterion does not apply, record the details that appear first.
1988	Do	Do	If the original publication details are covered by a label containing publication details relating to reproduction, reissue etc., give the publication details of the later publication in this area. Give the publication details of the original in a note (sec. 1.7B9) if they can be ascertained readily.
1998	Do	Do	Do
2004	Do	Do	Do
			Observations: The 1978 rule was deleted in 1988.
1978	1.4B6	Do	If the original publication details are covered by a label containing publication details relating to a reproduction, give the publication details of the reproductions this area. Give the publication details of the original in a note if they can be easily ascertained.
1988	Do	Do	If an item is known to have fictitious publications, distribution, etc., details, give them in the conventional order. Supply the real publication, distribution, etc., details as a correction if they are known.
1998	Do	Do	Do
2004	Do	Do	Do
			Observations: As the previous rule was deleted in 1988, the section number of this rule was brought one step ahead.
1978	1.4B7	Do	If an item is known to have fictitious publications, distribution, etc., details, record these in the conventional order. Supply the real publication, distribution, etc., details as a correction if these are known.

1988	N.P.	N.P.	Not Present
1998	N.P.	N.P.	Not Present
2004	N.P.	N.P.	Not Present
			Observations: This rule was moved forward in section number as one rule of 1978 was deleted.
1978	1.4B8	Do	It an item has two or more places of publication distribution etc., and / or names of publishers, distributors, etc., named in it, describe it in terms of the first named place of publication, distribution, etc., and the corresponding publisher, distributor, etc., Always add the place and name of a publisher if the first named place refers to a distributor, releasing agency, etc, If any subsequent place or name is distinguished by the layout of the source of information as being that of the principal publisher, etc., add that place and name. Follow this rule for items in more than one physical part when the place of publication, etc., and/ or the name of the publisher, etc., changes in the course of publication. If a place in the country of the cataloguing agency, with or without a corresponding publisher, etc., is named in a secondary position, add the information relating to it.
1988	N.P.	N.P.	Not Present
1998	N.P.	N.P.	Not Present
2004	N.P.	N.P.	Not Present
			Observations: This is the second deletion in this chapter.
1978	1.4C1	Place of Publication Distribution etc.,	Record the place of publication, etc., in the form and the grammatical case in which it appears.
1988	Do	Do	Transcribe a place of publication, etc., in the form and the grammatical case in which it appears. If the name of a place appears in more than one language or script, give the form in the language or script of the title proper. If this criterion does not apply,

			give th form that appears first.
1998	Do	Do	Do **Observations:** some additions were made in 1988 regarding place of publication in multiple language.
1978	1.4C3	Place of publication distribution etc.,	Add the name of the country, state, province etc., to the name of the place if it is considered necessary for identification, or if it considered necessary to distinguish the place from others of the same name. Use English form of name if there is one. Use abbreviations appearing in appendix B.
1988	Do	Do	If the name of the country, state province, etc., appears in the source of information, transcribe it after the name of place if it is considered necessary to distinguish the place from others of the same name. Supply the name of the country, state, province etc., if it does not appear in the source of information but is considered necessary for identification or distinction using the English form of name if there is one.
1998	Do	Do	Do
2004	Do	Do	Do **Observations:** Only one clause was added with this rule of 1978 in the 1988 revision. But the way it was done seems a havoc task. Language and syntax is unnecessarily complex, rather clumsy.
1978	1.4C5	Do	If a publisher, distributor, etc., has offices in more than one place and these are named in the item, always give the first named place, and the first of any subsequently named places that is in the home country of the cataloguing agency or is given prominence by the layout of the source of information. Omit all other places.
1988	Do	Do	If two or more places in which a publisher, distributor etc., has offices are named in the item, give the first named place. Give any subsequently named place that is given prominence by the layout or typography of the source of

			information. If the first named place and any place given prominence are not in the home country of the cataloguing agency, give also the first of any subsequently named places that is in the home country. Omit all other places.
1998	Do	Do	Do
2004	Do	Do	Do
			Observations: Instead of making cataloguing easier it's getting complex day by day. Here another place is asked to be added with the previous two, i.e., first place, prominent place & subsequently named place of home country. Construction of sentences is unnecessarily complex leading to huge wastage of energy, concentration and time.
1978	N.P.	N.P.	Not Present
1988	1.4C8	Place of publication distribution etc.,	Do not record a place of publication, distribution etc., for unpublished items (manuscripts, art originals, naturally occurring objects that have not been packaged for commercial distribution, unedited or unpublished films or video materials, stock shots, non processed sound recordings, unpublished computer files etc.,). Do not record a place of publication, distribution, etc., for unpublished collections (including those containing published item but not published as collections.) Do not give s. l. in either case.
1998	Do	Do	Do
2004	Do	Do	Do
			Observations: Question may arise, where does the place of publication be available for the item which is not published at all. Therefore, this rule is redundant.
1978	1.4D2	Name of publisher distributor etc.,	Give the name of a publisher, distributor, etc., in the shortest form in which it can be understood and identified internationally.
1988	Do	Do	Give the name of a publisher, distributor, etc in the shortest form in

			which it can be understood and identified internationally. If the shortest form of the name of the publisher, distributor etc., is in more than one language or script, give the form that is in the language or script of the title proper. If this criterion does not apply, give the shortest form in the language or script that appears first. Optionally, give the shortest form in each language or script. Precede each parallel statement by an equals sign. If the shortest form is same in all languages or scripts, give it once.
1998	Do	Do	Do
2004	Do	Do	Do
			Observations: Repetition of the same instruction in every section. It could be generalized in one place.
1978	1.4D4	Name of publisher distributor etc.,	If the name of the publisher, distributor, etc., appears in a recognizable form in the title and statement of responsibility area, give it in the publication, distribution, etc., area in the shortest form. If in such a case, the publisher, distributor, etc., is a person rather than a corporate body, give the initials and surname of the person.
1998	Do	Do	Do
2004	Do	Do	If an item has two or more publishers, distributors, etc., describe it in terms of the first named and the corresponding place(s). In the following cases, add subsequently named publishers distributors etc., and their corresponding places (If they are different from the place(s) already named): a) When the first and subsequently named entities are linked in a single statement b) When the first named entity is a distributor releasing agency, etc., and a publisher is named subsequently- c) When a subsequently named entity is clearly distinguished as the principal

			publisher, distributor, etc., by a layout typography d) When the subsequently named publisher, distributor, etc., is in the home country of the cataloguing agency and the first named publisher, distributor etc., is not. **Observations:** The 1978, 1988, & 1998 rule was deleted in 2004 and the subsequent rule was promoted in serial.
1978	1.4D5	Name of Publisher Distributor etc.,	If two or more agencies are named as performing the same function, always include the first named agency and add any agency given prominence by typography.
1988	Do	Do	If an item has two or more publishers, distributors, etc., describe it in terms of first named and corresponding place(s). In the following cases, add subsequently named publisher, distributors, etc., and their corresponding places (if they are different from the places(s) already named): a) When the first and subsequently named entities are linked in a single statement b) When the first named entity is a distributor releasing agency, etc., and a publisher is named subsequently- c) When a subsequently named entity is clearly distinguished as the principal publisher, distributor, etc., by a layout typography d) When the subsequently named publisher, distributor, etc., is in the home country of the cataloguing agency and the first named publisher, distributor etc., is not. Follow this rule for multipart items (sec. 1.0H2) when the publisher, etc., or the name of the publisher etc., changes in the course of publication.
1998	Do	Do	Do
2004	Do	Do	Optionally, give the name and, when appropriate, the place of a distributor when the first named entity is a

			publisher.
			Observations: Here the rule of 1978 was deleted and a new rule was introduced in 1988. In 2004 it was deleted and another rule was introduced.
1978	1.4D6	Do	If the name of the publisher distributor, etc., is unknown, give the abbreviation s.n. (sine nomine) or its equivalent in non roman scripts.
1988	Do	Do	Optionally, give the name and when appropriate, the place of a distributor when the first named entity is a publisher.
1998	Do	Do	Do
2004	Do	Do	If the name of the publisher, distributor, etc., is unknown, give s.n. (sine nominee) or its equivalent in a non roman script.
			Observations: AACR1 used 'n. pub.' in these cases, AACR2 replaced it with 's.n.'
1978	1.4D7	Name of Publisher Distributor etc.,	In case of doubt about whether a named agency is a publisher or a manufacturer, treat it as a publisher.
1988	Do	Do	If the name of the publisher, distributor, etc., is unknown, give s.n. (sine nominee) or its equivalent in a non roman script.
1998	Do	Do	Do
2004	Do	Do	In case of doubt about whether a named agency is a publisher or a manufacturer, treat it as a publisher.
1978	N.P.	N.P.	Not Present
1988	1.4D8	Do	In case of doubt about whether a named agency is a publisher or a manufacturer, treat it as publisher.
1998	Do	Do	Do
2004	Do	Do	Do not record the name of a publisher, distributor, etc., for unpublished items (e.g., manuscripts, art originals, naturally occurring objects that have not been packaged for commercial distribution, unedited or unpublished film or video materials, stock shots, non processed sound recordings, unpublished resources). Do not record the name of a publisher distributor, etc.. for unpublished collections (including those

			containing published items but not published as collections). Do not give s.n. in either case.
1978	N.P.	N.P.	Not Present
1988	1.4D9	Name of Publisher Distributor etc.,	Do not record the name of a publisher, distributor, etc., for unpublished items (e.g., manuscripts, art originals, naturally occurring objects that have not been packaged for commercial distribution, unedited or unpublished film or video materials, stock shots, non processed sound recordings, unpublished resources). Do not record the name of a publisher distributor, etc., for unpublished collections (including those containing published items but not published as collections). Do not give s.n. in either case.
1998	Do	Do	Do
2004	N.P.	N.P.	Not Present **Observations:** This rule has been promoted in serial number in 2004
1978	1.4F1	Date of pub., dist., etc.,	Give the date of publication, distribution, etc., of the edition named in the edition area. If there is no edition statement, give the date of first edition. Give dates in western style Arabic numerals. If the date found in the item is not of the Gregorian or Julian calendar, give the date as found and follow it with the year of the Gregorian or Julian calendar.
1988	1.4F1	Do	For published items, give the date of (i.e., year) of publication, distribution, etc., of the edition, revision etc., named in the edition area. If there is no edition statement, give the date of first publication of the edition to which the item belongs. Give dates in Western Style Arabic numerals. If the date found in the item is not of Gregorian of Julian calendar, give the date as found and follow it with the year(s) of Gregorian or Julian calendar. For unpublished items, see 1.4F9, for unpublished collections see 1.4F10
1998	Do	Do	Do

2004	Do	Do	Do
			Observations: Revision of 1988 seems redundant because some words added with the rule is quite unnecessary (e.g., 'for published items', if there is no edition statement ... belongs' – how can one ascertain the date of the edition in which the item belongs if no edition statement is there? Again the question of publication date does not arise in case of unpublished item.
1978	1.4F7	Date of pub., dist., etc.,	If no date of publication, distribution, etc., copy right date, or date of manufacture can be assigned to an item, give an approximate date of publication.
1988	Do	Do	If no date of publication, distribution, etc., copyright date or date of manufacture appears in an item, supply an approximate date of publication. Optionally, give an approximate date of publication if it differs significantly from the date(s) specified in 1.4F6 (i.e., date of copy right, manufacture or distribution)
1998	Do	Do	Do
2004	Do	Do	Do
			Observations: The word 'assigned' was confusing in 1978 edition. Reference of rule 1.4F6 from 1988 has increased the complexity, "the ., date of copy right, manufacture or distribution" could easily be added instead.
1978	1.4F8	Date of pub., dist., etc.,	If two or more dates are found in the various parts of a multipart item (e.g., if such item is published in parts over a number of years) give the earliest and the latest dates. In describing a multipart item that is not yet complete, give the earliest date only, and follow it with a hyphen and four spaces. Optionally, when the item is complete add the latest date.
1988	Do	Do	If two or more dates are found on the

various parts of a multipart item (e.g., when an item is published in parts over a number of years) give the earlier and later or earliest and latest dates, separated by a hyphen.

In describing a multipart item that is not yet complete, give the earliest date only, and follow it with a hyphen and four spaces.

Optionally, when the item is complete, add latest or later date.

1998	Do	Do	Do
2004	Do	Do	**Dates for serials, integrating resources and multipart items.**

If the first published issue, iteration, or part is available, give the beginning date followed by a hyphen. If the resource ceased or is complete and the last published issue, iteration, or part is available, give the ending date, preceded by a hyphen. If the first and last published issue, iterations, or parts are available, give the beginning and ending publication dates separated by a hyphen. If the publication date is the same for all issues, iterations, or parts, give only that date as the single date. For an updating loose leaf, supply the date of the last update if considered important.

If the first and /or last published issue, iteration, or part is not available, do not give the beginning and /or ending date; give information about the beginning and /or ending date in a note if it can be readily ascertained

Optionally, supply the beginning and / or ending publication date in the publication, distribution etc., area if it can be readily ascertained.

Observations: This rule in 2004 is given under new heading "Dates for serials, integrated resources and multipart items". But what is new in it? Major portion of the rule is re-written from the 1978 edition what was modified/ changed in 1988 and 1998

			edition. Newly added parts in the rule "If the publication date is the same for all issues, iterations, or parts, give only that date as the single date" bears no special significance at all.
1978	N.P.	N.P.	Not Present
1988	1.4F9	Date of pub., dist., etc.,	Do not record a date for naturally occurring objects that have not been packaged for commercial distribution. For other unpublished items (e.g., manuscripts, art originals, unedited or unpublished film or video materials, stock shots, non processed sound recordings, unpublished computer files), give the date of production (creation, inscription, manufacture, recording, etc.,).
1998	Do	Do	Do
2004	Do	Do	Do not record a date for naturally occurring object that have not been packaged for commercial distribution. For other unpublished items (e.g., manuscripts, art originals, unedited or unpublished film or video materials, stock shots, non processed sound recordings, unpublished **electronic resources**), give the date of production (creation, inscription, manufacture, recording, etc.,) . **Observations:** This rule which was introduced in 1988 used the term unpublished computer files. But in 2004 edition the term has been replaced with 'electronic resources'. This is probably done keeping in view the e-resources which have flooded the information society today.
1978	N.P.	N.P.	Not Present
1988	1.4F10	Date of pub., dist., etc.,	Give the date or inclusive dates of published collections (including those containing published items but not published as collections).
1998	Do	Do	Do
2004	Do	Do	Do
1978	1.5B1	Extent of Item	Record the number of physical units of the item being described by giving the

			number of parts in Arabic numerals and the specific material designation as detailed in the following chapters.
1988	Do	Do	Record the extent of the item by giving the number of physical units in Arabic numerals and the specific material designation as instructed in sub-rule .5B in the chapter dealing with the type of material to which the item belongs. If the units of the item are identical, add identical before the specific material designation.
1998	Do	Do	Do
2004	Do	Do	Do
			Observations: no significant changes took place only the language modified.
1978	1.5B4	Do	If the material being descried has a playing time, specify the later as detailed in the following chapters.
1988	Do	Do	If the item being described has a playing time as follows: a) If the playing time is stated on the item, give the playing time as stated b) If the playing time is not stated on the item but readily ascertainable, give it. c) Optionally, if playing time is neither stated on the item, nor readily ascertainable, give an approximate time. d) Optionally, if the parts of a multipart item have a stated uniform playing time or an approximate uniform playing time, give the playing time of each part followed by each. Otherwise give the total duration.
1998	Do	Do	Do
2004	Do	Do	Do
			Observations: The rules of 1978 was elaborated with more specifications and reorganized in 1988. Nothing new was added with much significance.
1978	N.P.	N.P.	Not Present
1988	1.5D2	Dimensions	Optionally, if the item is in a container, name the container and give its

			dimensions either after the dimensions of the item or as the only dimensions.
1998	Do	Do	Do
2004	Do	Do	Optionally, if the item is in a container, name ... of the item or as the only dimensions. Separate the dimensions by a comma.
			Observations: This was a new addition to the 1988 revision that is important for non book materials.
1978	1.5E1	Accompanying material	There are four ways of recording information about accompanying material: a) record the details of the accompanying material in a separate entry. b) record the details of the accompanying material in a multilevel description. c) record the details of the accompanying material in a note. d) record the name o accompanying at the end of physical description. Optional addition. If method (d) is applicable and further physical description is desired, add a statement of the extent, other physical details, and dimensions of the accompanying material as appropriate. Formulate such additional description in accordance with the rules for the material or type of publication. To which the accompanying material belongs.
1988	Do	Do	In 1988, point (d) was modified as below: give the number of physical units in Arabic numerals and the name of the accompanying materials and the name of the accompanying material designation) at the end of the physical description.
1998	Do	Do	Do
2004	Do	Do	Do
			Observations: Only the last point of earlier rule was modified with a new addition of the number of units accompanied. Adding the number of physical unit is more logical.

6.1.2. Overview of Chapter-1 (General Rules for Description) of AACR2

A lot of rules and sub-rules were added in 1988 revision in areas like the 'edition statement', 'parallel edition statement', 'statement relating to named revision of an edition' and 'SOR relating to a named revision of an edition'. But none of these are fundamental changes as far as the rules are concerned. These instructions were already in use in similar conditions before. Only some new cases were added here.

Sometimes, very simple modifications in rules were made in such a manner that it seemed a major change in the existing rules. For instance, in 1.4C3 only one sub-clause was added with the existing rule of 1978. That was "supply the name of the country, state, province, etc., if they do not appear in the source of information". It could be easily added with the existing rule. But the language and arrangement of the sentences were re-organised in such a manner that it seemed that a major revision had taken place there.

There is a significant addition in the rule 1.4F8 (Dates of publication and distribution etc.) under the sub-heading "Dates for serials, integrating resources and multipart items". It is significant because it was added during the 'comprehensive revision' of Chapter-12 in 2002. But after the thorough study of the rule it was found that the rule was only a rewritten version of the same rule of 1978 edition. Only the terms like 'integrating resources', 'loose-leaf' etc., was added with the kinds of documents dealt with in this chapter earlier.

Reflections of the revision and renaming of Chapter- 9 in 2001 can be seen in rules like 1.4C8 (Place of publication and distribution etc.), 1.4F9 (date of publication, distribution etc.) where the term 'computer files' was replaced by 'electronic resources'.

The comparative study among the 1978, 1988, 1998 and 2004 revisions of AACR2 shows that very few basic changes took place during the revisions. Most of the changes made were cosmetic in nature. They had nothing to do with the fundamental problems needed to be addressed during the revisions. They bear least significance to the cataloguing community. For example, changes found in most cases in the language and syntax of the rules like rule number: 1.1B2, 1.1B8, 1.1C4, 1.1D1, 1.1D3, 1.1E5, 1.1E6,1.1F2, 1.1F3, 1.1F4, 1.1F5, 1.1F8, 1.1G1, 1.4A2, 1.4B3, 1.4B6, 1.4C2, 1.4C3, 1.4C5, 1.4C7, 1.4D3, 1.4F8, 1.5B1, 1.5B3, 1.5B4, 1.5E, 1.6B2, 1.7A3, 1.8B2, 1.8D1, 1.8E1, 1.9A1, 1.10C, 1.10C1, 1.10C2, 1.11A). These revisions had hardly anything to do with the fundamental problems lies with the code.

Sometimes the changes of some common terms took place, as in rule numbers: 1.1F1, 1.1F4, 1.1F7, 1.1F10, 1.1G3 1.1G4, 1.2A2, 1.2B3, 1.2B5 1.2B6, 1.2C1, 1.2D1, 1.2E1, 1.6E1, 1.6F1, 1.6G1, 1.6H4, 1.6H5, 1.8C, 1.1B. Sometimes changes took place in section number and in the arrangement of parts within the rules (1.1E, 1.1G3, 1.4C3). Sometimes the later part of a rule is shifted and added to the preceding rule (1.1F14, 1.1F15) etc. Sometimes merger of two rules had also taken place to accommodate new rules (1.1F10, 1.1F11).

Very few deletions of out of context rules have taken place during the revisions of AACR2 from 1978 to 2004; only additions of new rules increased the size of the code. It has been found that in the 'General Rules for Description' chapter (Chapter-I) out of 60 modifications only 3 rules (1.4B5, 1.4B8, 1.4D5) were deleted during the said period. Here, in this comparative study of this chapter it has also been detected that out of these 60 (sixty) changes of rules in the selected areas of cataloguing, only 18 (eighteen) seemed to be basic changes.

There were occasions where major revisions of the rules took place like that of serials, e-resources, and in cartographic materials. In some cases changes in the examples has taken place. But that was not enough to address the problems and that too were done at the fag end of its life, in 2002 and 2004 revisions.

6.2. COMPARISON OF RULES OF CHAPTER- 3 (CARTOGRAPHIC MATERIALS) OF AACR2

6.2.1. Table of Comparison

Year	Rule No	Headings	Details
1978	1.1B1	Title Proper	Transcribe the title proper exactly as to wording, order, and spelling, but not necessarily as to punctuation and capitalization. Give accentuation and other diacritical marks that are present in the chief source of information.
1988	Do	Do	Do
1998	Do	Do	Do
2004	Do	Do	Transcribe the title proper exactly as to wording, order, and spelling, but not necessarily as to punctuation and capitalization. Give accentuation and other diacritical marks that are present in the chief source of information. For inaccuracies in the title proper of a serial or an integrating resource in any area except the series area, see 12.B1, (12.B1 says- Base the description of a serial on the first issue or part, lacking this on the earliest available issue or part.) **Observations:** Inadequacy of provisions in AACR2 regarding serials was addressed in 2004.
1978	N.P.	N.P.	Not Present
1988	N.P.	N.P.	Do
1998	N.P.	N.P.	Do
2004	1.1B1	Title Proper	Do not transcribe words that service as an introduction and are not intended to be part of the title. Give the title including those words in a note. **Observations :** This change did not bear much significance because the glossary of AACR2 defines title proper as "the chief name of an item..." No sensible cataloguer can treat introduction as title.
1978	N.P	N.P	Not Present
1988	1.1B1	Title Proper	If the title proper not taken from the

			chief source of information, give the source of the title in a note.
1998	Do	Do	Do
2004	Do	Do	Do
1978	N.P.	N.P.	Not Present
1988	1.1B10	Title Proper	If the chief source of information bears both a collective title and the title of individual works, give the collective title as the title proper and give the titles of individual in contents note.
1998	Do	Do	Do
2004	Do	Do	Do
			Observations: It's a significant development for the documents having both the collective title as well as titles for individual works
1978-2004	1.1D	Parallel Titles	No significant changes observed up to 2004. Only some changes noticed in language and syntax.
1978-2004	1.1E	Other Title Information	No changes in rule found till 2004, only some rearrangements found in case of examples.
1978	1.1F10	SOR	If an item has parallel titles but a statement or statements of responsibility in only one language or script, give the statement of responsibility after all the parallel titles or other title information.
1988	Do	Do	If an item has parallel titles but a ... other title information.
1998	Do	Do	If an item has parallel titles and a statement or statements of responsibility in more than one language or script, transcribe each statement after the title proper, parallel title, or other title information to which it relates.
2004	Do	Do	If it is not practicable to give the statements of responsibility after the titles to which they relate, transcribe the statement of responsibility in the language or script of the title proper and omit the others.
			Observations: In 1988, two section numbers, 1.1F10 & 1.1F11 merged. No significant changes observed except minor modifications in language. This

			merger was done to accommodate a new rule in between rule no 1.1F10 & 1.1F12.
1978	1.1F11	SOR	If an item has parallel titles and a statement or statements of responsibility in more than one language or script, give each statement after the title proper, parallel title, or other title information to which it relates.
1988	Do	Do	If it is not practicable to give the statements of responsibility after the titles to which they relate, give the statement of responsibility in the language or script of the title proper and omit the others
1998	Do	Do	If there are no parallel titles and a statement of responsibility appears in more than one language or script, transcribe the statement in the language or script of the title proper. If this criterion does not apply, transcribe the statement that appears first.
2004	Do	Do	Optionally, transcribe the parallel statements, each preceded by an equal sign.
			Observations: Rules of 1978 was shifted to earlier number in 1988 revision. And a new rule was added.
1978	1.1F14	SOR	Transcribe a statement of responsibility even if no person or body is named in that statement.
1988	Do	Do	Transcribe a statement of responsibility even if no person or body is named in that statement.
1998	Do	Do	A statement of responsibility may include words or phrases that are neither names, nor linking words.
2004	Do	Do	Do
			Observations: Minor addition with the existing rule was made. Actually, this was part of the next rule (1.1F15) in the 1978 edition. New arrangement is more logical than the previous one.
1978	1.1F15	SOR	Omit statements found in the chief source of information that neither constitutes other title information, nor form part of the statements of

			responsibility. A phrase such as "with spoken commentary by the artist" is a statement of responsibility. Statement of responsibility may include words or phrases which are neither names nor linking words.
1988	Do	Do	Omit statements found in the chief source of information that neither constitutes other title information nor form part of statement of responsibility.
1998	Do	Do	Do
2004	Do	Do	Do
			Observations: Later part of the rule of 1978 was shifted and added to the earlier rule (1.1F14) in 1988 revision, which is more logical.
1978	1.1G1	Items without a collective title	If in an item lacking a collective title, one work is the predominant part of the item, treat the title of that part as the title proper and name the other parts in a note.
1988	Do	Do	If in an item lacking a collective title, one work is the predominant part, treat the title of that work as the title proper and name the other work in a contents note.
1998	Do	Do	Do
2004	Do	Do	Do
			Observations: The minor parts in a work were earlier treated as general note. But 1988 revision onwards, it has been treated as contents note.
1978	1.1G2	Items without a collective title	If, in an item, lacking a collective title, no one predominates, record the title information, and statement of responsibility and a full stop followed by two sources of information, or in the order in which they appear in the item if there is no single chief source of information. Separate the titles of the parts by semicolons if the parts are all by the same person(s) or body (Bodies), even if the titles are linked by a connecting word or phrase. If the individual parts are by different persons or bodies, or in case of doubt, follow the

			title of each part by its parallel titles, other titles of the individually titled parts in the order in which they are named in the chief spaces.
1988	Do	Do	If in an item, lacking a collective title, no one work predominates, either describe the item as a unit or, optionally, in the case of cartographic materials (3.1G), sound recordings (7.1G1), computer files (9.1G1), and microforms (11.G1), make a separate description for each separately titled work, linking the separate descriptions with notes (1.7B21).
1998	Do	Do	If in an item lacking a collective title, no one work predominates, either describe the item as a unit (1.1G3) or make a separate description for each separately titled work, linking the separate descriptions with notes (1.7B21).
2004	Do	Do	Do
			Observations: The rule in 1978 was made a chaotic one with lots of unnecessary details. The same was a bit refined, but not completely done. It took 26 years to get it finally streamed lined! But there have not been many changes in the rules; mainly the language of the rule has been changed from time to time.
1978	1.1G3	Items without a collective title	Make the relationship between statements of responsibility and titles clear by additions, as instructed in 1.1F8
1988	1.1G3	Do	If describing the item as a unit, transcribe the titles of the individually titled works in the order in which they appear in the chief source of information, or if there is no single chief source of information, in the order in which they appear in the item, treating multiple sources of information as if they were one source.
1998	Do	Do	Separate the titles of the works by semicolons if the works are all by the same person(s) or emanate from the same body (bodies), even if the titles are linked by a connecting word or phrase. Follow the title of each work by its

			parallel title(s) and other title information.
2004	Do	Do	If the individual works by different persons or emanate from different bodies, or in case of doubt, follow the title of each work by its parallel title(s), other title information, and statement(s) of responsibility. Separate the groups of data with a full stop followed by two spaces. **Observations:** The rule of 1.1G2 & 1.1G3 of 1978 are recognised and rewrote in 1988 and followed in 1998 & 2004.
1978	1.2B5	Edition statement	If an edition statement appears in more than one language or script, record the statement that is in the language or script of the title proper. If this criterion does not apply, record the statement that appears first.
1988	Do	Do	If an edition statement appears in more than one language or script, record the statement that is in the language or script of the title proper. If this criterion does not apply, record the statement that appears first.
1998	Do	Do	Optionally, transcribe the parallel statement(s) each preceded by an equals sign.
2004	1.2B5	Do	Do **Observations:** The 1988 revision was followed till 2004.
1978	1.2C2	SOR relating to edition	In case of doubt about whether a statement of responsibility applies to editions or only to some, or if there is no edition statement, give such a statement in the title and statement of responsibility area.
1988	Do	Do	In case of doubt about whether a statement of responsibility applies to editions or only to some, or if there is no edition statement, give such a statement in the title and statement of responsibility area.
1998	Do	Do	When describing the first edition, give all statements of responsibility in the

			title and responsibility area.
2004	Do	Do	Do
			Observations: The 1988 addition to the old instructions seems superfluous because the first edition of a book is never treated from the edition point of view.
1978	N.P.	N.P.	Not Present
1988	1.2C3	SOR relating to edition	If an item has parallel edition statements that have been recorded and a statement of responsibility relating to the edition in only one language or script, give the statement of responsibility after all the parallel edition statements.
1998	Do	Do	Do
2004	Do	Do	Do
			Observations: Lapses of 1978 recovered in 1988.
1978	N.P.	N.P.	Not Present
1988	1.2C5	Do	If an item has an edition statement in only one language or script and a statement of responsibility relating to the edition in more than one language or script, give the statement of responsibility in the language or script of the title proper. If this criterion does not apply, give the statement that appears first.
1998	Do	Do	Optionally, transcribe the parallel statements of responsibility after the edition statement, each preceded by equals sign.
2004	Do	Do	Do
			Observations: Lapses of 1978 made up in 1988.
1978	1.2D1	Subsequent edition statement	If an item is designated as a reissue containing changes from a particular edition, give that statement following the edition statement and its statement of responsibility.
1988	Do	Statement relating to a named revision of an edition.	If an item is a revision of an edition (a named reissue of a particular edition containing changes from that edition), transcribe the statement relating to that

			revision following the edition statement and its statement of responsibility.
1998	Do	Do	Do
2004	Do	Do	Do
			Observations: Heading changed, but the rule was rewrote with additional clause- 'named revision'.
1978	N.P.	N.P.	Not Present
1988	1.2D2	Do	If the statement relating to the revision appears in more than one language or script, follow the instructions in 1.2B5
1998	Do	Do	Do
2004	Do	Do	Do
1978	N.P.	N.P.	Not Present
1988	1.2D3	Do	Do not record statements relating to a reissue of an edition that contains no changes unless the item is considered to be of particular importance to the cataloguing agency.
1998	Do	Do	Do
2004	Do	Do	Do
			Observations: Changes of 1988 hardly bears any significance.
1978	1.20E+01	SOR relating to subsequent edition statement	Record a statement of responsibility relating to one or more designated subsequent editions (but not to all subsequent edition) of a particular edition following the subsequent edition statement.
1988	Do	SOR relating to a named revision of an edition	Transcribe a statement of responsibility relating to one or more named revisions of an edition (but not to all such revisions) following the statement relating to the revision(s).
1998	Do	Do	Do
2004	Do	Do	Do
			Observations: Heading changed from 'designated subsequent editions' to 'named revision' and the terms were replaced in the rules also.
1978	N.P.	N.P.	Not Present
1988	1.20E+02	SOR relating to a named revision of an edition	If an item has parallel statements relating to revision of an edition that have been recorded and a statement of

			responsibility relating to that revision in only one language or script, give the statement of responsibility following all the parallel statements relating to the revision.
1998	Do	Do	Do
2004	Do	Do	Do
			Observations : Addition made in 1988 for parallel statements of responsibility and followed till 2004.
1978	N.P.	N.P.	Not Present
1988	1.2E3	Do	**Optional addition:** If the statement of responsibility referred to in 1.2E1 appears in more than one language or script, give each statement as instructed in 1.2c4 & 1.2c5
1998	Do	Do	Do
2004	Do	Do	Do
1978	1.4B1	Pub. dist. etc. (General rule)	This area is used to record all information about the place, name, and date of all types of publishing, distributing, releasing and issuing activities.
1988	Do	Do	This area, record information about the place, name and date of all types of publishing, distributing, releasing, and issuing activities.
1998	Do	Do	Do
2004	Do	Do	Do
			Observations: Nothing was said about unpublished materials.
1978	1.4B4	Do	Give names of places, persons, or bodies as they appear, omitting accompanying prepositions unless case endings would be affected.
1988	1.4B4	Do	Give names of places, persons or bodies as they appear, omitting accompanying prepositions unless case endings would be affected.
1998	Do	Do	Use abbreviations as instructed in Appendix-B.
2004	Do	Do	Do
			Observations: Important instruction regarding abbreviations added in 1988.

1978	1.4B5	General rules	If the publication, distribution, etc., details appear in more than one language or script, record the details that are in the language or script of the title proper. If this criterion does not apply, record the details that appear first.
1988	Do	Do	If the original publication details are covered by a label containing publication details relating to reproduction, reissue etc., give the publication details of the later publication in this area. Give the publication details of the original in a note (sec. 1.7B9) if they can be ascertained readily.
1998	Do	Do	Do
2004	Do	Do	Do
			Observations: The 1978 rule was deleted in 1988.
1978	1.4B6	Do	If the original publication details are covered by a label containing publication details relating to a reproduction, give the publication details of the reproductions this area. Give the publication details of the original in a note if they can be easily ascertained.
1988	Do	Do	If an item is known to have fictitious publications, distribution, etc., details, give them in the conventional order. Supply the real publication, distribution, etc., details as a correction if they are known.
1998	Do	Do	Do
2004	Do	Do	Do
			Observations: As the previous rule was deleted in 1988, the section number of this rule was brought one step ahead.
1978	1.4B7	Do	If an item is known to have fictitious publications, distribution, etc., details, record these in the conventional order. Supply the real publication, distribution, etc., details as a correction if these are known.
1988	N.P.	N.P.	Not Present
1998	N.P.	N.P.	Not Present

2004	N.P.	N.P.	Not Present **Observations:** This rule was moved forward in section number as one rule of 1978 was deleted.
1978	1.4B8	Do	It an item has two or more places of publication distribution etc., and / or names of publishers, distributors, etc., named in it, describe it in terms of the first named place of publication, distribution, etc., and the corresponding publisher, distributor, etc., Always add the place and name of a publisher if the first named place refers to a distributor, releasing agency, etc, If any subsequent place or name is distinguished by the layout of the source of information as being that of the principal publisher, etc., add that place and name.
1988	N.P.	N.P.	Follow this rule for items in more than one physical part when the place of publication, etc., and/ or the name of the publisher, etc., changes in the course of publication.
1998	N.P.	N.P.	If a place in the country of the cataloguing agency, with or without a corresponding publisher, etc., is named in a secondary position, add the information relating to it.
2004	N.P.	N.P.	Not Present **Observations:** This is the second deletion in this chapter.
1978	1.4C1	Place of Publication Distribution etc.,	Record the place of publication, etc., in the form and the grammatical case in which it appears.
1988	Do	Do	Transcribe a place of publication, etc., in the form and the grammatical case in which it appears.
1998	Do	Do	If the name of a place appears in more than one language or script, give the form in the language or script of the title proper. If this criterion does not apply, give the form that appears first.
2004	Do	Do	Do **Observations:** some additions were made in 1988 regarding place of publication in multiple language.

1978	1.4C3	Place of publication distribution etc.,	Add the name of the country, state, province etc., to the name of the place if it is considered necessary for identification, or if it considered necessary to distinguish the place from others of the same name. Use English form of name if there is one. Use abbreviations appearing in appendix B.
1988	Do	Do	If the name of the country, state province, etc., appears in the source of information, transcribe it after the name of place if it is considered necessary to distinguish the place from others of the same name. Supply the name of the country, state, province etc., if it does not appear in the source of information but is considered necessary for identification or distinction using the English form of name if there is one.
1998	Do	Do	Do
2004	Do	Do	Do
			Observations: Only one clause was added with this rule of 1978 in the 1988 revision. But the way it was done seems a havoc task. Language and syntax is unnecessarily complex, rather clumsy.
1978	1.4C5	Do	If a publisher, distributor, etc., has offices in more than one place and these are named in the item, always give the first named place, and the first of any subsequently named places that is in the home country of the cataloguing agency or is given prominence by the layout of the source of information. Omit all other places.
1988	Do	Do	If two or more places in which a publisher, distributor etc., has offices are named in the item, give the first named place. Give any subsequently named place that is given prominence by the layout or typography of the source of information. If the first named place and any place given prominence are not in the home country of the cataloguing agency, give also the first of any subsequently named places that is in the home country. Omit all other places.

1998	Do	Do	Do
2004	Do	Do	Do
			Observations: Instead of making cataloguing easier it's getting complex day by day. Here another place is asked to be added with the previous two, i.e., first place, prominent place & subsequently named place of home country. Construction of sentences is unnecessarily complex leading to huge wastage of energy, concentration and time.
1978	N.P.	N.P.	Not Present
1988	1.4C8	Place of publication distribution etc.,	Do not record a place of publication, distribution etc., for unpublished items (manuscripts, art originals, naturally occurring objects that have not been packaged for commercial distribution, unedited or unpublished films or video materials, stock shots, non processed sound recordings, unpublished computer files etc.,). Do not record a place of publication, distribution, etc., for unpublished collections (including those containing published item but not published as collections.) Do not give s. l. in either case.
1998	Do	Do	Do
2004	Do	Do	Do
			Observations: Question may arise, where does the place of publication be available for the item which is not published at all. Therefore, this rule is redundant.
1978	1.4D2	Name of publisher distributor etc.,	Give the name of a publisher, distributor, etc., in the shortest form in which it can be understood and identified internationally.
1988	Do	Do	Give the name of a publisher, distributor, etc in the shortest form in which it can be understood and identified internationally. If the shortest form of the name of the publisher, distributor etc., is in more than one language or script, give the form that is in the language or script of the title proper.

1998	Do	Do	If this criterion does not apply, give the shortest form in the language or script that appears first.
2004	Do	Do	Optionally, give the shortest form in each language or script. Precede each parallel statement by an equals sign. If the shortest form is same in all languages or scripts, give it once. **Observations:** Repetition of the same instruction in every section. It could be generalized in one place.
1978	1.4D4	Name of publisher distributor etc.,	If the name of the publisher, distributor, etc., appears in a recognizable form in the title and statement of responsibility area, give it in the publication, distribution, etc., area in the shortest form. If in such a case, the publisher, distributor, etc., is a person rather than a corporate body, give the initials and surname of the person.
1988	Do	Do	Do
1998	Do	Do	Do
2004	Do	Do	If an item has two or more publishers, distributors, etc., describe it in terms of the first named and the corresponding place(s). In the following cases, add subsequently named publishers distributors etc., and their corresponding places (If they are different from the place(s) already named): a) When the first and subsequently named entities are linked in a single statement b) When the first named entity is a distributor releasing agency, etc., and a publisher is named subsequently- c) When a subsequently named entity is clearly distinguished as the principal publisher, distributor, etc., by a layout typography d) When the subsequently named publisher, distributor, etc., is in the home country of the cataloguing agency and the first named publisher, distributor etc., is not.

			Observations: The 1978, 1988, & 1998 rule was deleted in 2004 and the subsequent rule was promoted in serial.
1978	1.4D5	Name of Publisher Distributor etc.,	If two or more agencies are named as performing the same function, always include the first named agency and add any agency given prominence by typography.
1988	Do	Do	If an item has two or more publishers, distributors, etc., describe it in terms of first named and corresponding place(s). In the following cases, add subsequently named publisher, distributors, etc., and their corresponding places (if they are different from the places(s) already named): a) When the first and subsequently named entities are linked in a single statement b) When the first named entity is a distributor releasing agency, etc., and a publisher is named subsequently- c) When a subsequently named entity is clearly distinguished as the principal publisher, distributor, etc., by a layout typography d) When the subsequently named publisher, distributor, etc., is in the home country of the cataloguing agency and the first named publisher, distributor etc., is not.
1998	Do	Do	Follow this rule for multipart items (sec. 1.0H2) when the publisher, etc., or the name of the publisher etc., changes in the course of publication.
2004	Do	Do	Do Optionally, give the name and, when appropriate, the place of a distributor when the first named entity is a publisher. **Observations:** Here the rule of 1978 was deleted and a new rule was introduced in 1988. In 2004 it was deleted and another rule was introduced.
1978	1.4D6	Do	If the name of the publisher distributor, etc., is unknown, give the abbreviation

			s.n. (sine nomine) or its equivalent in non roman scripts.
1988	Do	Do	Optionally, give the name and when appropriate, the place of a distributor when the first named entity is a publisher.
1998	Do	Do	Do
2004	Do	Do	If the name of the publisher, distributor, etc., is unknown, give s.n. (sine nominee) or its equivalent in a non roman script. **Observations:** AACR1 used 'n. pub.' in these cases, AACR2 replaced it with 's.n.'
1978	1.4D7	Name of Publisher Distributor etc.,	In case of doubt about whether a named agency is a publisher or a manufacturer, treat it as a publisher.
1988	Do	Do	If the name of the publisher, distributor, etc., is unknown, give s.n. (sine nominee) or its equivalent in a non roman script.
1998	Do	Do	Do
2004	Do	Do	In case of doubt about whether a named agency is a publisher or a manufacturer, treat it as a publisher.
1978	N.P.	N.P.	Not Present
1988	1 4D8	Do	In case of doubt about whether a named agency is a publisher or a manufacturer, treat it as publisher.
1998	Do	Do	Do
2004	Do	Do	Do not record the name of a publisher, distributor, etc., for unpublished items (e.g., manuscripts, art originals, naturally occurring objects that have not been packaged for commercial distribution, unedited or unpublished film or video materials, stock shots, non processed sound recordings, unpublished resources). Do not record the name of a publisher distributor, etc., for unpublished collections (including those containing published items but not published as collections). Do not give s.n. in either case.
1978	N.P.	N.P.	Not Present
1988	1.4D9	Name of Publisher Distributor etc.,	Do not record the name of a publisher, distributor, etc., for unpublished items (e.g., manuscripts, art originals.

			naturally occurring objects that have not been packaged for commercial distribution, unedited or unpublished film or video materials, stock shots, non processed sound recordings, unpublished resources). Do not record the name of a publisher distributor, etc., for unpublished collections (including those containing published items but not published as collections). Do not give s.n. in either case.
1998	Do	Do	Do
2004	N.P.	N.P.	Not Present **Observations:** This rule has been promoted in serial number in 2004
1978	1.4F1	Date of pub., dist., etc.,	Give the date of publication, distribution, etc., of the edition named in the edition area. If there is no edition statement, give the date of first edition. Give dates in western style Arabic numerals. If the date found in the item is not of the Gregorian or Julian calendar, give the date as found and follow it with the year of the Gregorian or Julian calendar.
1988	1.4F1	Do	For published items, give the date of (i.e., year) of publication, distribution, etc., of the edition, revision etc., named in the edition area. If there is no edition statement, give the date of first publication of the edition to which the item belongs. Give dates in Western Style Arabic numerals. If the date found in the item is not of Gregorian of Julian calendar, give the date as found and follow it with the year(s) of Gregorian or Julian calendar.
1998	Do	Do	For unpublished items, see 1.4F9, for unpublished collections see 1.4F10
2004	Do	Do	Do **Observations:** Revision of 1988 seems redundant because some words added with the rule is quite unnecessary (e.g., 'for published items'. if there is no edition statement ... belongs' – how can one ascertain the date of the edition in which the item belongs if no edition statement

			is there? Again the question of publication date does not arise in case of unpublished item.
1978	1.4F7	Date of pub., dist., etc.,	If no date of publication, distribution, etc., copy right date, or date of manufacture can be assigned to an item, give an approximate date of publication.
1988	Do	Do	If no date of publication, distribution, etc., copyright date or date of manufacture appears in an item, supply an approximate date of publication.
1998	Do	Do	Optionally, give an approximate date of publication if it differs significantly from the date(s) specified in 1.4F6 (i.e., date of copy right, manufacture or distribution)
2004	Do	Do	Do **Observations:** The word 'assigned' was confusing in 1978 edition. Reference of rule 1.4F6 from 1988 has increased the complexity, "the ., date of copy right, manufacture or distribution" could easily be added instead.
1978	1.4F8	Date of pub., dist., etc.,	If two or more dates are found in the various parts of a multipart item (e.g., if such item is published in parts over a number of years) give the earliest and the latest dates. In describing a multipart item that is not yet complete, give the earliest date only, and follow it with a hyphen and four spaces. Optionally, when the item is complete add the latest date.
1988	Do	Do	If two or more dates are found on the various parts of a multipart item (e.g., when an item is published in parts over a number of years) give the earlier and later or earliest and latest dates, separated by a hyphen. In describing a multipart item that is not yet complete, give the earliest date only, and follow it with a hyphen and four spaces.

			Optionally, when the item is complete, add latest or later date.
1998	Do	Do	Do
2004	Do	Do	**Dates for serials, integrating resources and multipart items.** If the first published issue, iteration, or part is available, give the beginning date followed by a hyphen. If the resource ceased or is complete and the last published issue, iteration, or part is available, give the ending date, preceded by a hyphen. If the first and last published issue, iterations, or parts are available, give the beginning and ending publication dates separated by a hyphen. If the publication date is the same for all issues, iterations, or parts, give only that date as the single date. For an updating loose leaf, supply the date of the last update if considered important. If the first and /or last published issue, iteration, or part is not available, do not give the beginning and /or ending date; give information about the beginning and /or ending date in a note if it can be readily ascertained Optionally, supply the beginning and / or ending publication date in the publication, distribution etc., area if it can be readily ascertained. **Observations:** This rule in 2004 is given under new heading "Dates for serials, integrated resources and multipart items". But what is new in it? Major portion of the rule is re-written from the 1978 edition what was modified/ changed in 1988 and 1998 edition. Newly added parts in the rule "If the publication date is the same for all issues, iterations, or parts, give only that date as the single date" bears no special significance at all.
1978	N.P.	N.P.	Not Present
1988	1.4F9	Date of pub., dist., etc.,	Do not record a date for naturally occurring objects that have not been packaged for commercial distribution.

			For o her **unpublished** items (e.g., **manuscripts, art** originals, unedited or **unpublished** film or video materials, **stock shots**, non processed sound **recordings,** unpublished computer files), **give the** date of production (creation, **inscription**, manufacture, recording, etc.,) .
1998	Do	Do	Do
2004	Do	Do	Do not record a date for naturally occurring object that have not been packaged for commercial distribution. For other unpublished items (e.g., manuscripts, art originals, unedited or unpublished film or video materials, stock shots, non processed sound recordings, unpublished **electronic resources**), give the date of production (creation, inscription, manufacture, recording, etc.,) . **Observations:** This rule which was introduced in 1988 used the term unpublished computer files. But in 2004 edition the term has been replaced with 'electronic resources'. This is probably done keeping in view the e-resources which have flooded the information society today.
1978	N.P.	N.P.	Not Present
1988	1.4F10	Date of pub., dist., etc.,	Give the date or inclusive dates of published collections (including those containing published items but not published as collections).
1998	Do	Do	Do
2004	Do	Do	Do
1978	1.5B1	Extent of Item	Record the number of physical units of the item being described by giving the number of parts in Arabic numerals and the specific material designation as detailed in the following chapters.
1988	Do	Do	Record the extent of the item by giving the number of physical units in Arabic numerals and the specific material designation as instructed in sub-rule .5B in the chapter dealing with the type of material to which the item belongs.

			If the units of the item are identical, add identical before the specific material designation.
1998	Do	Do	Do
2004	Do	Do	Do
			Observations: no significant changes took place only the language modified.
1978	1.5B4	Do	If the material being descried has a playing time, specify the later as detailed in the following chapters.
1988	Do	Do	If the item being described has a playing time as follows: a) If the playing time is stated on the item, give the playing time as stated b) If the playing time is not stated on the item but readily ascertainable, give it. c) Optionally, if playing time is neither stated on the item, nor readily ascertainable, give an approximate time. d) Optionally, if the parts of a multipart item have a stated uniform playing time or an approximate uniform playing time, give the playing time of each part followed by each. Otherwise give the total duration.
1998	Do	Do	Do
2004	Do	Do	Do
			Observations: The rules of 1978 was elaborated with more specifications and reorganized in 1988. Nothing new was added with much significance.
1978	N.P.	N.P.	Not Present
1988	1.5D2	Dimensions	Optionally, if the item is in a container, name the container and give its dimensions either after the dimensions of the item or as the only dimensions.
1998	Do	Do	Do
2004	Do	Do	Optionally, if the item is in a container, name ... of the item or as the only dimensions. Separate the dimensions by a comma.
			Observations: This was a new addition to the 1988 revision that is important

			for non book materials.
1978	1.5E1	Accompanying material	There are four ways of recording information about accompanying material: a) record the details of the accompanying material in a separate entry. b) record the details of the accompanying material in a multilevel description. c) record the details of the accompanying material in a note. d) record the name o accompanying at the end of physical description. Optional addition. If method (d) is applicable and further physical description is desired, add a statement of the extent, other physical details, and dimensions of the accompanying material as appropriate. Formulate such additional description in accordance with the rules for the material or type of publication. To which the accompanying material belongs.
1988	Do	Do	In 1988, point (d) was modified as below: give the number of physical units in Arabic numerals and the name of the accompanying materials and the name of the accompanying material designation) at the end of the physical description.
1998	Do	Do	Do
2004	Do	Do	Do **Observations**: Only the last point of earlier rule was modified with a new addition of the number of units accompanied. Adding the number of physical unit is more logical.

6.2.2. Overview of Chapter- 3 (Cartographic Materials) of AACR2

Like many other chapters of AACR2, Chapter- 3 (Cartographic Materials) was revised from time to time according to the requirements of the cataloguing world. Study shows that a lot of changes had taken place in this chapter due to the revision made by the JSC. Changes were made to address the contemporary issues in cataloguing of cartographic materials. But the effectiveness of the changes is not beyond question. For instance, along with smaller modifications of the rules in different areas, many rules were added in the publication and distribution area in 1988 revision. But most of these rules were available in Chapter-I (General Rules for Description). Therefore, instead of adding them in this chapter, they could easily be referred to Chapter-I with some more example of specific type (cartographic materials in this case) of items. Only a few revisions like addition of sub-clauses made to the rule 3.7B8 (mathematical and other cartographic data) with additional examples can be treated as effective changes. Almost no changes took place in 1998 revision, except a few minor changes in the language and examples of the rules.

'Cartographic Materials' is one of the three chapters which witnessed major changes in the revision of the code between 2001 and 2002. According to JSC three major types of changes took place in 2002 revision:

a. additional rules or additions to existing rules for the description of cartographic materials in electronic form;
b. miscellaneous changes to existing rules to bring them into line with current practice;
c. editorial changes;

The most significant among the above three is the first one. Three new rules were introduced in the 2002 revision in the 'Mathematical and other material specific details' area (formerly- Mathematical data area) to enable more accurate description of cartographic materials of electronic origin and/or that bears the features of continuing resources. But interestingly the first among the three rule 3.3E (types and extent of resource) was deleted within two years, in 2004 revision. This certainly may go against the efficiency of the judgment made by the JSC.

Moreover, although it was claimed that a major revision had taken place in the chapter 'Cartographic

Materials' in 2002 revision, reality seemed something different. Only three (one deleted in 2004 out of the three) new rules were added with the existing rules of 1988 & 1998 revisions (1998 edition was almost unchanged from that of 1988). Some minor changes in the existing rules with negligible modifications like the replacement of old terms, change of language and examples of the previous revisions failed to fulfill the need of the cataloguers and make AACR2 adjustable to the contemporary information world.

6.3. COMPARISON OF RULES OF CHAPTER- 9 (MACHINE READABLE DATA FILES/ COMPUTER FILES/ ELECTRONIC RESOURCES) OF AACR2

6.3.1. Table of Comparison

Year	Rule	Heading	Details
1978	9.0B1	Chief Source of Information	The chief source of information for a machine readable data file with an adequate internal user label. If the information required is not available from the chief source, take it from the following sources (in this order of preference): Documentation issued by the creator, etc, of the file Other published descriptions of the file Other sources (including the container of the file and its labels)
1988	Do	Do	The chief source of information for computer files is the title screen(s). If there is no title screen, take the information from other formally presented internal evidence (e.g., main menus, program statements). If the information required is not available from internal sources, take it from the following sources (in order of preference): the physical carrier or its labels information issued by publisher, creator etc., with the file (sometimes called documentation) information printed on

			the container issued by the publisher, distributor etc. In case of variation in fullness of information found in these sources, prefer the source with the most complete information. If the item being described consists of two or more separate physical parts, treat a container or its permanently affixed label that is the unifying element as the chief source of information if it furnishes a collective title and the formally presented information in, or the labels on, the parts themselves do not. If the information required is not available from chief source or the sources listed above, take it from the following sources (in this order of preference): other published descriptions of the file other sources
1998	Do	Do	The chief source of information for computer files is the title screen(s). If there is no title screen, take the information from other formally presented internal evidence (e.g., main menu, program statement, first display of information, the header to the file including 'subject' lines, information at the end of the file). In case of variation in fullness of information found in these sources, prefer the sources with the most complete information. If the computer file is unreadable without processing (e.g., compressed file, printer- formatted file), take the information from the file after it has been uncompressed, printed out, or otherwise processed for use. If the information required is not available from the chief source or the sources listed above, take it from the following sources (in this order of preference): ... The chief source of information for electronic resources is the resource itself. Take the information from formally

			presented evidence (e.g., title screen(s), main menus, program statements, initial display(s) of information, home page(s), the file header(s) including 'subject' lines, encoded metadata (e.g., TEI headers, HTML/XML meta tags), and the physical carrier or its labels, including information that has been uncompressed, printed out, or otherwise processed for use. If the information in these sources varies in degree of fullness, prefer the source that provides the most complete information. If the information requested is not available from the resource itself, take it from the following sources(in this order of preference):
2004	Do	Do	Printed or online documentation or other accompanying material (e.g., publisher's letter, 'about' file, publisher's web page about an electronic resource) Information printed on a container issued by the publisher distributor etc. If the item being described consists of two or more separate physical parts, treat a container or its permanently affixed label that is the unifying element as the chief source of information if it furnishes a collective title and the formally presented information in or the labels on, the parts themselves do not. If the information required is not available from the chief source or the sources listed above, take it from the following sources (in this order of preference): Other published descriptions of the resource Other sources (e.g., metadata records) **Observations:** Nothing had been changed since the 1988 revision except replacement of some of the terms used and modifications in language and arrangement of sentences. Too much elaboration made in the instructions overcrowded.

1978	9.0B2	Prescribed Sources of Information	The prescribed source(s) of information for each area of the description of machine readable data files is set out below. Enclose information taken from outside the prescribed source(s) in square brackets.
1988	Do	Do	Do
Do	Do	Do	Do
Do	Do	Do	Do
			Observations: Among the areas some changes are seen 'file description' of 1978 because file characteristic. This again changed to "type and extent of resource". One new addition 'container' is made in the list of prescribed sources of information in 1988.
1978-2004	9.1B1	Title Proper	**Observations:** Rule remain unchanged only examples increased from 1978-2004
1978	9.1B2	Do	Do not treat a locally assigned data set name as title proper, unless the creator, etc., of the file has assigned a data set name that is also the title of the file. If desired, record a data set name in a note.
1988	Do	Do	Always give the source of the title proper in a note. If the title has been supplied, give the source of the supplied title in a note.
1998	Do	Do	Do
2004	Do	Do	Do
			Observations: 1978 rule was modified and source of title proper was asked to include in note section in 1988. The same rule continued till 2004.
1978	9.1B3	Do	If neither the internal user label nor the documentation supplied by the creator, etc., of the file contains a title for the file, supply a brief descriptive title and enclose it in squire brackets. Indicate in a note that the title has been supplied.
1988	Do	Do	Do not record a file name or a data set name as the title proper unless it is the only name given in the chief source. If desired, give a file name or data set name not used as the title proper in a note.

1998	Do	Do	Do
2004	Do	Do	Do
			Observations: The 1978 rule was modified. It has similarity with the rule that belonged to the earlier section of 1978.
1978	9.1F1	SOR	Record statements of responsibility relating to those persons or bodies responsible for the content of the file as instructed in 1.1F. Give statements relating to those persons or bodies responsible for the preparation of the file in the machine readable form in the note area.
1988	Do	Do	Transcribe statements relating to those persons or bodies responsible for the content of the file as instructed in 1.1F. Give statements relating to sponsors, etc., or to persons or bodies who have prepared or contributed to the production of the file, in a note.
1998	Do	Do	Transcribe statements of responsibility relating to those persons or bodies credited with a major role in creating the content of the file as instructed in 1.1F. Give all other statements of responsibility in notes.
2004	Do	Do	Do
			Observations: Only jugglery of words. Nothing changed in the essence of the rules. Only the language modified with new terms/ words in last two revisions.
1978	9.1G1	Item without a collective title	If an item lacks a collective title, record the titles of the individual parts as instructed in 1.1G
1988	Do	Do	If a computer file lacks a collective title, either describe the item as a unit or make a separate description of each separately titled part.
1998	Do	Do	Do
2004	Do	Do	If an electronic resource lacks a collective title, either describe the item as a unit or make a separate description for each separately titled part.

			Observations: No changes took place except the name of the item 'computer file' has changed to 'electronic resources'
1978	9.1G2	Do	Make relationship between the statements of responsibility between and the parts of an item lacking a collective title clear by additions as instructed in 9.1F2
1988	Do	Do	In describing as a unit a computer file lacking a collective title, transcribe the titles of the individual parts as instructed in 1.1G3
1998	Do	Do	Do
2004	Do	Do	In describing as a unit an electronic resource lacking a collective title, transcribe the titles of the individual parts as instructed in 1.1G3
			Observation: only name of item changed
			Observations: Only name of the item changed from 'computer file' to 'electronic resources'.
1978	N.P	N.P	Not Present
1988	9.1G3	Items without a collective Title	Make the relationship between statements of responsibility and the parts of an item lacking a collective title and described as a unit clear by additions as instructed in 9.1F2
1998	Do	Do	Do
2004	Do	Do	Do
			Observations: New rule added in 1988 and followed till 2004.
1978	N.P.	N.P.	Not Present
1988	9.1G4	Do	Optionally, make a separate description for each separately titled part of an item lacking a collective title. For the statement of the extent in each of these descriptions, see 9.5B2. Link the separate descriptions with notes (see9.7B21). For instructions on sources of information see 9.0B
1998	Do	Do	Do
2004	Do	Do	Do
1978	9.2B1	Edition Statement	Transcribe a statement relating to an edition of a machine readable data file

			that contains differences from other editions, or that is a named reissue of that file, as instructed in 1.2B
1988	Do	Do	Transcribe a statement relating to an edition of a computer file that contains differences from other editions of that file, or to a named reissue of a file, as instructed in 1.2B. Give the source of the edition statement in a note (see9.7B7) if it is different from the source of the title proper.
2004	9.2B1	Do	Transcribe a statement relating to an edition of an of an electronic resource that contains differences from other editions of that resource, or to a named reissue of a resource, as instructed in 1.2B Give the source of the edition statement in a note if it is different from the source of the title proper. **Observation:** No basic deference took place among the rules. Only the name of the item changes.
1978	9.2B5	Do	This rule was shifted to the next number in 1988 revision
1988	Do	Do	Transcribe an edition statement appearing accompanying materials only if it also refers to the file. In case of doubt, do not record such an edition statement.
1998	Do	Do	Do
2004	Do	Do	If an item consists of multiple physical carriers, including accompanying materials, and there are multiple edition statement relating to the whole as well as parts of the resource, transcribe only the edition statement(s) relating to the whole resource in the edition area. Edition statement(s) relating to parts may be given in a note. **Observation:** New rule added here in 1988 and the 1978 rule was shifted one step down for this.
1978	9.2D1	Subsequent edition statement	If the item is a named version of a particular edition containing changes from that edition, give the subsequent

			edition statement as instructed in 1.2D Do not record statements relating to subsequent editions that contain no changes unless the item is considered to be of particular importance to the cataloguing agency.
1988	Do	Statement relating to a named revision of an edition	If the item is a named version of a particular edition containing changes from that edition, give the subsequent edition statement as instructed in 1.2D
1998	Do	Do	Do not record statements relating to subsequent editions that contain no changes unless the item is considered to be of particular importance to the cataloguing agency.
2004	Do	Do	Do **Observations**: Heading of the rule was changed in 1988.
1978	9.3	Material (or type of publication) specific details area	This is not used for machine readable data file.
1988	Do	File characteristics Area	A detailed work is done on the heading here. Two rules with 3 sub-rules were added here with detailed examples.
1998	Do	Do	Do
2004	Do	Material (or type of publication) specific details area	This area is not used for electronic resources.
			Observations: This 9.3 section was not used in 1978. In 1988 a very detailed rules and regulations were added in this section. It continued till 1998. Surprisingly it was dropped in 2004 again.
1978	9.4B	Publication production distribution etc. Area	For items with multiple places and names of publishers, producers, distributors etc., follow the instructions in 1.4B
1988	9.4B1	Publication distribution etc., area	Follow the instructions in 1.4B for items with multiple or fictitious places and names of publishers, distributors etc.,
1998	Do	Do	Record information about the place,

			name, and date of all types of publishing, distributing, etc., activities as instructed in 1.4B
2004	Do		Do
			Observations: Instructions remain unchanged, only the language and syntax varies from year to year.
1978	N.P	N.P	N.P
1988	Do	Do	Do
1998	Do	Do	Do
2004	9.4B2	Publication distribution etc., area	Consider all remote access electronic resources to be published
			Observations: New provision for electronic resources made.
1978	N.P	N.P	N.P
1988	9.4C2	Place of publication distribution, etc.,	Do not record a place of publication, distribution etc., for an unpublished computer file. Do not record s.l. in such case.
1998	Do	Do	Do
2004	Do	Do	Do
			Observations: This rule was added in 1988
1978	N.P.	N.P.	N.P.
1988	9.4D2	Name of publisher, distributor etc	Do not record the name of publisher, distributor, etc., for an unpublished computer file. Do not record s.n. in such a case.
1998	Do	Do	Do
2004	Do	Do	Do not record the name of a publisher, distributor, etc., for an unpublished electronic resource. Do not record s.n. in such a case.
			Observations: This rule was added in 1988 and the term 'computer file' was replaced with 'electronic resources in 2004.
1978	9.4F2	Date of publication, production, distribution	Give any other useful dates (e.g. dates of collection of a data and dates of supplementary files) in the note area.
1988	Do	Do	Give the date of creation of an

			unpublished computer file.
1998	Do	Do	Do
2004	Do	Do	Do
			Observations: The rule of 1978 has been shifted to the next number and one new rule inserted in between in 1988.
1978	N.P.	N.P.	Not Present
1988	9.4F3	Do	Give the useful dates (e.g. dates of collection of data) in a note.
1998	Do	Do	Do
2004	Do	Do	Do
			Observations: This rule was in 9.4F2 section no. in 1978. Shifted here in 1988.
1978	N.P.	N.P.	N.P.
1988	N.P.	N.P.	N.P.
1998	N.P.	N.P.	N.P.
2004	9.4F4	Date of publication distribution etc.	If there is no publication distribution etc., date which applies to the item as a whole, and the item has multiple copyright dates which apply to various aspects of the production (e.g. programming, sound, production, graphics, documentation) transcribe only the latest copyright date. Optionally, transcribe the other dates in a note or in a contents note.
			Observations: In absence of publication, distribution date copyright date is given like the same of the books. It could be referred to chapter -1.
1978	9.5B1	Extent of file	Record the number of files making up a machine readable data file by giving the number of parts in Arabic numerals and one of the following terms as appropriate: data file, program file, object program.
			Record the number of files... as appropriate.
1988	Do	Do	When new physical carriers are developed for which none of these terms is appropriate, give the specific name of the physical carrier as consciously as possible, preferably qualified by computer.

			If the information is readily available and if desired, indicate the specific type of physical medium. Optionally, if general material designations are used, omit computer from the specific material designation. Give a trade name or other similar specification in a note.
1998		Do	Do
2004		Do	For direct access, electronic resources, record the number of physical units of the carrier by giving the number of them in Arabic numerals and one of the following terms as appropriate: When new physical carriers are developed for which none of these terms is appropriate, give the specific name of the physical carrier as consciously as possible, preferably qualified by computer. Optionally, use a term in common usage to record the specific format of the physical carrier. Optionally give in addition to the physical carrier, an appropriate term preferably taken from subrule.5B of one of the chapters of part I if considered to be important. Give a trade name or other similar specification in a note. **Observations:** These rule revisions in 1988and 2004 are all hotchpotch. Too much detail is given in the instructions which are all very confusing. Confusion increased while supplying standard vocabulary also.
1978	9.5B2	Do	Add in parenthesis to the designation for a data file the number of logical records. Add in parentheses to the designation for a program file the number statements and the name of programming language. Do not add the number of statements to the designation of an object program.
1988	Do	Do	If the description is of a separately titled part of an item lacking a collective title

			(see 9.1G4), express the functional extent in the form on rule 2, on rule 3 of 5 disks, n 1 disk, etc.
1998	Do	Do	Do
2004	Do	Do	Do
			Observations: The 1988 revision is more logical than the previous rule as it gives better specifications for the extent of the electronic resources.
1978	9.5B3	Extent of file	Add to the designation for a multipart file the number of logical records or statements in each file.
1988	N.P	N.P	Deleted
1998	N.P.	N.P.	N.P.
2004	9.5B3	Extent of item	Optionally, record the extent of an electronic resource that is available only by remote access. Use the appropriate term preferably taken from sub-rule 5B of one of the chapters of part-I or a term in common usage.
			Observations: This rule was there in 1978 but deleted in 1988 and again reintroduced in 2004 with modifications.
1978	9.5B4	Extent of the file	Add the designation for an object program the name, number etc., of the machine in which it runs
1988	N.P.	N.P.	N.P.
1998	N.P.	N.P.	N.P.
2004	Do	Do	Give the number or approximate number of files that make up the content (use file or files preceded by an Arabic numeral) and/ or the number or approximate number of records (use records), statements (use statements), or types (give the term in either abbreviated or full form), if readily available and considered to be important. Enclose additions in parentheses.
			If such characteristics cannot given succinctly, give them in a note.
			Observations: Unnecessary details supplied made the rule clumsy.
1978	9.5C1	Other title details	Give other characteristics of the file in the note area.

1988	Do	Do	If the file is enclosed to produce sound, give 'sd'. If the file is enclosed to display in two or more colours, give col. Give details of the requirements for the production of sound or the display of colour in a note.
2004	Do	Do	If the resource is specified to have sound, or is known to produce sound, give 'sd'. If the file is encoded to display in two or more colours, give col. Give details of requirements for the production of sound or display of colour in a note. **Observations:** This section was modified in 1988 and 1998 a bit. But it was thoroughly revised in 2004. There was one sub-rule 1978. In 2004 it was increased to three.
1978-2004	9.6	Series area	**Observations:** This area remained unchanged till 2004
1978	9.7	Note area	20 rules were there in this area in 1978. The number of rules increased to 21 in 1988. One new rule 'with' note was added with the existing rules.
1988	Do	Do	Do
1998	Do	Do	Do
2004	Do	Do	The number of rules increased to 22 in 2004. Another new rule "item described" was added in 2004 revision. **Observations:** One new rule with the existing 20 rules was added in 1988. This continued with minor modifications till 2004. But strangely, the rule 9.7B15 was dropped in 1988, but the number remained vacant till 2004. Probably, it was overlooked because in other chapters it was seen that the preceding or the succeeding rule was shifted to replace the deleted rule. But in this case, there was no mention of the number even. Question might not arise if it was kept vacant. There was no mention of the number. This was probably an editorial error.

6.3.2. Overview of Chapter-9 (Machine Readable Data Files/ Computer Files/ Electronic Resources) of AACR2

The title of the chapter was assigned 'Machine readable Data Files' in 1978. It was modified and renamed in 1988 as 'Computer Files'. In 2001 revision this title was again changed and the new title for the chapter assigned was 'Electronic Resources'.

It is said that a comprehensive revision of the chapter was made in 2001 revision. No doubt the horizon was expanded very much by the change of the title from 'Computer Files' to 'Electronic Resources'. The sources of information, mainly the chief source of information had to redefine as the number and variety of documents covered had increased to a great extent. Changes in rules were made in number of cases, but they were just simple modifications, no fundamental changes could be seen. In most cases one or two clauses of the existing rules were modified and reused in the revised code. Some new examples were also added with the introduction of new kinds of documents.

The JSC claimed it to be a comprehensive revision. Revision made here were much more in number in comparison with that of other chapters or the previous revisions of the code. But whether it can be called comprehensive revision or not may be debated.

6.4. COMPARISON OF RULES OF CHAPTER- 12 (SERIALS/ CONTINUING RESOURCES) OF AACR2

6.4.1. Table of Comparison

Year	Rule	Heading	Details
1978	12.1B1	Title Proper	Record the title proper as instructed in 1.1B
1988	Do	Do	Transcribe the title proper as instructed in 1.1B. If the title proper is not taken from the chief source of information or if in a printed serial, it is taken from a title page substitute, give the source in a note.

1998	Do	Do	Do
2004	Do	Do	Transcribe the title proper as instructed in 1.1B Correct obvious typographic errors when transcribing the title proper and give the title as it appears on the resource in a note. In case of doubt about whether the spelling of a word is incorrect, transcribe the spelling as found. If the title proper includes any statement that mentions an earlier title, title absorbed etc., that may or may not be grammatically linked to the rest of the title, do not transcribe such a statement as part of the title. Do not give the mark of omission. Give relationship with other bibliographic resources in a note. For omissions from the title proper for dates, names, numbers etc., that can be expected to vary. Give the source of title proper in a note as instructed in 12.7B3. **Observations:** Most of the additions in 2004 is unnecessarily overburdened. Those instructions which are in the "General Rules for Descriptions" Chapter can be referred from here.
1978	12.1B2	Title Proper	In case of doubt about whether a corporate body's name or an abbreviation of that name is part of the title proper, treat the name as such only if it is consistently so presented in various locations in the serial (cover, caption, masthead, editorial pages etc.,) and/ or, when cataloguing retrospectively, in indexes, abstracts, or other lists. When the title appears in full and in the form of an acronym or initialism in the chief source of information, choose the full form as title proper unless the acronym or initialism is the only form of title presented in other locations in the serial.
1988	Do	Do	Do
1998	Do	Do	Do

2004	Do	Do	When the title appears in full and in the form of an acronym or initialism in the chief source of information, choose the full form as the title proper. **Observations :** New rule inserted in 12.1B2 in 1988 and continued till 2004 with slight revision. The existing rule of 1978 was shifted in the next section no. i.e., one step down in the chronology.
1978	N.P	N.P	Not Present
1988	12.1B8	Title proper	If the title proper of a serial changes, make a new description.
1998	Do	Do	Do
2004	Do	Changes in title proper	a) serials. If a major change in the title proper occurs, make a new description. If a major change occurs in the title proper on a subsequent issue or part, in general, give the later title in a note. b) Integrating resources. If any change in the title proper occurs on a subsequent iteration, change the statement of responsibility area to reflect the current iteration and in general, give the earlier title in a note. **Observations**: The two divisions were hardly needed. Section b was not needed to be given separately. The instruction can be conveyed through part a, only in general.
1978	N.P	N.P	Not Present
1988	N.P	N.P	Not Present
1998	N.P	N.P	Not Present
2004	12.1D3	Change in parallel title	a) serials. If a parallel title is added, deleted, or changed on a subsequent issue or part, make a note if the change is considered to be important. b) Integrating resources. If a parallel title is added, deleted, or changed on a subsequent iteration, change the title and statement of responsibility area to reflect the current iteration and give any earlier parallel title in a note if considered to be important.
1978	12.1.E1	Other title information	Record other title information as instructed in 1.1E. Treat the fuller form

			of an acronym or initialism that is, or is part of , the title proper s other title information if it is given in the chief source of information.
1988	Do	Do	Transcribe other title information as instructed in 1.1E When an acronym or initialism of the title and its full form appear in the chief source of information, treat the one not chosen as the title proper as other title information.
1998	Do	Do	Do
2004	Do	Do	Transcribe other title information as instructed in 1.1E if considered to be important. Always transcribe or supply other title information if it falls within one of the categories below: a) If an acronym or initialism of the title appears in the chief source of information with the full form of the title, transcribe the acronym or initialism as other title information. b) If a statement of responsibility of the name of a publisher, distributor etc., is an integral part of the other title information, transcribe it as such. c) If the title proper considers solely of the name of a corporate body, conference, etc., supply a brief addition in the language of the title proper as other title information to explain the title. Do not transcribe other title information that consists solely of words relating to the currency of the contents or the frequency of updating. If other title information has not been transcribed in the title and statement of responsibility area, give it in a note or ignore it.
1978	N.P	N.P	Not Present
1988	N.P	N.P	Not Present
1998	N.P	N.P	Not Present

2004	12.1E2	Change in other title information	a) Serials. If other title information has been recorded in the title and statement of responsibility area and that information changes on a subsequent issue or part, make a note if the change is considered to be important. b) Integrating resources. If other title information is recorded in the title and statement of responsibility area and that information changes on a subsequent iteration, change the title and statement of responsibility area to reflect the current iteration and make a note if the changes is considered to be important. **Observations:** This rule was added in 2004 where obvious redundancy is seen in the instructions. The two sections can easily be merged in one and the message can easily be conveyed in one section.
1978	12.1F3	SOR	Do not record as statement of responsibility statements relating to personal editors of serials. If a statement relating to an editor is considered necessary by the cataloguing agency, give it in a note.
1988	Do	Do	Do
1998	Do	Do	Do
2004	Do	Do (Editors)	a) Serials. Do not record as statements of responsibility statements relating to persons who are editors. If a statement relating to an editor is considered necessary by the cataloguing agency, give it in a note. b) Integrating resources. Record statements relating to persons who are editors as statements of responsibility if considered to be important. **Observations :** There was hardly any need to rewrite the rule of the previous revision, There was no need to add the heading 'Editor' as it in under the heading "statement of Responsibility". The rule related to the integrating resources can easily be referred to the chapter-1 (General Rules for Descriptions) rule 1.1F1

			Therefore, major part of the rule is redundant. The redundancy could easily be avoided.
1978	N.P	N.P	Not Present
1988	N.P	N.P	Not Present
1998	N.P	N.P	Not Present
2004	12.1F5	Change in Statements of Responsibility	a) Serials. If a person or body recorded in a statement of responsibility is added or deleted on a subsequent issue or part and this change does not require a new description, give the name of the later person or body in a note or make a note of the deletion. (see 12.7B7.2) If the change is only in the presentation of the name of the person or body, make a note if the change is considered to be important. b) Integrating resources. If the statement of responsibility is added, deleted or changed on a subsequent iteration, change the title and statement of responsibility area to reflect the current iteration and make a note if the change is considered to be important. (see 12.7B.2) **Observations:** Again the redundancy is seen in use of wards or sections. The second part of the rule could easily be merged with the first part. There would not be any deviation from the message it wanted to convey in the second part of the rule. These superfluous characteristics are abundantly seen in this chapter revision. The use of the different kinds of notation is another unusual addition. One chapter in a code numbered in a different way hampers the uniformity of the arrangement of rules and causes inconveniences in the use of rules.
1978	N.P.	N.P.	Not Present
1988	N.P	N.P	Not Present
1998	N.P	N.P	Not Present
2004	12.1G1	Items without collective title	For resources that lack a collective title see 1.1G

1978	12.2B1	Edition area	Record the edition statement as instructed in 1.2B if it belongs to one of the following types: a) local edition statement b) special interest edition statements c) special format or physical presentation statement d) language edition statements e) reprint or reissue statements indicating a reissue or revision of the serial as a whole.
1988	Do	Do	Do
1998	Do	Do	Do
2004	Do	Do	a) Serials. If an edition statement belongs to one of the types below, transcribe it as instructed in 1.2B i) local edition statement ii) special interest edition statements iii) special format or physical presentation statement iv) language edition statements v) reprint or reissue statements indicating a reissue or revision of the serial as a whole. b) Integrating resources. Transcribe an edition statement as instructed in 1.2B if considered to be important. **Observations**: Where is the necessity of making two heads?
1978	12.2B4	Do	For serials published in numerous editions see 12.7B7J
1988	Do	Do	Do
1998	Do	Do	Do
2004	N.P	N.P.	Not Present **Observations**: This rule was deleted in the 2004 revision.
1978	12.2.D1	Subsequent edition statement	Record a subsequent edition statement as instructed in 1.2D
1988	Do	Statement relating to a named revision of an edition	If the item is a named revision of an edition, transcribe the statement relating to that revision as instructed in 1.2D

			Do not record statements relating to a reissue that contains no changes unless the item is considered to be of particular importance to the cataloguing agency.
1998	Do	Do	Do
2004	Do	Do	Do
			Observations : Title of the rule or heading changed and one almost insignificant sub-clause was added in the 1988 revision and continued till 2004. A reissue is not an edition; therefore, question does not arise to record statements relating to the reissue in the edition area.
1978	12.2E1	Statement of responsibility relating to subsequent edition statement.	Record a statement of responsibility relating to one or more designated subsequent editions, but not to all subsequent editions, of a particular edition as instructed in 1.2E.
1988	Do	Statement of responsibility relating to a named revision of an edition	Transcribe a statement of responsibility relating to one or more named revisions of an edition 9 but not to all such revisions) as instructed in 1.2E and 12.1F.
1998	Do	Do	Do
2004	Do	Do	Do
			Observations: Heading changed to 'named revisions' from 'subsequent revision'. In description, instead of 'designated subsequent edition', 'named revision' has been used.
1978	12.3B1	Numeric and/ or alphabetic designation	Give the numeric and/or alphabetic designation of the first issue of a serial as given in that issue. Use standard abbreviations (see appendix B) and numerals in place of words (see appendix C). In describing a facsimile or other reprint give the numeric and/ or alphabetic designation of the original. Follow the hyphen with four spaces (see also 12.3F)
1988	Do	Do	Do
1998	Do	Do	Do

2004	Do	Do	Give the numeric and/ or alphabetic designation of the first and/ or last issue or part of a serial in the same terms, but not necessarily with the same punctuation, used in that issue or part. Use abbreviations as instructed in appendix B and numerals as instructed in appendix C. In describing a facsimile or other reprint, give the numeric and/ or alphabetic designation of the original. For serials that have ceased publication, see 12.3F. If the sequence of numbering is continued from a previous serial, give the numbering of the first issue or part of the serial presented by the new description. **Observations:** Merger of the rule 12.3B1 & 12.3B3 takes place in 2004. Regarding punctuation, standard instruction was there in 1978 which need not to be rewritten again.
1978	12.3B3	Do	If serial has changed its title, but has continued the sequence of numbering etc., used under the previous title, record the numbering etc., of the first issue under the new title
1988	Do	Do	Do Do
1998	Do	Do	Not Present
2004	N.P.	N.P.	**Observations:** In 2004 this rule was merged with the rule in 12.3B1
1978	12.3C4	Chronological designation	If the first issue of a serial is identified both by numbering etc., and a chronological designation, give the numbering etc., before chronological designation
1988	Do	Do	Do
1998	Do	Do	Do
2004	Do	Do	If the first and/ or last issue or part of a serial is identified by both a numerical and/ or alphabetic designation and a chronological designation, give the numeric and/ or alphabetic designation before the chronological designation.

			However, if the designation consists of a year and a number that is a division of the year, give the year before the number **Observations**: This rule was edited slightly. With the existing rule 'last issue' was added in 2004.
1978	12.3F	Completed serials	In describing a completed serial, give the designation of the first issue followed by the designation of the last issue.
1988	Do	Do	Do
1998	12.3F1	Do	Do
2004	Do	Ceased serials	In describing a serial that has ceased publication, give the designation of the first issue or part followed by the designation of the last issue or part. If information about the first issue or part is not available, give only the designation of the last issue or part. **Observations :** Heading changed from completed serials to ceased serials. Rest of the rule is more or less the same as before.
1978	12.3G	Successive designations	If a serial starts a new designation system without changing its title proper, give the designation of the first and last issue under the old system, followed by the designation of the first issue under the new system.
1988	12.3G1	Do	Do
1998	Do	Do	If a serial starts a new designation ... first issue under the new system. Distinguish between a serial with a common title and a section title and a serial with a new designation system indicated by new series or similar wording.
2004	Do	Change in numbering	If the numbering starts a new sequence with a different system, give the designation of the first and/ or last issue or parts under the old system, followed by the designation of the first issue or part under the new system. If a new sequence is accompanied by wording to differentiate the sequence, such as new series, include this wording.

			Distinguish such wordings from that of a section title that is to be placed after a common title. If a new sequence with the same system before is not accompanied by wordings such as new series, supply [new ser.] or another appropriate term (or its equivalent in the language of the title proper). Give a note for other variations in designations that do not constitute a new sequence if the change is considered to be important. **Observations :** Lack of precision haunts everywhere. Descriptions are overcrowded with cases instead of conditions.
1978	N.P.	N.P.	Not Present
1988	N.P.	N.P.	Not Present
1998	N.P.	N.P.	Not Present
2004	12.4C2	Change of place of publication distribution etc.	a) serial. If the place of publication, distribution etc., changes in a subsequent issue or parts, give the later place in a note if considered to be important. b) Integrating resources. If the place of publication distribution etc., changes on a subsequent iteration, change the publication distribution etc., area to refer the current iteration and give the earlier place in a note if considered to be important.
1978	N.P.	N.P.	Not Present
1988	N.P.	N.P.	Not Present
1998	N.P.	N.P.	Not Present
2004	12.4D2	Change in name of publication distribution etc.	a) Serials. If the name of publication distribution etc., changes on a subsequent issue or part and this change does not require a new description, give the later name in a note if considered to be important. b) Integrating resources. If the name of the publisher distributor etc., changes on a subsequent iteration, change the publication distribution etc., area to

			reflect the current iteration and give the earlier name in a note if considered to be important.
1978	12.4F1	Date of publication distribution etc.	Record the date of publication of the first issue as instructed in 1.4F. Follow the date with a hyphen and four spaces.
1988	Do	Do	Give the date of publication of the first issue as instructed in 1.4F. Follow the date with a hyphen and four spaces. Give the date of publication even if it coincides, wholly or in part, with the date given as the chronological coverage.
1998	Do	Do	Do
2004	Do	Beginning date of publication distribution etc.	Give the beginning date of publication, distribution, etc., as instructed in 1.4F
			Observations: Second part of the 1988 rule is taken from 12.4F2 of 1978.
1978	12.4F2	Date of publication distribution etc.	Record the date of publication even if it coincides, wholly or in part, with the date given as the chronological coverage.
1988	Do	Do	In describing a completed serial, give the dates of publication of the first issue and the last issue separated by a hyphen.
1998	Do	Do	Do
2004	Do	Ending date of publication distribution etc.,	a) Serials. In describing a serial that has ceased publication, give the date(s) of publication as instructed in 1.4F. b) In describing an integrating resource that is complete, give the date(s) of publication as instructed in 1.4F. **Observations:** The 1978 rule is merged with the previous rule in 1988. Obviously, the next rule 12.4F3 becomes 12.4F2 in 1988. But the rules of 2004 here are not very much at par with the spirit of the previous rules.
1978	12.4G2	Place of manufacture, name of manufacturer, date of manufacture	Optional addition. Give the place, name of manufacturer, and/ or date of manufacture if they are found in the serial and differ from the place, name of publisher, etc., and date of publication, etc., and are considered important by the cataloguing agency.

1988	Do	Do	Do
1998	Do	Do	Do
2004	Do	Change in place and/ or name of manufacturer	a) Serials. If the place and/ or name of the manufacturer changes on a subsequent issue or part and the name of the publisher continues to be unknown, give the later place and/ or name of the manufacturer in a note if considered to be important. b) Integrating resources. If the place and/ or name of the manufacturer changes on a subsequent iteration and the name of the publisher continues to be unknown, change the publication, distribution etc., area to reflect the current iteration and give the earlier place and/ or name of the manufacturer in a note if considered to be important. **Observations :** The rules in 2004 were new addition. The existing rule in this section number was demoted a step to accommodate the rule here. The subheading is not at par with the arrangement of rules here.
1978	N.P.	N.P.	Not Present
1988	N.P.	N.P.	Not Present
1998	N.P.	N.P.	Not Present
2004	12.4G3	Place of manufacturer, name of manufacturer, date of manufacture	Optional addition. Give the place, name of manufacturer, and/ or date of manufacture if they are found in the resource and differ from the place, name of publisher, etc., and date of publication, etc., and are considered important by the cataloguing agency. Make a note of changes as instructed in 12.4G2 if the place and/ or name of the manufacturer changes on a subsequent issue, part, or iteration. **Observations :** The rule of 12.4G2 (1978) had been shifted to 12.4G3 in 2004 with little modifications.
1978	12.5B1	Extent of item (including specific material designation)	For a serial that is still in progress, give the relevant specific material designation (taken from rule 5B in the chapter dealing with the type of material to which the serial belongs, e.g., 11.5B

			for microform serials) preceded by three spaces. In the case of printed serials, the specific material designation is 'v'.
1988	Do	Do	For a serial that is still in progress... the specific material designation is 'v', 'no', or 'pt'.
1998	Do	Do	Do
2004	Do	Do	For a resource that is still in progress give the relevant specific material designation (taken from sub rule 5B in the chapter dealing with the type of material to which the resource belongs, e.g., 11.5B for microform resources). For printed resources, use the specific material designation 'v' for updating loose-leafs, add the qualifier (loose-leaf).
			Observations: The rule of 1978 was adopted in 1988 with minor modifications and in 2004 'loose-leaf' was added.
1978	N.P.	N.P.	Not Present
1988	12.5B3	Extent of item (including specific material designation)	If a serial consists of or contains, Braille or another tactile system, make additions to the statement of extent as indicated in the sub-rule 5B in the chapter dealing with the type of material to which the serial belongs.
1998	Do	Do	Do
2004	Do	Do	If a resource consists of or contains, Braille or another tactile system, make additions to the statement of extent as indicated in the sub-rule 5B in the chapter dealing with the type of material to which the resource belongs.
			Observations : The rule added in 1988 was continued till 2004. But in 2004 instead of 'serial' 'resource' is used.
1978	N.P.	N.P.	Not Present
1988	N.P.	N.P.	Not Present
1998	N.P.	N.P.	Not Present
2004	12.5C2	Change in other physical details	a) Serials. If other physical details are added on a subsequent issue or part, change the physical description area to reflect all the issues or part as instructed in 12.5c1. If other physical details are

			omitted or changed on a subsequent issue or part, make a note if the change is considered to be important. b) Integrating resources. If the other physical details are added, omitted, or changed on a subsequent iteration, change the physical description area to reflect the current iteration and make a note if the change considered to be important. **Observations:** Redundancy in the use of rules is quite obvious. Both the points could easily be merged into one.
1978	N.P.	N.P.	Not Present
1988	N.P.	N.P.	Not Present
1998	N.P.	N.P.	Not Present
2004	12.5D2	Change in dimensions	If dimensions of a resource change, or multiple parts differ in size, give the dimensions from the smallest or smaller to largest or larger separated by a hyphen unless otherwise instructed in sub-rule 5D in the chapter dealing with the type of material to which the resource belongs
1978	12.5E1	Accompanying material	Record the name, and optionally the physical description of any material that is intended to be issued regularly and is intended to be used in conjunction with the serial, as instructed in 1.5E. Give a note on the frequency, etc., of accompanying material. If accompanying material is issued irregularly or issued once, describe it in a note or ignore it.
1988	Do	Do	Give as instructed in 1.5E, the details of accompanying material that is intended to be issued regularly. If using 1.5E1d and if the serial is still in progress, give the name of the accompanying material preceded by three spaces. Make a note on the frequency of accompanying material. If accompanying material is issued irregularly or issued only once. describe it in a note or ignore it.
1998	Do	Do	Do

2004	Do	Do	Give details of accompanying material in one of the following ways: a) Make a separate entry b) make a multilevel description or c) make a note d) give the number of physical units in Arabic numerals and the name of the accompanying materials at the end of physical description. Optional addition. If method d) is used and if more detail is desired, give the physical description of accompanying material as instructed in the following chapters. **Observations:** Although it seems that many changes happened in 2004 revision, in reality very insignificant changes had taken place during the revisions of the rules.
1978	N.P.	N.P.	Not Present
1988	N.P.	N.P.	Not Present
1998	N.P.	N.P.	Not Present
2004	12.6B2	Change in series statement	a) Serials. If a series is added, deleted, or changed on a subsequent issue or part and this change cannot be stated clearly in this series area, make a note if the change is considered to be important. b) Integrating resources. If a series is added, deleted, or changed on a subsequent iteration change the series area to reflect the current iteration and make a note if the change is considered to be important. **Observations:** Theses two rules could easily be merged into one. Moreover, this instruction is hardly needed because those things which cannot be analysed by the defined rules are always noted in the note area of catalogue.
1978-2004	12.7	Note area	**Observations:** Minor changes took place in this area which is very insignificant. Although some extra rules were added in 2004 like 'change in title proper', 'change in statement of responsibility', 'change in edition information', 'change in numbering', 'change in publication distribution etc.,'

'change in series' etc. These are all useless redundancy. Almost all these peculiarities were included in the previous rules. There were provisions for these rules in the previous revisions of the code, although not explicitly stated like that of 2004 revision. Another thing which seems very inappropriate is the separate rules for integrating resources. It was not needed at all. It is a superfluous addition in 2004 revision which in most cases only increased the bulk of the code.

6.4.2. Overview of Chapter -12 (Serials/ Continuing Resources) of AACR2

This chapter of AACR2 was named as 'Serials' at the very first edition of AACR2 in 1978. In 2002 this title was changed to 'Continuing Resources'. This was done to include the resources that had never been covered in the rules adequately. Those included updating websites, updating loose leafs etc.

The rules were expanded to include separate provisions for continuing printed resources, updating electronic resources and updating loose leafs. The comparative study among different revisions of the code shows that most of the changes that took place due to the revision were superfluous. Those rules which were part of 'General Rules for Description' chapter were in most cases included in this chapter in the 2002 revision. For instances, inaccuracies in title, be it typographical error or error in spelling etc., could easily be referred to Chapter 'General Rules for Description'.

Another instance of redundancy was found in this revision. New rules were incorporated in this revision for each of the following changes- changes in title proper, in parallel title, in other title information, in statement of responsibility, in place of publication and distribution, in name of publisher and distributor etc., in place and/or name of manufacturer, in other physical details, in series statement. Specific rules were provided for the said changes in the concerned areas of the code. But the instructions given in each of these rules were almost the same, i.e., repetition of the same instructions everywhere. All these rules could easily be incorporated in one single general instruction given at the beginning of the chapter to avoid redundancy.

Let us quote one rule from the code here to see yet another superfluous treatment of the same kind. Rule 12.2B1 (edition area) instructed to follow 1.2B (1978). This rule was introduced in a different way in 2004- two sub-rules were made under two subheadings like this:

(a) Serials : If an edition statement belongs to one of the types below, transcribe it as instructed in 1.2B.

(b) Integrating resources : Transcribe an edition statement as instructed in 1.2B if considered to be important.

This could easily be written in one instruction. More precision was also possible with little revision of the language here. Therefore, two separate headings were not necessary at all. There were so many instances of the same which marred the flavour of the comprehensive revision of the chapter.

Moreover, the two subdivisions in the rules, a) serials and b) Integrating resources were hardly needed in most of the cases. As the title of the chapter was changed from 'Serials' to 'Continuing Resources' it was implied that all the rules were meant for both types of resources. It has also been found that almost all the rules noted under 'integrating resources' are the repetition of the same rules noted under the subheading 'serials'. Therefore, both of them could easily be merged and made one compact rule.

The use of the word 'resources' instead of 'serials' unlike the earlier revisions might be another strong logic in support of this argument. By using the term 'resources' the documents, both physical and electronic were generalized here and the scope and coverage of the rules were increased many folds at one stroke. The uncontrolled use of the rules and sub-rules under two different categories (serials and integrating resources), and the lack of precision in the use of language spoiled the cataloguers' long expectations of incorporating the integrating resources like the loose leafs and websites in the cataloguing purview of AACR2.

6.5. CONCLUSION

Revisions had been made throughout the whole life span of AACR2. It has been updated almost every year, with a number of thorough revisions; but in most cases the revisions remains confined within the cosmetic changes. The language, syntax, arrangements of rules, sequences or preferences of rules and examples, all have been modified frequently. Segregation or merger of more than one rule has also taken place in a lot of cases. But the burning issues containing the basic concepts mentioned below have hardly been addressed in time.

Some of the most discussed issues like 'main entry', 'content verses carrier', 'rule of three', 'unpublished items' etc. are much discussed almost since the introduction of AACR2 in 1978. In due course of time, problems like dealing with serials and electronic documents appeared as major difficulties to catalogue properly with AACR2. Rules have been modified to address these problems, new rules added, sometimes old and out of context rules deleted (although very few in numbers), new and contemporary examples introduced, but the fundamental changes in the concepts and their reflections in the newly added rules were not found resulting to the dissatisfaction of the cataloguers.

REFERENCES

Anglo-American Cataloging Rules. (1967). Prepared by the American Library Association the Library of Congress, the Library Association, and the Canadian Library Association. British Text. General editor C. Sumner Spalding. London: The Library Association.

Anglo-American Cataloguing Rules. (1978). Prepared by the American Library Association, the British Library, the Canadian Committee on Cataloguing, the Library Association and the

Library of Congress; edited by Michael Gorman and Paul W. Winkler. 2nd. ed. Chicago: American Library Association.

Anglo-American Cataloguing Rules. (1988). Prepared under the direction of the Joint Steering Committee for the Revision of AACR; edited by Michael Gorman and Paul W. Winkler. 2nd. ed. 1988 revision. Chicago: American Library Association.

Anglo-American Cataloguing Rules. (1998). Prepared under the direction of the Joint Steering Committee for the Revision of AACR. 2nd. ed. 1998 revision. Chicago: American Library Association.

Anglo-American Cataloguing Rules. (2002). Prepared under the direction of the Joint Steering Committee for the Revision of AACR .- 2nd. ed., 2002 revision, 2004 update. Chicago: American Library Association.

7

Rules of AACR2 and RDA

7.0. INTRODUCTION

This chapter deals with a comparative study in detail between AACR2 and RDA. The principles and objectives of AACR2 as well as that of RDA along with the basic structures of both the codes are compared here. Comparison and analysis of different rules that are changed in RDA in respect to the rules of AACR2 is made in detail here to establish the differences between the rules of AACR2 and RDA.

RDA is a new cataloguing code designed on the entity relationship concept of FRBR model devised by IFLA. It's a departure from its predecessor, AACR2. RDA is a principle-based cataloguing code designed for the online environment. Significant changes are made in the new code in respect to the rules of AACR2. Major changes have taken place in the conceptual foundation of the code, along with numerous changes in the rules for description and access points in different areas of cataloguing. This changes are made to resolve the long pending unresolved issues of AACR2 like the 'content versus carrier', 'rule of three' problems with 'seriality' etc.

Rule 0.24 of AACR2 says, "It is a cardinal principle of the use of part I that the description of a physical item should be based in the first instance of the chapter dealing with the class of materials to which that item belongs... In short, the starting point for the description is the physical form of the item in hand, not the original or any previous form in which the work has been published" (AACR2, 1987: 8). Obviously, cataloguing done following AACR2 is based on the carrier rather than the intellectual or the artistic content of the work.

In RDA cataloguing is done according to the FRBR concept which treats a book/ document/ resource as an 'item' that is a single representation of a 'distinct intellectual or artistic creation' i.e., 'work'. In RDA the 'entity relationship' concept of FRBR ('work', 'expression', 'manifestation' and 'item') ensures the consideration of the work in case of giving description. Thus the long discussed issue of AACR2 'content versus carrier' has been resolved in RDA.

Absence of explicit principles and objectives was a serious lapse in AACR2. The cataloguers hardly have any other alternative but to follow the AACR2 rules without knowing why they are doing so. Unlike the codes of Cutter and Ranganathan, it bears no clearly stated principles & objectives which makes it more a rule book, rather than a cataloguing code.

RDA has introduced explicit principles and objectives of cataloguing at the beginning of the code. This is to facilitate the "cataloguer's judgment" during practical cataloguing. RDA has resolved the issues of 'rule of three' by keeping provision of recording more than three persons or bodies in the statement of responsibility area. Thus the long debated issues of AACR2 have been taken care of in the new code. A comparative study of the rules between the two codes is made in a tabular form below:

7.1. TABLE OF COMPARISON

7.1.1. Descriptions

Heading	AACR2	RDA
Inaccuracies	AACR2 1.0F1...transcribe an inaccuracy or a misspelled word as it appears in the item. Follow such an inaccuracy either by [sic] or i.e. and the correction within square brackets. Supply a missing letter or letters in square brackets.	In RDA 1.7.9 When instructed to transcribe an element as it appears on the source of information, transcribe an inaccuracy or a misspelled word as it appears on the source, except where instructed otherwise.
	The wolrd [sic] of television *The Paul Anthony Buck [i.e. Brick] lectures*	Make a note correcting the inaccuracy if it is considered to be important for identification or access.
	Observations: It's more logical to point out the inaccuracy immediately followed by [sic] as AACR2. The provision of RDA in this regard is unnecessary lengthy.	If the inaccuracy appears in a title, record a corrected form of the title as a variant title if it is considered to be important for identification or access.
	If a word is misspelled in the title, there is ample chance for the users to get misled, because unless the word is a proper noun people will search the document with the correct spelling. Moreover, Average users hardly go through the note section.	*The wolrd of television* *The Paul Anthony Buck lectures*
Title Proper	AACR2 1.1B1. If the title proper as given in the chief source of information includes the punctuation marks ... or [ ], replace them by – and ( ), respectively. **Observations:** This rule has been modified in RDA, but the language is too clumsy to understand.	RDA 1.7.3. Transcribe punctuation as it appears on the source, omitting punctuation on the source that separates data to be recorded as one element from data to be recorded as a different element, or as a second or subsequent instance of an element.
Do	AACR2 1.1B10 If the chief source of information bears both a collective title and the	RDA 2.3.2.10 When preparing a comprehensive description for a resource that has a source of

	titles of individual works, give the collective title as the title proper and give the titles of the individual works in a contents note.	information for the title proper bearing both a collective title and the titles of individual contents within the resource, record the collective title as the title proper.
	Three notable stories	*Three notable stories*
	Note: Contents: Love and peril /Marquis of Lorne - To be or not to be / Mrs. Alexander – The melancholy hussar / Thomas Hardy	Source of information also bears the titles of the three stories contained in the resource: Love and peril by the Marquis of Lorne; To be or not to be by Mrs. Alexander; and The melancholy hussar by Thomas Hardy
	Observations: The AACR2 approach was more pragmatic because it records all the individual works at the same time very precisely.	**Optional Addition** Record the titles of the individual contents as titles of related works.
GMD	**AACR2** 1.1C1 Choose one of the lists of general material designation given below and use terms from the chosen list in all descriptions for which general material designations are desired.	**RDA** The General Material Designation has been replaced by RDA Media type (3.2), Carrier type (3.3), and Content type (6.10).
	GMD: *computer file, motion picture, music, multimedia, slide, video recording, globe, braille, model, film strip, map, manuscript etc.*	**Media type:** *audio, computer, microform, microscopic, projected, stereographic, unmediated, video* **Carrier type:** Audio carriers, Computer carriers, Microform carriers, Microscopic carriers, Projected image carriers, Stereographic carriers, Unmediated carriers, Video carriers **Content type**: cartographic dataset, cartographic image, computer dataset, computer program, notated music, performed music, sounds, still image, three-dimensional moving image, two-dimensional moving image

Parallel titles	**AACR2** 1.1D1. Transcribe parallel titles in the order indicated by their sequence on, or by the layout of, the chief source of information. **Observations:** The RDA approach is a clear cut violation of the Canon of Ascertainability in case of books. Restriction on sources of information is removed in RDA probably to accommodate electronic documents.	**RDA** 2.3.3.1 defines parallel title as the title proper in another language and/or script, but there is no restriction on sources for this information. 2.3.3.2 says to take parallel titles from any source within the resource.
Do	**AACR2** 1.1D2 In preparing a second-level description, give the first parallel title. Give any subsequent parallel title that is in English **Observations:** AARC2 gives instructions on which ones and how many parallel titles to record. This is absent in RDA.	**RDA** doesn't have the concept of first-level, second-level, and third-level of description.
Other title information	**AACR2** 12.1E1 specifies that other title information for continuing resources is only recorded if it is considered to be important. It lists three categories where it is always considered important.	**RDA** does not have this limitation, although in RDA other title information is not a core element. **Observations:** As it is not a core element in RDA, therefore, it can be treated as optional.
Do	**AACR2** 12.1E1. Transcribe other title information as instructed in 1.1E if considered to be important. Always transcribe or supply other title information if it falls within one of the categories below: a) If an acronym or initialism of the title appears in the chief source of information with the full form of the title, transcribe the acronym or initialism as other title information. b) If a statement of responsibility or the name of	**RDA** 2.3.4.3 Record other title information appearing on the same source of information as the title proper applying the basic instructions on recording titles given under 2.3.1. **Observations:** RDA core elements recommend that as a minimum, a record describing a resource should include all of the core elements that are applicable to that entity. Other title information in RDA is not a core element. Therefore, although there are no restrictions as AACR2, it can be treated as optional here.

	AACR2	RDA
	a publisher, distributor, etc., is an integral part of the other title information, transcribe it as such. c) If the title proper consists solely of the name of a corporate body, conference, etc., supply a brief addition in the language of the title proper as other title information to explain the title.	
Do	**AACR2** 1.1E6. If the title proper needs explanation, supply a brief addition as other title information, in the language of the title proper. (12.1E1c) If the title proper consists solely of the name of a corporate body, conference, etc., supply a brief addition in the language of the title proper as other title information to explain the title. *Longfellow [GMD]: [selections]* *Conference on Industrial Development in the Arab Countries [GMD]: [proceedings]*	In RDA there is no equivalent, as it goes against the principle of representation. However, other title information may be supplied for cartographic resources (AACR2 3.1E2, RDA 2.3.4.5) and moving image resources (AACR2 7.1E2, RDA 2.3.4.6). **Observations:** Sometimes titles need explanation, which is missing in RDA. As usual, RDA has kept the provision open partially, here for cartographic resources and moving image resources.
Do	**AACR2** 3.1E2. If the title proper does not include an indication of the geographic area covered by the item and if the other title information does not include such an indication or if there is no other title information, supply, as other title information, a word or brief phrase indicating the area covered. **Observations:** RDA instructs to supply words indicating geographical area covered as other title information and, if required, the subject portrayed along with the indication that the information was taken from	**RDA** 2.3.4.5 If the title proper of a cartographic resource does not include an indication of the geographic area covered and/or the subject portrayed, and a) the other title information does not include such an indication or b) if there is no other title information supply as other title information a word or brief phrase indicating the area covered and, if applicable, the subject portrayed. Indicate that the information was taken from a source outside the resource itself as instructed under 2.2.4.

	a source outside the resource itself.	
Do	**AACR2** 7.1E2.If the item is a trailer containing extracts from a larger film, add [trailer] as other title information.	**RDA** 2.3.4.6 If the resource is a trailer containing extracts from a larger moving image resource, and the title proper does not indicate this, supply trailer as other title information. Indicate that the information was taken from a source outside the resource itself as instructed under 2.2.4.
Statement of respon- sibility	**AACR2** 1.1A2 says that a statement of responsibility taken from outside the chief source of information must be enclosed in square brackets. **Observations:** According to ACR2, information should be taken from the chief source of information, where as RDA allows to collect information from anywhere of the resource. This is against the canon of Ascertainability.	**RDA** 2.4.2.2 Take statements of responsibility relating to title proper from the following sources (in order of preference): a) the same source as the title proper b) another source within the resource itself c) one of the other sources of information specified under 2.2.4. 2.2.4 If information required to identify the resource does not appear on a source forming part of the resource itself, take it from one of the following sources (in order of preference): a) accompanying material (e.g., a leaflet, an "about" file) b) a container that is not issued as part of the resource itself (e.g., a box case) c) other published descriptions of the resource d) any other available source (e.g., a reference source). If information taken from a source outside the resource itself is supplied in any of the elements listed below, indicate that fact either by means of a note or by some other means (e.g., through coding or the use of square brackets).

	AACR2	RDA
Do	**AACR2** 1.1F5. If a single statement of responsibility names more than three persons or corporate bodies performing the same function, or with the same degree of responsibility, omit all but the first of each group of such persons or bodies. Indicate the omission by the mark of omission (...) and add et al. (or its equivalent in a nonroman script) in square brackets. *Roger Colbourne... [et al.]* *Chief Source of information reads: Roger Colbourne, Suzanne Bassett, Tony Billing, Helen McCormick, John McLennan, Andrew Nelson and Hugh Robertson* **Observations: RDA** has no limitation like the rule of three of AACR2. It has kept open the option for recording more than three persons or bodies in statement of responsibility area. But at the same time it has kept open the option of limiting the number of persons responsible for any work for economy, omitting all but the first of each group of such persons, families, or bodies.	**RDA** 2.4.1.5. Record a statement of responsibility naming more than one single statement regardless of whether the persons, families, or corporate named in it perform the same function or different functions. *Roger Colbourne, Suzanne Bassett, Tony Billing, Helen McCormick, John McLennan, Andrew Nelson and Hugh Robertson* Source of information reads: Roger Colbourne, Suzanne Bassett, Tony Billing, Helen McCormick, John McLennan, Andrew Nelson and Hugh Robertson **Optional Omission** If a single statement of responsibility names more than three persons, families, or corporate bodies performing the same function, or with the same degree of responsibility omit all but the first of each group of such persons, families, or bodies. Indicate the omission by summarizing what has been omitted in the language and script preferred by the agency preparing the description. Indicate that the summary was taken from a source outside the resource itself as instructed under 2.2.4. *Roger Colbourne [and six others]* *Source of information reads: Roger Colbourne, Suzanne Bassett, Tony Billing, Helen McCormick, John McLennan, Andrew Nelson and Hugh Robertson* ***RDA** 2.2.4 If information taken from a source outside the resource itself is supplied in any*

		of the elements listed below, indicate that fact either by means of a note or by some other means (e.g., through coding or the use of square brackets).
Do	**AACR2** 1.1F12. Treat a noun phrase occurring in conjunction with a statement of responsibility as other title information if it is indicative of the nature of the work. *Characters from Dickens [GMD]: dramatised adaptations / by Barry Campbell* **If the noun or noun phrase is indicative of the role of the person(s) or body (bodies) named in the statement of responsibility rather than of the nature of the work, treat it as part of the statement of responsibility.** *Roman Britain [GMD]/ research and text by Colin Barham* **In case of doubt, treat the noun or noun phrase as part of the statement of responsibility.**	**RDA** 2.4.1.8 **If a noun or noun phrase occurs with a statement of responsibility, treat the noun or noun phrase as part of the statement of responsibility.** **Observations:** **Whereas AACR2 treats a noun or a noun phrase as part of other title information as well as part of statement of responsibility, RDA treats them all as part of statement of responsibility only. The AACR2 provision was more logical than that of RDA.**
Edition statement	**AACR2** 1.2.B1. Transcribe the edition statement as found on the item. Use abbreviations as instructed in appendix B and numerals as instructed in appendix C. *Nyudg.* *(Source of information reads: Ny udgave)* *2nd ed.* *(Source of information reads: Second edition)*	In **RDA**, edition statement is a transcribed element and no abbreviations are used unless they appear on the source used for the edition statement. **Observations**: Law of parsimony is violated immensely here. RDA's decision not to use abbreviations in the descriptions is not well appreciated because it has not only violated the laws of parsimony but also against the general law of economy in cataloguing.

Do	**AACR2** B.5A1. Abbreviate words, or substitute one form of abbreviation with the prescribed abbreviation, in the edition statement, according to B.9-B.12, B.14-B.15. **Observations**: RDA is against the use of abbreviations in cataloguing.	**RDA 2.5**.1.4. Transcribe an edition statement as it appears on the source of information. Apply the general guidelines on transcription given under 1.7. **RDA** B.4. For transcribed elements, use only those abbreviations found in the sources of information for the element.
Do	**AACR2** C.2B1. Substitute Arabic numerals for roman in the following areas and elements of the bibliographic description: a) in an edition statement.	**RDA** 1.8.1. When recording numbers expressed as numerals or as words in a transcribed element, transcribe them in the form in which they appear on the source of information. Apply the general guidelines on transcription, as applicable.
Do	**AACR2** C.3B1. Substitute Arabic numerals for numbers expressed as words in the following areas and elements of the bibliographic description: a) in an edition statement b) in the material c)... etc.	Since edition statement is not listed in 1.8.1, none of the special rules on recording numbers in 1.8.2-1.8.5 apply, so no substitutions will be made in edition statements.
Inaccuracies in edition statement	**AACR2** 1.0F1. In an area where transcription from the item is required, transcribe an inaccuracy or a misspelled word as it appears in the item. Follow such an inaccuracy either by [sic] or by i.e. and the correction within square brackets. Supply a missing letter or letters in square brackets.	In **RDA,** inaccuracies are transcribed as they appear on the source of information. If necessary, a note may be made correcting the inaccuracy. In case of doubt about whether the spelling of a word is incorrect, transcribe the spelling as found.
Edition statement	**AACR2** 1.2B2. If the edition statement consists solely or chiefly of characters that are neither numeric nor alphabetic, give the statement in words in the language and script of the title proper and enclose them in square brackets. *[Three asterisks] ed.*	**RDA** 2.5.1.4 Transcribe an edition statement as it appears on the source of information. Apply the general guidelines on transcription given under 1.7. If a designation of edition consists of a letter or letters and/or a number or numbers without accompanying words, add an appropriate word,

	If the edition statement consists of a letter or letters and /or a number or numbers without accompanying words, add an appropriate word or abbreviation. *3e[éd.],* *[State] B*	enclosed in square brackets. Indicate that the information was taken from a source outside the resource itself as instructed under 2.2.4. *3e[éd.],* *[State] B* *[Version] 1.1*
Do	**AACR2** 1.2B4. **Optional addition.** If an item lacks an edition statement but is known to contain significant changes from other editions, supply a suitable brief statement in the language and script of the title proper and enclose it in square brackets. *[New ed.]* [3eéd.] [2nd ed., partly rev.]	There is no equivalent in RDA to this AACR2 rule, but information required to identify the resource may be supplied for the edition statement (RDA 2.2.4) and therefore it could be given in square brackets.
Publication distribution etc., area	**AACR2** 1.4B4 and 1.4C3 says to use abbreviations found in appendix B. **Observations:** Economy in cataloguing has not been observed in RDA.	**RDA** 2.8.1.4. Transcribe places of publication and publishers' names in the form in which they appear on the source of information. Apply the general guidelines on transcription given under 1.7. **Optional Omission** Omit levels in a corporate hierarchy that are not required to identify the publisher. Do not use a mark of omission (...) to indicate such an omission.
Do	**AACR2** 1.4D2 says to give the name of a publisher, distributor, etc., in the shortest form in which it can be understood and identified internationally. *Penguin* *(Source of information reads: Penguin Books)* **Observations:** Economy in cataloguing has never been	**RDA** 2.8.1.4. Transcribe places of publication and publishers' names in the form in which they appear on the source of information. Apply the general guidelines on transcription given under 1.7. *Penguin Books* RDA 2.8.2.3. Include both the local place name (city, town, etc.) and the name of the larger jurisdiction or jurisdictions

	maintained in RDA. Shortest form of Publisher and distributor can be used here. Regarding place RDA's instruction is nothing new, in AACR2 wherever needed name of the larger jurisdictions were added. But here it has become mandatory.	(state, province, etc., and/or country) if present on the source of information.
Do	**AACR2** 1.4B6, 1.4C2, 1.4C3, 1.4C4 all specify the addition of information in square brackets. **Observations:** Instead of giving within square brackets in the publication area, RDA asks to put addition of information in the note area.	**RDA** 2.20.6-2.20.9 the element is transcribed as it appears, and notes are used to record additional/different information if considered important. **RDA** 2.20.7.3 Make notes on details relating to place of publication, publisher, or date of publication not recorded in the publication statement element, if they are considered to be important for identification or access.
Do	**AACR2** 1.4C5. If two or more places in which a publisher, distributor, etc., has offices are named in the item, give the first named place. Give any subsequently named place that is given prominence by the layout or typography of the source of information. If the first named place and any place given prominence are not in the home country of the cataloguing agency, give also the first of any subsequently named places that is in the home country. Omit all other places.	In **RDA**, the place names are recorded in the order indicated by the sequence, layout, or typography of the names on the source of information (2.7.2.4, 2.8.2.4, 2.9.2.4, 2.10.2.4). Only the first place on the source is required.
Do	**AACR2** 1.4C6. If no place or probable place can be given, give s.l. (sine loco), or its equivalent in a nonroman script. *[s.l]: New Age Press* **Observations:** In AACR1 in this case it was written that	**RDA** 2.8.2.6. If neither a known nor a probable local place or country, state, province, etc., of publication can be determined, record *Place of publication not identified*. (RDA 2.7.2.6, 2.8.2.6, 2.9.2.6, 2.10.2.6). *[Place of publication not*

	'[n. p.]' for "no place". AACR2 had some pedantic affection-it used [s. l.] (sine loco) instead of [n. d.]. Now, RDA has written [Place of publication not identified].	*identified]: New Age Press*
Do	1.4D6. If the name of the publisher, distributor, etc., is unknown, give s. n. (sine nominee) or its equivalent in a nonroman script. **Observations:** In AARC 1 in this case it was written [n. pub.] for "no publisher". AACR2 wrote 's. n.' (sine nominee). Now, RDA has written "publisher not identified."	2.8.4.7. For a resource in a published form, if no publisher is named within the resource itself, and the publisher cannot be identified from other sources as specified under 2.2.4, record publisher not identified.
Date of publication, distribution, etc.	**AACR2** 1.4F6 says that if dates of publication, distribution, etc. are unknown, give the copyright date or, in its absence, the date of manufacture. *C1953* 1989 printing 1995 pressing **Observations:** In RDA dates of publication, distribution, copyright, or manufacture are given separately.	Following **RDA** 2.8.6.6, if no approximate date of publication can be supplied, the date of publication element will contain 'date of publication not identified'. If dates of distribution, copyright, or manufacture are known they will be recorded in the respective elements.
Do	**AACR2** 1.4F7. If no date of publication, distribution, etc., copyright date, or date of manufacture appears in an item, supply an approximate date of publication. *,[1971 or 1972] one year or the other* *,[1969?] probable date* *,[between 1906 and 1912] use only for dates fewer than20 years apart* *,[ca. 1960] approximate date* *,[197-] decade certain* *,[197-?] probable decade* *,[18—] century certain*	**RDA** 2.8.6.6. For a resource in a published form, if the date of publication is not identified in the resource, supply the date or approximate date of publication. Apply the instructions on supplied dates given under 1.9.2. If an approximate date of publication for a resource that is in a published form cannot reasonably be determined, record 'date of publication not identified.' **Observations:** AACR2 had a provision of giving approximate

	,[18–?] probable century **AACR2** 2.16G. If the item is undated and the date of publication is unknown, give an approximate date. *[1492?]* *[not after Aug. 21, 1492]* *[between 1711 and 1719]*	date, decade even century. RDA has removed theses provisions.
Do	**AACR2** 1.4F6. If the dates of publication, distribution, etc., are unknown, give the copyright date or, in its absence, the date of manufacture (indicated as such) in its place. *, c1967* *, 1967 printing* *, p1983* *, 1979 pressing*	In RDA, copyright date is a separate element, as are date of production, date of publication, date of distribution, and date of manufacture. Copyright date is a core element in RDA, if neither the date of publication nor the date of distribution is identified. **RDA** 2.11.1.3. Record copyright dates applying the general guidelines on numbers expressed as numerals or as words given under 1.8. Precede the date by the copyright symbol (©) or the phonogram symbol (!), or by copyright or phonogram if the appropriate symbol cannot be reproduced.
Do	**AACR2** 1.4F6. If the dates of publication, distribution, etc., are unknown, give the copyright date or, in its absence, the date of manufacture (indicated as such) in its place. *, c1967* *, 1967 printing* *, p1983* *, 1979 pressing*	**RDA** 2.10.6. Date of manufacture is a core element for a resource in a published form if neither the date of publication, the date of distribution, nor the copyright date is identified.
Do	**AACR2** 1.4F7 provides a few formats for supplied dates. *[1971 or 1972] one year or the other* *[1969?] probable date* *[between 1906 and 1912] used only for dates fewer than 20 years apart* *[ca.1960] approximate date*	**RDA** 1.9 Here different format is specified. Ranges of years will be recorded using the format "[between XXXX and XXXX]", and if the dates are probable a question mark will be added. If the earliest and/or latest possible dates are known "not before" and "not after" will be used.

	[197-] decade certain *[197-?] probable decade* *[18—] century certain* *[18—?] probable century*	*[between 1846 and 1853?]* *[not after August 21, 1492]* **Observations:** Format of dates supplied is changed in RDA.
	AACR2 C.2B1 says to substitute Arabic numerals for roman in the date of publication, distribution, etc., element.	**RDA** 1.8.2 instructs to record numerals in the form preferred by the agency creating the data, with alternatives to record numerals in the form in which they appear on the source of information, or to record them both ways.
Physical description	In **AACR2**, the system of measurement used to record dimensions varies depending on the type of resource.	In **RDA,** metric units are used, although there is an alternative to use the system of measure preferred by the agency preparing the description.
Do	In **AACR2**, metric units are considered abbreviations and followed by a full stop (e.g., cm.)	In **RDA** they are considered to be symbols and are not followed by a full-stop
	AACR2 Appendix B contains a number of abbreviations that are used in recording the physical description, e.g., "p." for "pages" and "v." for "volumes", "ill." for "illustrations".	In **RDA**, the only abbreviations that are used in describing carriers or content are in dimensions, e.g., "in." for "inch", and duration, e.g., "hr." for "hour".
Numbering within series	**AACR2** 1.6G1 specifies the use of abbreviations found in Appendix B. AACR2 B.5B1 says that abbreviations can be substituted	**RDA** does not have this provision. However, the "Numbering of part" element (RDA 24.6) does specify use of abbreviations and substitution of abbreviations.
	AACR2 C.2B1 says to substitute Arabic numerals for roman in series numbering.	**RDA** 1.8.2 instructs to record numerals in the form preferred by the agency creating the data, with alternatives to record numerals in the form in which they appear on the source of information, or to record them both ways.
Sub-series	**AACR2** 1.6H7 instructs to omit the ISSN of the main series if the ISSN of the sub-series is given.	At **RDA** 2.12.8.3 and 2.12.16.3 this is an optional omission.

7.1.2. Choice of Access Points

Heading	AACR2	RDA
Choice of Access Points	AACR2 21.2 and 21.3 gives detail how to handle changes in title proper and changes of persons or bodies responsible for a new work, and specify when a new description is made for serials.	RDA 1.6 lists some additional situations where a new description is needed for multipart monographs, serials, and integrating resources: change in mode of issuance; and, change in media type. A new set of base volumes for an updating loose-leaf also requires a new description. **Observations:** Some additional clauses added to cope up with the changing media type and changing environment.
Do	AACR2 21.0D lists some designations of function, and there is reference to designations used in other rules. According to AACR2 abbreviated designation of function should be added as the list provided.	RDA lists, in Appendix I, relationship designators for relationships between a resource and persons, families, and corporate bodies associated with a resource. **Observations:** Instead of abbreviated form of designations, full form of the designation of function performed is added in RDA.
Do	AACR2 21.6B and 21.6C make a distinction between when two or three, or four or more persons or bodies share responsibility (i.e., the rule of three). **Observations**: The much debated 'rule of three' has been removed in RDA.	Whilst RDA continues to provide instructions on inclusion of the authorized access point representing the person, family, or corporate body with principal responsibility for the work in the authorized access point for the work, it does not place any limitations on what in AACR would be the added entries (RDA Section 6). In addition, there is an alternative at RDA 6.27.1.3 to include the name of more than one collaborator in the access point representing the collaborative work.

Do	AACR2 21.6C2. If responsibility is shared among more than three persons or corporate bodies and principal responsibility is not attributed to any one, two, or three, enter under title. Make an added entry under the heading for the first person or corporate body named prominently in the item being catalogued. If editors are named prominently, make an added entry under the heading for each if there are not more than three. If there are more than three named prominently, make an added entry under the heading for the principal editor and/or for the one named first. *Biochemistry / Lubert Stryer ... [et al.]* *Main entry under the title* *Added entry under the heading for Stryer*	RDA 6.27.1.3 If principal responsibility for the work is not indicated, construct the authorized access point representing the work using the authorized access point representing the first-named person, family, or corporate body followed by the preferred title for the work. *Tracey, John Paul. Managing bird damage to fruit and other horticultural crops* *Resource described: Managing bird damage to fruit and other horticultural crops / John Tracey, Mary Bomford, Quentin Hart, Glen Saunders, Ron Sinclair* *Cage, John. Double music* *Resource described: Double music: percussion quartet / John Cage and Lou Harrison. Composed jointly by Cage and Harrison, each writing two of the four parts* **Observations**: The 'rule of three' has been dropped. Here in case where principal responsibility is not defined, the authorized access point is to be constructed like the name-title added entry of AACR2.
Do	AACR2 21.7B1... If there are more than three compilers/ editors named prominently, make an added entry under the heading for the principal compiler/ editor and/ or for the one named first. Thus, AACR2 limits the number of added entries that can be made for collections of works by different persons or bodies.	RDA does not have this limitation. 6.27.1.4 If the work is a compilation of works by different persons, families, or corporate bodies, construct the authorized access point representing the work using the preferred title for the compilation, formulated according to the instructions given under 6.2.2. **Observations**: AACR2 limits the number of added entries for collections of works by different

		persons or bodies; RDA does not have this limitation.
Do	21.7C1. If a work falling into one of the categories given in 21.7A1 lacks a collective title, enter it under the heading appropriate to the first work named in the chief source of information of the item being catalogued. If the item lacks a collective chief source of information, enter it under the heading appropriate to the first work in the item. Make added entries for editors/ compilers and for the other works as instructed in 21.7B1, in so far as it applies to works without a collective title.	6.27.1.4 Compilations of works by different persons, families, or corporate bodies says, if the compilation lacks a collective title, construct separate access points for each of the works in the compilation **Alternative** Instead of (or in addition to) constructing access points for each of the works in the compilation, construct an authorized access point representing the compilation using a devised title formulated according to the instructions given under 2.3.2.11.
Do	The **alternative** rule at AACR2 21.28 allows for librettos to be entered under the heading appropriate to the musical work.	In RDA librettos are not treated as musical works. (Note: RDA 6.19.1.7 and 6.28.1.10 deleted at March 2009 meeting)
Do	AACR2 21.35A makes a distinction between treaties, etc. between two or three governments, and those between four or more governments.	In RDA the first part of the access point representing the work (the AACR2 main entry) is the corporate body named first on resources embodying the treaty, or in reference sources (or if these are inconsistent, the one named first on the first resource received) (RDA 6.29.1.15). There is an exception for situations where there is only one government on one side of the treaty, etc., and two or more governments on the other side, to use the authorized access point representing the single government on one side as the first part of the access point representing the work.
Do	AACR2 21.36C6 and 21.36C7 limit added entries to the "first named party on each side".	RDA 19.3.2 does not have this limitation.

Do	21.37A. Enter a work that is accepted as sacred scripture by a religious group, or part of such a work, under title. When appropriate, use a uniform title as instructed in 25.17-25.18. Make an added entry under the heading for one, two, or three persons associated with the work and/or the item being catalogued. If there are four or more such persons, do not make added entries.	RDA 6.30.1.2 has an exception for creating the authorized access point for some sacred scriptures by combining the authorized access point for the person creating the work and the preferred title for the work. **Observations:** AACR2 says to enter all sacred scriptures under title. RDA has an exception for creating the authorized access point for person creating the work combined with the preferred title of the work.

7.1.2.1. Headings for Persons

Heading	AACR2	RDA
Headings for Persons	AACR2 22.2B includes specific instructions on the choice of name to be used as the basis for the heading for persons whose works all appear under one pseudonym, those who have established separate bibliographic identities, contemporary authors, and others.	RDA 9.2.2.8 says if an individual has more than one identity, choose the name associated with each identity as the preferred name for that identity. Consider an individual who uses one or more pseudonyms, or his or her real name as well as one or more pseudonyms, to have more than one identity. **Observations:** In AACR2 specific instructions were given for pseudonym used by any person where as in RDA persons with more than one identity have been generalized with only one exception.
Do	AACR2 22.3D1 says that if variant spellings of a person's name are found and these variations are not the result of different Romanization, choose the form resulting from an official change in orthography, or, if this does not apply, choose the predominant spelling.	RDA 9.2.2.5.4 If variant spellings of a person's name are found, and these variations are not the result of different transliterations, choose the form found in the first resource received. **Observations:** AACR2 says to choose from variant spellings of a person's name or of an official

		change in orthography, or, to choose the predominant spelling. RDA says to choose the form found in the first resource received. This is not very pragmatic approach because the library may have resources which bear spellings which the author/ creator used very rarely or which is officially changed. Therefore, the AACR2 rules were better in this case.
Do	AACR2 22.5C contains detailed instructions on compound surnames.	Instructions specific to certain languages have been replaced in RDA by a reference to IFLA *Names of persons: national usages for entry in catalogues* (RDA 9.2.2.10.2)
Do	AACR2 22.15C Do not add other titles or terms associated with names entered under surname unless they are required to distinguish between two or more persons with the same name and neither dates nor fuller forms of name are available. However, people who use terms such as "Jr." identify themselves this way and users may look for them with the term included.	In RDA terms indicating relationship, such as "Jr.", are treated as part of the name (RDA 9.2.2.9.5) *Saur, Karl-Otto, Jr.* Brown, George, Rev. Welch, Denton, Ph.D. **Observations:** AACR2 follows the Cannon of Individualisation in this case, which RDA does not.
Do	The AACR2 rule includes use of the abbreviations "cent.", "ca.", "b.", "d." and "fl.".	RDA Appendix B does not include these abbreviations. "Century" will be spelled out. Instead of "ca.", "approximately" will be used. The abbreviations "b.", "d." and "fl." are not necessary if the date is recorded as RDA element sub-types, and could be generated for display based on the encoding format
Do	AACR2 22.17 specifies that years of activity are not to be used for dates in the twentieth century.	RDA does not have this limitation on recording period of activity.
Do	AACR2 22.19B1 allowed	In RDA, additions to access

	terms of address (e.g., "Rev.", "Sir"), titles of position or office, initials of an academic degrees (e.g., "Ph.D."), and initials denoting membership in an organization to be used as distinguishing terms. **Observations:** Unlike RDA, AACR2 has used the terms to follow the Cannon of Individualisation in this case to distinguish among the similar names.	points representing persons are limited to those given in RDA 9.19.1.2. A term indicating profession or occupation is only added for a person whose name consists of a phrase or appellation not conveying the idea of a person. Terms of address are not used as additions to names, but may be included as part of the name when the name consists only of the surname, is for a married person identified only by a partner's name and a term of address (RDA 9.2.2.9.4), or is part of a phrase consisting of a forename or forenames preceded by a term of address (RDA 9.2.2.23). *Pius XII, Pope* *Dositheos, Patriarch of Jerusalem* *Arundel, Philip Howard, Earl of, Saint* *Stone Mountain (Writer)* *Taj Mahal (Musician)* *Davis, Maxwell, Mrs.* *Read, Miss* *Seuss, Dr.*

7.1.2.2. Headings for Corporate Bodies

Heading	AACR2	RDA
Headings for Corporate Bodies	AACR2 24.2C If variant spellings of the name appear in items issued by the body, use the form resulting from an official change in orthography or, if this does not apply, use the predominant spelling. In case of doubt, use the spellings found in the first item catalogued.	RDA 11.2.2.5.1 If variant spellings of the name appear in resources associated with the body, choose the form found in the first resource received. *African Centre for Fertilizer Development not* *African Center for Fertilizer Development Resource received first has spelling "Centre" resource received second has spelling "Center"*

Do	AACR2 24.7B4 instructs that if the sessions of a conference, etc. were held in three or more locations, to follow the first named place by "etc." *International Conference on Alternatives to War (1982: Paris, France, etc.)*	RDA instructs to list all of the locations (11.3.2.3). When included in an access point, multiple locations will be separated by a semi-colon (RDA E.2.2.4). *International Conference on Alternatives to War (1982: Paris, France; London, England; Dundee, Scotland)*

7.1.2.3. Uniform Titles

Heading	AACR2	RDA
Uniform Titles	AACR2 25.3B Says if no title in the original language is established as being the one by which the work is best known, or in case of doubt, use the title proper of the original edition. It also says to omit introductory phrases and statement of responsibility that are part of title proper. *Wodehouse, P.G.* *[Ring for Jeeves]* *The return of Jeeves*	Title proper of the original edition is used as the preferred title, and accordingly the instructions at RDA 2.3.1.5 and 2.3.1.6 will apply.
Do	In the case of simultaneous publication in the same language under different titles AACR2 25.3C1 prefers the title of the edition published in the home country of the cataloguing agency. AACR2 25.3C2 and 25.3C3 provide additional guidance. *Cataloguing agency in United States:* *Joesten, Joachim* *Rats in the larder: the story of Nazi influence in Denmark. (published in New York. 1939)* *Joesten, Joachim* *[Rats in the larder]* *Denmark's day of doom (published in London. 1939)*	In RDA, the choice of the preferred title is based on the title of the resource first received (RDA 6.2.2.4). *Rats in the larder* *Preferred title for work by Joachim Joesten for use in an access point based on the title of the edition published in New York: Rats in the larder: the story of Nazi influence in Denmark.* *Simultaneously published in London under the title: Denmark's day of doom. The resource published in New York is the first received* **Observations:** According to this rule title of the resource

		first received should be considered as preferred title which may not always be appropriate.
Do	AACR2 25.5C1 says do not add the name of the language to a uniform title for a motion picture with subtitles.	RDA 6.12.1.4 does not have this limitation when recording the languages in a single expression.
Do	AACR2 25.5C1 uses "Polyglot" as an addition to the uniform title if an item is in three or more languages.	RDA specifies naming each of the languages as an addition to the access point when a single expression of a work involves more than one language. When there are multiple language expressions of the same work RDA specifies creating a separate access point for each language expression.
Do	AACR2 25.9 covers when the term "Selections" is used as the uniform title.	Following RDA, "Selections" is not used alone as the preferred title, "Works Selections" is used instead (RDA 6.2.2.11).

7.1.2.4. Sacred Scriptures

Heading	AACR2	RDA
Sacred Scriptures	AACR2 25.18A2 Enter the Old Testament as Bible. O.T. and New Testament as Bible. N.T.	In RDA the Old and New Testaments are referred to by their spelled out forms, not the existing AACR2 abbreviations "O.T." and "N.T.".
Do	According to AACR2 25.18A11, when a version of the Bible is identified by the name of the translator, and there are more than two, the name of the first is followed by 'et al.'	According to RDA 6.25.1.4, if the version is identified by the name of the translator, use a short form of the translator's name. If there are two translators, hyphenate their names. If there are more than two, use the name of the first followed by *and others.*
	Bible. English. Gordon et al. An English translation of the Old Testament by Alexander R. Gordon, Theophile J. Meek, J.M. Powis Smith, Leroy Waterman	*Gordon and others An English translation of the Old Testament by Alexander R. Gordon, Theophile J. Meek, J.M. Powis Smith, Leroy Waterman*

Observations: RDA is using fuller form of names/ words everywhere throughout the code. But surprisingly it has used the shorter form of names of the translators and says to hyphenate the names if there are two translators. This is definitely misleading for the users because it will create difficulties in searching by the name of the translators. Another important development can be seen here "and others" was used in AACR1 in case of multiple persons responsible for works. It was replaced with [... et al.] in AACR2 and again "and others" reintroduced in RDA.

7.2. CONCLUSION

The Joint Steering Committee for the Development of RDA has designed the new code which is based on clearly defined principles and reorganization of the rules. Despite bringing significant changes in conceptual level and in cataloguing rules, it seems that RDA is unable to full fill the expectations of the cataloguing community. Most of the changes brought here in RDA, are at the conceptual level, but implementing them in practical cataloguing is very difficult. Perhaps, Gorman (2007: 64) was right when he said that FRBR (on which RDA is based) may have some merit as a way of looking at the theory of cataloguing- it has little as a foundational document for creating a cataloguing code. Moreover, the necessity of adapting the new code has been questioned many times by the cataloguing experts throughout world. Study shows that there are very negligible numbers of resources in most of the libraries which bears more than one manifestations or multiple manifestations. Therefore, switching over to RDA hardly bears any meaning to them.

During the comparative study between AACR2 and RDA some peculiarities have also been noticed. Firstly, new rules are introduced to resolve the long pending issues of AACR2 like the 'rule of three'. But the old rule of AACR2 has also been kept as an optional one with little or almost no modification. RDA has no limitation like the rule of three of AACR2. It instructs to record more than three persons or bodies in statement of responsibility area. But at the same time it has kept open the option (2.4.1.5) of limiting the number of persons responsible for any work for 'economy' omitting all but the first of each group of such persons, families, or bodies. Likewise, sometimes keeping the old concepts almost intact, changes are brought in the nomenclature of the terms of cataloguing. Main-entry Heading- Uniform Heading gone, Preferred Access Point comes, Added-entry gone, comes the Variant Access Point.

Secondly, echoes of the first edition of AACR (AACR1) can be heard in some cases. When the place of publication was not available in the item, AACR1 (Rule 139C) used '[n. p.]' for "no place". RDA's use of "Place of publication not identified" in this cases seems almost similar. The same is true to the name of publisher also. In AACR1 in this case it was written [n. pub.] for "no publisher" (Rule 139C). Now, RDA has written "publisher not identified." Another instance of the same kind can be seen where AACR1 used first person, or body followed by 'and others' omitting multiple persons or bodies responsible for any work (Rule 134D), AACR2 used [...et al.] for the same (1.1F5), and now RDA is using 'and others' (2.4.1.5) to fulfill the same purpose again. This certainly bears a special significance. (Biswas & Rath, 2013: 251) Some may even call it 'looking back in despair'.

Thirdly, economy in cataloguing is not at all followed in RDA. It instructs to write the fuller forms of standard abbreviations like 'p.', 'vol.' etc. and many more. RDA says to use fuller form of terms/ names everywhere throughout the code. But surprisingly in the headings of sacred scriptures, it has asked to use the shorter form of names of the translators and says to hyphenate the names if there are two translators. This is definitely misleading for the users because it will create difficulties in searching the document by the name of the translators. Moreover, it has asked to use the name of the first, followed by "and others", if there are more than two translators. This is a significant development because RDA never goes for the precisions or economy in cataloguing, if it is at all followed anywhere, it is kept as optional rule. It has dropped the 'rule of three' of AACR2, but here it goes for direct omission which certainly may stand against its consistency.

Another notable inconsistency which can be mentioned here is in case of supplying the other title information. AACR2 1.1E6 says, if the title proper needs explanation, a brief addition can be supplied as other title information, in the language of the title proper. RDA discourages this as it goes against the 'principle of representation' (0.4.3.4). But it has asked to supply as other title information a word or brief phrase in case of cartographic resources and supply the word 'trailer' as other title information for moving image resources if needed for better clarification. Thus lots of inconsistencies can be traced throughout the new code RDA which certainly needs immediate attention.

REFERENCES

Anglo-American Cataloging Rules. (1967). Prepared by the American Library Association the Library of Congress, the Library Association, and the Canadian Library Association. British Text. General editor C. Sumner Spalding. London: The Library Association.

Anglo-American Cataloguing Rules. (1978). Prepared by the American Library Association, the British Library, the Canadian Committee on Cataloguing, the Library Association and the Library of Congress; edited by Michael Gorman and Paul W. Winkler. 2nd. ed. Chicago: American Library Association.

Anglo-American Cataloguing Rules. (1988). Prepared under the direction of the Joint Steering Committee for the Revision of AACR; edited by Michael Gorman and Paul W. Winkler. 2nd. ed. 1988 revision. Chicago: American Library Association.

Anglo-American Cataloguing Rules. (1998). Prepared under the direction of the Joint Steering Committee for the Revision of AACR. 2nd. ed. 1998 revision. Chicago: American Library Association.

Anglo-American Cataloguing Rules. (2002). Prepared under the direction of the Joint Steering Committee for the Revision of AACR .- 2nd. ed., 2002 revision, 2004 update. Chicago: American Library Association.

Biswas, Subhankar and Rath, Durga Sankar. (2013). *Novelty in RDA: a Comparative Analysis of the Rules of AACR2 and RDA*. IASLIC Bulletin, 58(4) 242-252.

Gorman, Michael. (2007). RDA: *Imminent Debacle*. American Libraries, 38. (11) 64-65.

IFLA (1997). *Functional Requirements for Bibliographic Records: final report* .Retrieved September 7, 2011 from www.ifla.org.

Joint Steering Committee for Revision of AACR. *(2008). RDA prospectus*. Retrieved on September 20, 2008 from www.collectionscanada.ca/jsc/rdaprospectus.html.

Joint Steering Committee for Development of RDA. (2013). *RDA Resource Description and Access*. Chicago: American Library Association.

8

Implementation of RDA

8.0. INTRODUCTION

RDA has brought revolutionary changes in the descriptive cataloguing. But the real challenge lies in the practical implementation of the code in the libraries and information centers. Libraries which are accustomed with the conventional cataloguing since the inception of modern cataloguing are sure to stumble while taking the initiative of adopting RDA for its far off move from AACR2. RDA has gone far away from AACR2 in the description of documents by changing the basic concept of cataloguing and introducing FRBR in its place. The description of documents based on item in hand has now been shifted to work, the artistic or intellectual content of any document. This change of concept demands radical changes in the descriptive cataloguing, which no doubt has brought revolution in the concept of cataloguing we are acquainted with till today. Obviously, differences of opinion have emerged regarding the implementation of RDA. Studies conducted in the USA have given opinions which are not very encouraging. Most of the countries are waiting to get a clear picture of its implementation in USA before they move towards a decision.

This chapter deals with the background and

improvements of implementation of RDA in developed countries and the prospects in developing countries along with the alternative plans that can be adopted to make the transition smoother without hampering the day-to-day activities of libraries.

8.1. IMPLEMENTATION OF RDA IN USA

Before we discuss about the implementation of RDA in other countries, let us see what the RDA constituent member countries are thinking about implementing it. The senior management at the *Library of Congress (LC), National Agricultural Library (NAL),* and *National Library of Medicine (NLM) charged the U.S. RDA Test Coordinating Committee* to devise and conduct a national test of *Resource Description and Access* (RDA). The Coordinating Committee made its evaluation of RDA by testing it within the library and information environment, assessing the technical, operational, and financial implications of the new code and submitted its recommendations in June 2011.

The committee recommended that contingent on the satisfactory progress/ completion of the tasks and action items pointed by the Coordinating Committee, it recommended that RDA should be implemented by LC, NAL, and NLM no sooner than January 2013. The three national libraries should commit resources to ensure progress is made on the issues mentioned.

The *Report and Recommendations of the U.S. RDA Test Coordinating Committee* says that The U.S. RDA Test amassed an unexpectedly huge amount of data that provided the Coordinating Committee a wealth of RDA records and survey responses to analyse. This wealth of data helped to inform the ultimate decision to recommend that the three U.S. national libraries implement RDA no sooner than January 2013. The 26 test partners (including LC, NAL, and NLM) created 10,570 bibliographic records and 12,800 authority records. More than 8,000 surveys were submitted.

A key question was asked of each test partner

institution, each record creator, and anyone in the U.S. community who wished to complete a survey: "Do you think that the U.S. community should implement RDA?" Answers from institutional test partners were as follows: 34% 'yes'; 28% 'yes with changes'; 24% 'ambivalent'; 14% 'no'. Record creators were somewhat more negative: 25% 'yes'; 45% 'yes with changes'; 30% 'no' ('ambivalent' was not offered as a choice for record creators).

The survey report clearly shows reluctance of cataloguing or 'record creating' communities to implement RDA. RDA, whenever stating its relationship to other standards for resource description and access (RDA 0.2) says that RDA is built on foundations established by the *Anglo-American Cataloguing Rules* (AACR) and the cataloguing traditions on which it was based. Instructions derived from AACR have been reworked to produce a standard that will be easier to use, more adaptable, and more cost-efficient in its application. But in reality, it is neither 'easier to use', nor 'more adaptable' and not even 'more cost-efficient in it application'. Therefore, it's obvious that there's a huge gap between its words and deeds. It has raised doubt of many about the future of RDA and the practicability of adapting RDA in libraries and information centers.

8.1.1. Findings of the RDA Test Coordinating Committee

Some of the most important findings of the RDA Test Coordinating Committee pertinent to our study are summarized below:

8.1.1.1. Use of RDA Toolkit

There were several positive comments related to the RDA Toolkit. The overall impression from the comments, however, was that users struggled to use the Toolkit effectively. Many respondents found the Toolkit to be clunky and difficult to navigate.

8.1.1.2. RDA Content

The text of RDA was compared with AACR2, ISBD,

and the CONSER Cataloging Manual using two common readability tools. The comparison indicated that RDA text was the least readable. A larger number of participants reported confusion about the structure, organization, and vocabulary in RDA and commented that the order of the rules in RDA did not match current cataloguing workflows. The text was described as redundant, circular, and complicated, rather than being a simplified set of rules. Suggestions for improving the text came from both those who had positive and negative reactions to the content.

8.1.1.3. Local Operations

A majority of test partner institutions anticipate some negative impact on local operations in acquisitions, copy cataloging, original cataloging, and bibliographic file maintenance. Nevertheless, a majority of test partner institutions felt that the U.S. community should implement RDA.

8.1.1.4. Costs and Benefits

Costs of implementing RDA occur in various areas: subscription to the RDA Toolkit, development of training materials and creation/ revision of documentation, production time lost due to training and the learning curve, and impact on existing contracts.

Based on the test findings, the summary statements below indicate that a lot of goals were not met. The body of the report presents the findings that led the Coordinating Committee to these conclusions:

- Be compatible with internationally established principles and standards.
  - This goal was partially met. The Coordinating Committee looks forward to increased harmonization efforts among JSC, ISBD, and ISSN communities.
- Enable users to find, identify, select, and obtain resources appropriate to their information needs.

— This goal was partially met. User comments on RDA records indicate mixed reviews on how well new elements met user needs. The test did not fully verify all the user tasks above.

- Be optimized for use as an online tool.
  — This goal was not met.
- Be written in plain English, and able to be used in other language communities.
  — This goal was not met.
- Be easy and efficient to use, both as a working tool and for training purposes.
  — This goal was not met.

The Coordinating Committee believes that RDA should be accountable to its own goals and has drafted a plan that postpones implementation until these goals are substantially met.

It can be noted here that none of the said libraries, even none of the constituent member (of *JSC for Development of RDA*) libraries of other countries also implemented RDA till the end of March 2013. The first move came from the Library of Congress and the British Library who implemented RDA on April 1, 2013. According to LC announcement made on March 2, 2013, in its website, "The U.S. RDA Test Coordinating Committee issued its first quarterly update on progress towards carrying out the recommendations made in the Committee's Final Report issued in June 2011. The progress is promising..." Here they announced the target RDA Implementation Day to be March 31, 20013. As of April 1, 2013 the U.S. Library of Congress and the British Library are using RDA as their official descriptive cataloging standard. Since then, a number of libraries in the USA, the UK and many other countries have implemented the new code of cataloguing. They are as follow:

8.2. LIBRARIES CURRENTLY CATALOGING IN RDA

8.2.1. National Libraries

- Bibliothèque et Archives nationales du Québec
- British Library
- Library and Archives Canada
- Library of Congress (US)
- National Agricultural Library (US)
- National Library Board, Singapore
- National Library of Australia
- National Library of Malaysia
- National Library of Medicine (US)
- National Library of the Philippines

8.2.2. Other Notable Institutions

- Brigham Young University (US)
- Cambridge University (UK)
- Courtauld Institute (UK)
- North Carolina State University (US)
- OLIS/Bodleian Library (UK)
- University of Chicago (US)
- University of Warwick (UK)
- U.S. Government Printing Office

Report shows that a few libraries have already implemented RDA as their official descriptive cataloguing standard leading by Library of Congress. Although Library of Congress implemented RDA as their official descriptive cataloging standard on April 1, 2013, it had kept the old AACR2 catalogues as their main searching option till April 2014, where as the new RDA catalogues were kept as second option to their patrons. This may be seen from three different angles- firstly the library authority is too much concerned about the conveniences of the users. They are thinking that the users may feel uneasy with the new catalogues which may hamper their search for the desired document in time. The second thought may be that gathering experiences from the previous cataloguing code implementations Library of Congress has decided to wipe out the ill reputation of 'superimposition' as it did in 1967 for AACR1, 1974 for ISBD and 1981 for AACR2. It may be noted here that the implementation of AACR1 occurred 60 days after the date of publication. AACR2 was published in 1978 but implementation was first postponed to 1980, then to 1981. Whereas RDA was published in June 2010 and implemented in April 2013.

And the last thought may be that the library authority was not confident enough about the acceptance and the effectiveness of the RDA catalogues to the library users in general. Therefore, they were in dilemma to replace the old AACR2 catalogues with the new RDA catalogues. RDA declares that instructions derived from AACR have been reworked to produce a standard that will be easier to use, more adaptable, and more cost-efficient in its application. If it was the fact, then there should not have any doubt about its acceptance and effectiveness. It took thirteen months to get it streamlined and replace the old catalogue. Then the old catalogue had been kept as the second option to the library users. Hence, one may reasonably doubt about the future of RDA as effective cataloguing standard of the new era.

8.3. IMPLEMENTATION OF RDA IN THE DEVELOPING COUNTRIES

8.3.1. Present Scenario

Implementing RDA in the developing countries faces numerous barriers. Firstly, RDA is a complex cataloging standard that is built on the significant development over what has gone before. But most of the libraries in these countries are still at an early stage. They hardly have the technological and financial capabilities to study the new standard thoroughly and consider seriously about its adaptation

Secondly, full RDA text is available online (printed version, if available, is not very convenient for use) on subscription basis against a payment of huge amount of money ($ 325 annually, for single users since January, 2014). It's a costly affair for these libraries to afford this recurring cost with their limited financial capabilities. Training library staff/ cataloguers in RDA is another field where they are also facing hardship. Training facilities too are not easily available and affordable for the libraries of these countries.

Lastly, the most valid point against implementing RDA in developing countries comes from the documents itself. RDA catalogues are good for the works having multiple manifestations. But survey conducted here proves that majority of these libraries possess very negligible percentage of documents/ resources which have multiple manifestations. Libraries in general hardly possess any documents with several manifestations, only a very few specialized libraries and some research libraries possess some documents of this kind, that too very negligible in number. Therefore, the best way is to wait and watch till more development takes place in RDA cataloguing which proves more beneficial and cost effective to them.

They should definitely wait till things get settled down at those countries which took direct part in the design and development of RDA. They should keep a close vigil on their activities regarding implementation, responses / feedback of the users, acceptances to the library community as well as to other metadata communities as RDA intended for them also, and browsing their databases to assess the necessity and compatibility of RDA in the libraries of these countries in its present form. This may prove beneficial for them because they hardly possess enough money and man power to do experiments in their own with RDA catalogues in their libraries which always runs through a lot of constrains due to lack of sufficient resources.

Hasty decision in favour of direct implementation of RDA in the developing countries at this moment is nothing but sheer wastage of the limited money and man power they possess. Survey conducted by different institutions shows that they have hardly any need for immediate switching over to RDA catalogues as there are very few documents with more than one manifestation in these libraries at present. Even if they take the risk of implementing RDA in these libraries now who can say that this is the right and positive development at least for coming few years?

We have not forgotten the experiences of MACR21 retro conversion. The amount of money spent for that project will go astray and another lot of fresh investment in computer hardware and software will require at the outset. This is hardly affordable for these countries who are always struggling due to lack of sufficient resources. Although RDA MARC21 mapping is done, still it needs a lot of editing work to make the records RDA compatible. If these financially weak countries again go for another phase of conversion into RDA catalogues, who will bear the huge expenses needed for these projects? It will be nothing but unnecessary generosity shown to the software and the retro-conversion vendors. Moreover, even if they could manage to afford the expenses, should they go for the implementation immediately? It requires more introspection to answer this question, as data received till date shows that implementation of RDA is not at all satisfactory even in the member countries of Joint Steering Committee for the Development of RDA (JSC).

Therefore, the developing countries should restrain themselves from taking hasty decisions in this regard. Rather, they should keep a constant vigil over the developments till the turmoil boils down to a certain point. Let things settle down because it's not the end of RDA, it's just the beginning, and I thing, more development of it will be followed very soon. Therefore, they should refrain from wasting their hard earn resources and take time till RDA gets matured.

8.3.2. Application of the Principles of Osmosis

The other alternative may be the application of Ranganathan's Principle of Osmosis. The principles states, when a change in the catalogue code becomes necessary in deference to the canon of context, on and after a chosen date

i. all the new accessions be catalogued according to new catalogue code

ii. just those old collections which are known to be in much use can be re-catalogued

iii. The new accessioned books and re-catalogued books be kept in a new collection, and similarly their catalogue cards are kept in a new collection

iv. The rest of the old collection be kept as old collection, similarly their catalogue cards to be kept as old collection.

This principle can be applied in libraries of our country to those works which have more than one manifestation or those documents which are used frequently. As we know works with multiple manifestations are negligible in number in all over the Libraries of the world. Several studies made worldwide have shown that percentage of the works possessed by the libraries with single manifestation is maximum. In our country the number is much higher. The very few works with multiple manifestations our library possess, or the number of documents in active use in these libraries can easily be re-catalogued and kept in the new cataloguing system following Ranganathan's Principles of Osmosis.

Support in favour of this alternative option can be strengthened with the logic shown by Ranganathan in his Law of Osmosis. In his opinion there are two alternatives in situations like this i) either change over to new code or ii) living in dead past.

8.3.2.1. Present Practice

The present practice is of changing of catalogue code is met in the following ways:

8.3.2.1.1. Wasteful Practice

In the first way, the entire collection of a library is re-catalogued. The cost is enormous. Often to find the necessary money, active service is starved, reference service is cut out, book-fund is depleted. All this amounts nearly to a criminal waste of library fund. Law of Parsimony is therefore chagrined.

8.3.2.1.2. Capitulation to the Past

In the second way, eyes are closed to the changes. The obsolete code and the obsolete scheme are perpetuated in defiance of the Canon of Context and of the Laws of Library Science, and to the neglect of readers' unexpressed needs. This amounts to tying up the future with the dead past. This capitulation to the dad past is fatal to any social institution; and library is a life-giving social institution.

8.3.2.2. Living in the Present

The right way shown by the canon of context is to live the present. We should neither waste the library fund nor do disservice to readers. The Principle of Osmosis helps us to chalk out the right way. (Ranganathan, 1976: 137) According to it, the documents of a library fall into three groups:

i. New documents

ii. Documents- usually or mostly of recent past- continuing to be in active use ; and

iii. Old documents rarely, or occasionally in use.

When the catalogue code has to be changed, the three groups should be treated differently.

8.3.2.2.1. New Documents

From the date of change over, all the new documents

should be catalogued by the new code. These should be kept as 'New Collection'. Their catalogue cards also should be kept as 'new collection' (now a separate database for online catalogue can be made). This does not mean any extra cost.

8.3.2.2.2. Recent Documents in Active Use

Within a short period after the date of change over to the new catalogue code the active documents of recent past should be rapidly re-catalogued. In some cases, no serious change will be necessary. The only work to be done will be to pick out their cards from the old collection, and insert them in the new collection (in online environment exporting data of the concerned items to the new database). The documents themselves should be similarly transferred from old to new collection, as and when the cards are transferred. A suitable mark should be put at the back of the title page to indicate the absorption of the document in the new collection.

8.3.2.2.3. Osmotic Pressure of Use

After first few months of high-pressure of absorption, the daily quota of absorption will become small. It will go on thinning almost to a vanishing point in about five years. By the time all the 'live-books' would have been transferred by the 'Osmotic Pressure of Use' from old collection to the new collection. The 'dead books' will forever remain in the old collection, without any harm to any reader. (Ranganathan, 1988: 73)

8.4. CONCLUSION

Thus, instead of taking huge projects of conversions into RDA catalogues, the developing countries can do the same on a trial basis with other alternative means. The Principle of Osmosis can play the most significant role in the transformation of the existing catalogues (or metadata) of AACR2 in to that of RDA. It may be the safest and cheapest (obeys the Law of Parsimony) way of adopting new cataloguing code in the libraries of the developing countries which always pass through lots of financial and other constrains. Where re-cataloguing according to the new code is a mere dream to some libraries due to lack of sufficient fund and additional manpower, library of any stature can think of changing over, following this scientific principle of library science.

REFERENCES

Ranganathan, S. R. (1976). *Prolegomena to library classification.* 3rd ed. Bombay: Asia Publishing House.

Ranganathan, S. R. (1988). *Classified catalogue code: with additional rules for dictionary catalogue code. 5th ed.* Bangalore: Sarada Ranganathan Endowment for Library Science.

U.S. RDA Test Coordinating Committee. (2011). *Full Report.* Retrieved on August 2, 2011 from http://www.loc.gov/bibliographic-future/rda/rdatesting-finalreport-20june2011.pdf

U.S. RDA Test Coordinating Committee. (2012). *First Quarterly updates.* Retrieved on February 25, 2012 from http://www.loc.gov/aba/rda/pdf/RDA_updates_16jan12.pdf

Bibliography

Adamich, Tom. (2008). RDA (Resource Description and Access): the new way to say AACR2. *Knowledge Quest, .36* (4), 64-69.

American Library Association. (1949). *Cataloguing Rules for Author and Title Entries*. 2nd ed. edited by Clara Beetle. Chicago: ALA.

Andersen, Leif. (2004). After MARC- what then? *Library Hi Tech, 22* (1), 40-51.

Anglo-American Cataloging Rules. (1967). Prepared by the American Library Association the Library of Congress, the Library Association, and the Canadian Library Association. British Text. General editor C. Sumner Spalding. London: The Library Association.

Anglo-American Cataloguing Rules. (1978). Prepared by the American Library Association, the British Library, the Canadian Committee on Cataloguing, the Library Association and the Library of Congress; edited by Michael Gorman and Paul W. Winkler. 2nd. ed. Chicago: American Library Association.

Anglo-American Cataloguing Rules. (1988). Prepared under the direction of the Joint Steering Committee for the Revision of AACR; edited by Michael Gorman and Paul W. Winkler. 2nd. ed. 1988 revision. Chicago: American Library Association.

Anglo-American Cataloguing Rules. (1998). Prepared under

the direction of the Joint Steering Committee for the Revision of AACR. 2nd. ed.. 1998 revision. Chicago: American Library Association.

Anglo-American Cataloguing Rules. (2002). Prepared under the direction of the Joint Steering Committee for the Revision of AACR. 2nd. ed., 2002 revision, 2004 update. Chicago: American Library Association.

Arlene G Taylor. (2007).*Introduction to cataloguing and classification.* New Delhi: Atlantic Publishers.

Ball, Katharine L. (1969). The Paris Conference. In Rowland, Arthur Ray (ed.). *The catalogue and Cataloguing* (pp. 190- 195). London: Crosby Lockwood & Sons.

Baughaman, B and Svenonius, E. (1984) Main entry free? *Cataloguing and Classification, 5,* 1-15.

Beall, Jeffrey. (2006). Some Reservations about FRBR. *Library Hi Tech News, 23* (2), 15-16.

Bhattachariya, Ganesh. (1969). *Cataloguing Research in India.* Bangalore: DRTC.

Bierbaum, E.G. (1994). A modest proposal: no more main entry. *American Libraries, 25*(1), January. 81-84.

Biswas, Subhankar. (2015). Reflections of Ranganathan's Normative Principles of Cataloging in RDA. Cataloging & Classification Quarterly. 53(8), 948-963

Biswas, Subhankar and Rath, Durga Sankar. (2013). *Novelty in RDA: a Comparative Analysis of the Rules of AACR2 and RDA.* IASLIC Bulletin, 58(4) 242-252.

Biswas, Subhankar and Rath Durga Sankar. (2014) From Maunsell to Lubetzky: a journey back in search of the root of FRBR among the cataloguing codes of Anglo American origin. Annals of Library and Information Studies, 61(1), March 2014, 7-14.

Boeuf, Patrick Le. (2001). *The Impact of the FRBR Model on the Future Revisions of the ISBDs: A Challenge for the IFA Section on Cataloguing.* 67th IFLA Council and General Conference August 16-25, 2001, Boston.

Retrieved from http://www.ifla.org

-.(2005). FRBR: hype or cure-all? Introduction. *Cataloging & Classification Quarterly, 39* (3-4), 1-13.

Boll, John J. (1990). The Future of AACR2. *Cataloging and Classification Quarterly* 12 (1): 3-34.

Bowen, Jennifer; Lindahl, David and Mayo, Jan. (2011). Cataloging News. *Cataloging & Classification Quarterly, 49* (5), 431-440.

Bowman, J.H (2003).*Essential cataloguing.* London: Facet Publishing.

-. (2006). The Development of Description in Cataloguing Prior to ISBD. *Aslib Proceedings, 58* (1-2), 34-48.

Breeze, H. (2000). Cataloging remote electronic resources. *Law Library Journal, 92* (1), 91-97.

Brian Schottlaender.(ed). (1998) *The Future of the Descriptive Cataloging Rules.* Chicago : American Library Association.

(The) British National Bibliography. (2001). Boston Spa, West Yorkshire: The British Library.

Brown, Georgia L. (1981). AACR2: OCLC's implementation and database conversion. *Journal of Library Automation, 14* (3), 161-173.

Brunt, Rodney. (1998). Old Rules for a New Game: Cutter Revisited. *Library Review, 47*(2), 82–90.

Brunt, Rodney M. (1992). The Code and the catalogue: a return to compatibility. Library *Review 41* (3): 21-32.

Buckland, Michael L. (1988). Bibliographies, library records, and the redefinition of the library catalog. *Library Resources and Technical Services* 32 (4): 299-311.

Burton, P. A. and A. M. Hawkins. (1993). Attitudes to an online public access catalogue in an academic library. *Library Management* 14 (5): 13-15.

Byrum John D. and Coe, D. Whitney. (1979). AACR as applied by research libraries for serials cataloging.

Library Resources and Technical Services, 23 (2), 139-146.

Carter, Ruth C. and Kascus Marie A. (1991). Cataloging and Classification Quarterly 1980-1990: Content, Change, and Trends. *Cataloging and Classification Quarterly, 12* (3/4), 69-79.

Chan, Lois Mai. (1985). *Cataloging and classification: an introduction*. New York: McGraw-Hill.

Chaplin, A. H. (1956). A Universal Cataloging Code. *The Library Quarterly, 26* (4), 337-347.

Chaplin, Arthur H. (1957). A universal cataloging code. In *Toward a Better Cataloging Code,* edited by R. F. Strout, 78-97. Chicago: the University of Chicago, Graduate Library School.

Chapman, Ann. (2010). The Case of AACR2 Versus RDA. *Legal Information Management, 10* (3), 210-213.

Choi, Yunseon. (2012). A Practical Application of FRBR for Organizing Information in Digital Environments. *Knowledge Organization, 39* (4), 233-254.

Clark, John Wills. (1909). *The Care of Books*. Cambridge: Cambridge University Press.

Clarke, A. L. (1933). *Manual of practical indexing: including arrangement of subject cataloguing*. London: Grafton.

Cockshutt, Margaret E. and Cook, C. Donald. (1983). Decision logic for Anglo-American Cataloguing Rules, Chapter 21: 'Choice of Access Points'. *Library Resources and Technical Services, 27* (4), 371-390.

Cole, Jim E. AACR2 and ISBD(S): correspondence or divergence? (1982). *Serials Review, 8* (3), 67-69.

Conners, David. (2008). A Ghost in the Catalog: the Gradual Obsolescence of the Main Entry. *The Serials Librarian Serials Librarian, 55* (1), 285-97.

Cook, C. Donald. (1986). Cataloguing in the International Arena. *Library Resources and Technical Services, 30* (1), 23-30.

Croissant, Charles R. (2012). FRBR and RDA: What They are and How They May Affect the Future of Libraries. *Theological Librarianship: An Online Journal of the American Theological Library Association, 5* (2), 6-22.

Croissant, Charles R. (2012). FRBR and RDA: What They are and How They May Affect the Future of Libraries. *Theological Librarianship: An Online Journal of the American Theological Library Association, 5* (2), 6-22.

Cutter, C. A. (1904). *Rules for a dictionary catalogue.* 4th ed. Washington: Government Printing Office.

Danskin, Alan. (1998). International initiatives in authority control. *Library Review, 47* (4), 200–205.

Danskin, Alan. (2004). Mature consideration: Developing Bibliographic Standards and Maintaining Values. *New Library World, 105* (1198/1199), 113-117.

-. (2006). *Tomorrow never knows: the end of cataloguing?* World Library And Information Congress: 72nd IFLA General Conference And Council 20-24 August 2006, Seoul, Korea. Retrieved from http://www.ifla.org.

Davis-Brown, B. and Williamson, D. (1996). Cataloging at the Library of Congress in the digital age. *Cataloging and Classification Quarterly, 22* (3/4), 171-196.

Dawson, Alan. (2004). Digital Directions: Creating Metadata that work for Digital Libraries and Google. *Library Review, 53* (7), 347-350.

Delsey, Tom. (1998). Modeling the Logic of AACR. In Jean Weihs (ed.) *the principles and Future of AACR: proceedings of the International Conference on the Principles and Future Development of AACR, Toronto, Ontario, Canada, October 23-25, 1997* (pp.1-16). Ottawa: Canadian Library Association.

Denton, William. (2011). Implementing FRBR in Libraries: Key Issues and Future Directions. *Cataloging & Classification Quarterly, 49* (1), 47-49.

Dunkin, Paul S. (1956). Criticisms of current cataloging

practice. *The Library Quarterly, 26* (4), 286-302.

Dunkin, Paul S. (1972). Cataloging & Classification - The Big IF, *American Libraries, 3* (7), 775-783.

Dunsire, Gordon and Willer, Mirna. (2011). Standard Library Metadata Models and Structures for the Semantic Web. *Library Hi Tech News, 28* (3), 1-12.

Edgar, N.L (1975). What Every Librarian should Know about Proposed Changes in Cataloguing Rules: a Brief Over view. *American Libraries, 6* (10), 602-607.

Edgar, Neal L., Spalding C. Summer, Richmond, Phyllis A. & Hagler, Ronald. (1975). What Every Librarian Should Know about Proposed Changes in Cataloging Rules: A Brief Overview, *American Libraries, 6* (10), 602-607.

Elrod, J. McRee (Mac). (2008). The Case for Cataloguing Education. *The Serials Librarian Serials Librarian, 55* (1-2), 1-10.

El-Sherbini Magda and Klim,George. (2004). Metadata and cataloging practices, *The Electronic Library, 22* (3), 238-248.

El-Sherbini, Magda and Curran, Megan. (2011). Resource Description and Access 'RDA': New Code for Cataloging. *Serials Librarian 60* (1-4), 7-15.

Escreet, P.K.(1971). *Introduction to Anglo-American Cataloguing Rules.* London: Andre Deutsch.

Fasana, Paul. (1975). AACR, ISBD(S) and ISSN: a comment. *Library Resources and Technical Services, 19* (4), 333-337.

Fattahi, R. (1996). Cataloguing at the Crossroads: Cataloguers have a lot to offer the Information Age. *Cataloguing Australia, 22* (3/4), 59-67.

Fattahi Rahmat.1998. Library cataloguing and abstracting and indexing services: reconciliation of principles in the online environment? *Library Review, 47* (4), 211–216.

Fattahi, Rahmatollah. (1996). Super records: an Approach towards the Description of Works appearing in various Manifestations. *Library Review, 45* (4), 19-29.

Fattahi, Rahmatollah (1998). AACR2 and Catalogue Production Technology: Relevance of Cataloguing Principles to the Online Environment. In Jean Weihs (ed.) *the principles and Future of AACR: proceedings of the International Conference on the Principles and Future Development of AACR, Toronto, Ontario, Canada, October 23-25, 1997* (pp.17-43). Ottawa: Canadian Library Association.

Ford, Bruce E. (1980). New attempts to resolve old conflicts: chapter 22 of AACR 2. *Library Resources and Technical Services, 24* (3), 214-216.

Foxon, David. (1955).*The Technique of Bibliography*. London. National Book League.

Francis, Frank. (1963). Addresses. In A. H. Chaplin (ed.) *International Conference on Cataloguing Principles: report, Paris, 9th – 18th October, 1961* (pp.13-15). London: Organizing Committee of the ICCP.

Fritz, D. A. (1998). Cataloging with AACR2R and USMARC for Books, Computer files, Serials, Sound recordings, Video recordings. *Library Resources and Technical Services, 42* (4), 318-320.

Fritz Deborah. A. (2009). *Cataloging with AACR2 & MARC 21 for books, electronic resources, sound recordings, video recordings, and serials.* New Delhi: Pentagon Press.

Frost, Carolyn O. (1976). The Bodleian Catalogs of 1674 and 1738: an Examination in the Light of Modern Cataloguing Theory. *The Library Quarterly, 46*(3), 248-270.

Frumkin, Jeremy. (2006). Digital Libraries: Modern Practices, Future Visions in Our Cages with Golden Bars. *OCLC Systems & Services: International digital library perspectives, 22* (4), 247-248.

Garnett, Richard. (1899). *Essays in Librarianship and Bibliography*. New York: F. P. Harper.

Genetasio, Giuliano. (2012).*The Statement of International Cataloguing Principles and their Future*. Retrieved September 7, 2012 from http://leo.cilea.it/index.php/jlis/issue/view/326

Gerhard, K. H. (1997). Cataloging Internet Resources: Practical Issues and Concerns. *Serials Librarian, 32* (1/2), 123-37.

Gorman, Michael. (1977).Changes in Cataloguing Codes: Rules for Entry and Heading. *Library Trends, 25* (3), 587-601.

-. (1978). The Anglo American Cataloguing Rules, Second edition. *Library Resources and Technical Services, 22* (3), 209-226.

-. (1978). Toward Bibliographic Control: and Now, from the Wonderful Folks Who Gave You Superimposition. *American Libraries, 9* (10), 620-621.

-. (1997). What is the Future of Cataloguing and Cataloguers? in *63rd IFLA General Conference - Conference Programme and Proceedings - August 31- September 5, 1997* Retrived October 9, 2007, from http://www.ifla.org/IV/ifla63/63gorm.htm

-. (2000). *From Card Catalogues to Webpacs: Celebrating Cataloguing in the 20th Century*. Retrieved August 9, 2011 from http://lcweb.loc.gov/catdir/bibcontrol/gorman_paper.html.

-. 2006. *Cataloguing the Web: an oxymoron*. Retrieved August 9, 2009 from http:// mg.csufresno.edu/papers/Metadata.pdf

-. (2007). RDA: Imminent Debacle. *American Libraries, 38*. (11) 64-65.

Gorman, Michael and Pat Oddy (1998). The Anglo-American Cataloguing Rules, Second Edition: their history and principles. In Jean Weihs (ed.) *the principles and Future of AACR: proceedings of the International Conference on the Principles and Future Development of AACR, Toronto, Ontario, Canada, October 23-25, 1997* (pp.158-165). Ottawa: Canadian Library Association.

Graham, Crystal. (1990). Definition and scope of multiple versions. *Cataloging & Classification Quarterly* 11 (2): 5-32.

Gredley, Ellen J. (1980). Standardising bibliographical data: AACR2 and international exchange. *Journal of Librarianship* 12 (2): 84-101

Gregor, Dorothy and Mandel, Carol. (1991). Cataloguing must Change. *Library Journal, 116* (6), 42-47.

Guha, B. & Prashad, H. N. (1986). Ranganathan's normative principles and AACR-II. In T. S. Rajagopalan (Ed.) *Ranganathan's philosophy: assessment, impact, and relivance.* (pp. 352-362) New Delhi: Vikas Publishing House.

Gull, C. D. (1963). The Impact of Electronics upon Cataloguing Rules. In A. H. Chaplin (ed.) *International Conference on Cataloguing Principles: report, Paris, 9th – 18th October, 1961* (pp.281-290). London: Organizing Committee of the ICCP.

Harden, Jean. (2012). Inadvertent RDA: New Catalogers' Errors in AACR2. *Journal of Library Metadata, 12* (2-3), 264-278.

Haskins, Susan M. (1960). Moving toward international cataloging agreement. *ALA Bulletin, 54* (3), 194-196.

Haynes, Elizabeth. (2005). *Unlocking the mysteries of cataloging: a Workbook of examples.* London: Libraries Unlimited.

Henderson, K.L. (1976).Treated with a degree of uniformity and common sense: descriptive cataloging in the United States 1876-1975. Library Trends, *25*(1), 227-71.

Hepfer, Cindy and Hepfer, Will. (1987). AACR2's effect on public services. *Serials Librarian, 12* (1/2), 19-25.

Hider Philip and Huthwaite Ann. (2006). *The Potential Impact of RDA on OPAC Displays.* Retrieved November 2, 2007, from http://www.nla.gov.au/lis/stndrds/grps/acoc/papers2006.html

Hill, Janet Swan (ed.). (2004). *Education for cataloging and the organization of information : Pitfalls and the pendulum.* New Delhi: Viva Books.

Hine, Betsy N. (2011). Introducing RDA: a Guide to the Basics. *Technical Services Quarterly, 28* (4), 470-472.

Hirons, J; Hawkins, L and French, P. (2000): AACR2 and you: Revising AACR2 to Accommodate Seriality. *Serials Librarian,38* (3-4), 249-256.

Hirons, Jean and Reynolds, Regina. (1999). Seriality: it's not just for serials any more. Library Review. 48, (4), 163-168.

Hirons, Jean and Graham Crystal. (1998). Issues related to Seriality. In Jean Weihs (ed.) *the principles and Future of AACR: proceedings of the International Conference on the Principles and Future Development of AACR, Toronto, Ontario, Canada, October 23-25, 1997* (pp.180-212). Ottawa: Canadian Library Association.

Hitchens, Alison and Symons, Ellen.(2009). Preparing Catalogers for RDA Training. *Cataloging & Classification Quarterly, 47* (8), 691-707.

Hoffman, Halen K. (1977). Cataloguing Codes & Non-book Materials. *Research Librarian, 8* (3), 129-146.

Hoffman Herbert H. (1983). AACR2 and the level of description principle. *Library Resources and Technical Services, 27* (4), 395-396.

Hopkins, Judith. (1993). One-stop information store: the catalog beyond Cutter. *Cataloging and Classification Quarterly* 16 (3): 127-31.

Horner, John. (1970). *Cataloguing.* London: Association of

Assistant Librarians.

Howarth, Lynne. (1998).Content versus Carrier. In Jean Weihs (ed.) *the principles and Future of AACR: proceedings of the International Conference on the Principles and Future Development of AACR, Toronto, Ontario, Canada, October 23-25, 1997* (pp.148-156). Ottawa: Canadian Library Association.

Howarth, Lynne C and Weihs, Jean. (2008). Enigma variations: parsing the riddle of main entry and the "rule of three" from AACR2 to RDA *Cataloging & Classification Quarterly, 46* (2), 201-220.

Hunter, E J and Graham, M. (1994). Guide to the AACR2 1988 revision: a programmed instruction. *Australian Library Review,11* (4), 515.

Hunter, Eric J. (1968). *Cataloguing: a guide book.* London: Clive Bingley.

Huthwaite, Ann. (2000). AACR2 and its place in the Digital World: Near-Term Solutions and Long-Term Direction. Retrieved on December 10, 2007 from http:// .lcweb.loc.gov/catdir/bibcontrol/huthwaite_paper.html.

Huthwaite, Ann. (2003). AACR2 and other Metadata Standards: the Way Forward. *Cataloging and Classification Quarterly,36* (3-4), 87-100.

ICCP. (1963). *Report: International Conference on Cataloguing Principles Paris, 9th – 18th October, 19961.* London: Organizing Committee of the ICCP.

IFLA (1997). *Functional Requirements for Bibliographic Records: final report* .Retrieved September 7, 2011 from www.ifla.org.

IFLA. (2002). *International Standard Bibliographic Description for Serials and Other Continuing Resources. 2002.* Retrieved December 2, 2007, from http://www.ifla.org/VII/s13/pubs/isbdcr-final.pdf

IFLA. (2009). *The Statement of International Cataloguing Principles.* Retrieved September 7, 2012 from www.ifla.org.

(The) *Indian National Bibliography*. (1994). Calcutta: Central Reference Library, Government of India, Ministry of H. R.D., Department of Culture.

Intner, Sheila S. (1983). A Survey Explores: Equality of Cataloging in the Age of AACR2. *American Libraries, 14* (2). 102-103.

Intner, Sheila S, Fountain, Joanna F. and Weihs, Jean. (eds.). (2011). *Cataloging correctly for kids : an Introduction to the tools*. Chicago: American Library Association

Intner, Sheila S., Lazinger, Susan S. and Weihs, Jean. (2006). *Metadata and its Impact on Libraries*. Westport: Libraries Unlimited.

Jewett, Charles C. (1852). *Smithsonian Report on the Construction of Catalogues of Libraries, and of a General Catalogue; and their Publication by Means of Separate, Stereotyped Titles, with Rules and Examples*. Washington: Smithsonian Institution

Joint Steering Committee for Revision of AACR. (2008). RDA prospectus. Retrieved on September 20, 2008 from www.collectionscanada.ca/jsc/rdaprospectus.html.

Joint Steering Committee for the Development of RDA. (2008). *RDA Final Draft*. Retrieved on December 7, 2008 from www.rdaonline.org.

Joint Steering Committee for Development of RDA. (2013). *RDA Resource Description and Access*. Chicago : American Library Association.

Jolley. L. (1960). *The Principles of Cataloguing*. London: Crosby Lockwood & Sons

-. (1967) [Review of] Anglo-American Cataloguing Rules, North American Text. *Journal of Documentation, 23* (4), 349.

Jolley, L. J. (1963). Function of the Main Entry in the Alphabetical Catalogue: a Study of the Views put Forward by Lubetzky and Verona. In A. H. Chaplin (ed.) *International Conference on Cataloguing Principles: report, Paris, 9th – 18th October, 1961* (pp.159-163). London: Organizing Committee of the ICCP.

Jul E. (1998). Cataloging Internet Resources: an Assessment and Prospectus. *Serials Librarian, 34* (1/2) 91-104.

Kelm, Carol R. (1978). The Historical Development of the second edition of Anglo American Cataloguing Rules. . *Library Resources and Technical Services 22* (1), 22-33.

Kidane, Resoum. (2013). Cataloguing in the Digital Age: Cataloguers' and Library Schools' Opinions on RDA and AACR2R. *ALISS Quarterly, 8* (4), 24-34.

Kiorgaard, Deirdre and Huthwaite Ann. (2005). Authority control in AACR3. *ACOC seminar 2005.* Retrieved December 2, 2007, from http://www.nla.gov.au/lis/stndrds/grps/acoc/papers2006

Kiorgaard, Deirdre. (2006). *A Rose by any other Name? from AACR2 to Resource Description and Access.* Retrieved December 19, 20010 from *www.valaconf.org.au/vala2006/papers2006/83_Kartus_Final.pdf*

Knowlton, Steven A. (2006). A Preview of the New Cataloging Code. *MLA Forum, 5(1).* Retrieved October 01, 2012 from http://www.mlaforum.org/volumeV/issue1/article2.htm

Koehler, Wallace. (2004). Digital libraries, digital containers, library patrons, and visions for the future. *The Electronic Library, 22* (5), 401-407.

Kraus, Daniel. (Oct 2007). Controversies in cataloging. *American Libraries, 38* (9), 66-67.

Kraus, Daniel. (2007). Controversies in Cataloging. *American Libraries38* (9), 66-67.

Kuhagen, Judith A. and Mering, Margaret. (2013). RDA and Serials: Theoretical and Practical Applications. *Serials Librarian,64* (1-4), 5-14.

Kumar, Krishan (1986). Ranganathan's Canons of Cataloguing and Scientific Method. In T. S. Rajagopalan (Ed.) *Ranganathan's Philosophy: Assessment, Impact, and Relivance.* (pp. 383-394). New Delhi: Vikas Publishing House.

Lam, V.T. (2000). Cataloging Internet resources: why, what, how. *Cataloging and Classification Quarterly, 29* (3) 2000, 49-61.

LeBlanc, J. D. (1993). Cataloging in the 1990s: Managing the Crisis (mentality). *Library Resources and Technical Services, 37* (4), 423-433.

Library of Congress. (1946). *Studies of Descriptive Cataloging.* Library of Congress: Washington D.C.

Lubetzky, S. (1953). Development of cataloging rules. Retrieved August 9, 2011 from https://www.ideals.illinois.edu/bitstream/handle/2142/5511/librarytrendsv2i2c_opt.pdf?

Lubtzky, Seymour. (1963). The Function of the main entry in the alphabetical catalogue: one approach. In A. H. Chaplin (ed.) *International Conference on Cataloguing Principles: report, Paris, 9th – 18th October, **1961*** (pp.139-143). London: Organizing Committee of the ICCP.

-. (1969) *Descriptive Cataloging: problems and principles: report 3 of a series on the principles of cataloguing.* Los Angeles: California University.

-. (1999). On the Use of Form Headings in an Alphabetical Catalog. *The Library Quarterly, 69* (2), 222-236.

Madison, Olivia M. A. (2005). The origins of the IFLA study on Functional Requirements for Bibliographic Records. *Cataloging & Classification Quarterly, 39* (3-4), 15-37.

Mandel, Carol. (1991). Cataloguing for Access. *Reference Librarian,* (34), 61-68.

Manning, Ralph. (1998). Introduction. In Jean Weihs (ed.) *the principles and Future of AACR: proceedings of the*

International Conference on the Principles and Future Development of AACR, Toronto, Ontario, Canada, October 23-25, 1997 (pp.ix-xi). Ottawa: Canadian Library Association.

Maxwell, Margaret F. (1977). The Genesis of the Anglo American Cataloguing Rules. *Libri, 27* (3), 238-262.

McIntosh, Joyce. (2011). *Cataloging and indexing: Challenges and solutions.* Oakville: Apple Academic Press.

Meador Roy and Wittig, Glenn R.(1991).AACR2 rules used in assigning access points for books in two subjects: implications for automatic cataloguing expert systems. *Library Resources and Technical Services, 35* (2), 135-140.

Medeiros, Norm. (2005). The future of the Anglo-American cataloguing rules. *OCLC Systems & Services, 21* (4), 261-263.

Miller, Liz. (2011). Resource Description and Access (RDA): an Introduction for Reference Librarians. *Reference & User Services Quarterly, 50* (3), 216-222.

Molto, M and Svenonius, E. (1998). An electronic interface to AACR2. *Cataloging and Classification Quarterly, 26* (1), 3-24.

Moore, Julie Renee. (2006). RDA: New cataloguing Rules, coming soon to a library near you. Library Hi Tech News, November 9, 12-16.

Morris, D. E. and Wool, G. (1999). Cataloging: Librarianship's best Bargain. *Library Journal, 124* (11), 44-46.

Murtomaa, E. (1999). The impact of the functional requirements for bibliographic records: recommendations on the ISBD(ER). *Cataloging and Classification Quarterly, 28* (1), 33-41.

Myer, S A. (2003). AACR2 Revisions and Electronic Resources: Chapters 9 and 12: report on the Electronic Resources Discussion Group. *Serials Review, 29* (1), 60-62.

Needham, C. D. (1971). *Organizing Knowledge in Libraries: an introduction to information retrieval.* London: Andre Deutsch.

Needleman, Mark. (2008). The Resource Description and Access Standard. *Serials Review, 34* (3), 233-234.

Oddy, Pat. (1996). Bibliographic Standards for the New Age. *Library Review, 45* (2), 30-40.

Oder, N. (1998) Cataloging the Net: can we do it? *Library Journal, 123* (16), 47-51.

Oliver, Chris. (2010). *Introducing RDA : a Guide to the basics.* London: Facet Publishing.

-. (2004). FRBR is everywhere, but what happened to the format variation issue? Content versus carrier in FRBR. *Serials Librarian, 45* (4), 27-36.

Olson, Hope A. (2006). Codes, costs, and critiques: the organization of information in Library Quarterly, 1931-2004. *Library Quarterly, 76* (1), 19-35.

Olson, N. B. and Swanson, E. (1993). Cataloguing Computer files. *Cataloging and Classification Quarterly, 18* (2), 101-102.

Omekwu Charles O., Egberongbe, H.S. and John-Okeke, Rita (2007). Shared Catalogues and Cataloguing Tools: Information and Communication Technology as Catalyst, *Library Hi Tech News,* (3), 19-25.

Osborn, Andrew. (1941). Crisis in cataloging. *The Library Quarterly, 11* (4) 393-411.

Osborn, Andrew D. (1956). Cataloguing and Cataloguing Codes in other countries today. In *Toward a Better Cataloguing Code: Papers presented before the Twenty-first Annual Conference of Graduate Library School of the University of Chicago June 13-15, 1956.*(pp.26-35). Chicago: The University of Chicago Graduate Library School.

Palmer, B. (2002). Cataloguing Practices of Public Libraries in England. *Catalogue and Index, 144,* 1-4.

Panizzi, A. (1841). *Rules for the Compilation of Catalogue. In the Catalogue of Printed Books in the British Museum.* London: British Museum.

Parameswaran, M. (1989). *AngloAmerican Cataloguing Rules (II) and CCC (5): a comparative study.* New Deihi: Ess Ess Publications

Pardo, Carol E. (2012), Practical Cataloging: AACR2, RDA and MARC21, *Journal of Archival Organization, 10* (3-4), 249-250.

Peregoy, Marjorie. (1978). AACRII and Serials Cataloguing. *Serials Librarian, 3* (1), 15-30.

Perry, Asheleigh A. (2013). Demystifying FRAD: Functional Requirements for Authority Data. *The Journal of Academic Librarianship, 39* (2), 116.

Petersen, E. N. (1963). Addresses. In A. H. Chaplin (ed.) *International Conference on Cataloguing Principles: report, Paris, 9th – 18th October, 1961* (pp.13-15). London: Organizing Committee of the ICCP.

Pettee, Julia. (1936). The Development of authorship entry and the formulation of authorship rules as found in the Anglo-American Code. *Library Quarterly, 6*(3), 270-90.

-. (1946). *Subject Headings: the History and Theory of the Alphabetical Approach to Books.* New York: H. W. Wilson.

Piggot, Mary. (1963).*Uniformity in descriptive cataloguing.* Libri, 13(1), 45-54

Pisanski, Jan. and Z ¡ umer, Maja. (2007). Functional requirements for bibliographic records: an investigation of two prototypes. *Program: electronic library and information systems, 41* (4), 400-417.

Randall, Kevin M. (2011). RDA: End of the World Postponed. *Serials Librarian, 61* (3-4), 334-345.

Ranganathan, S. R. (1938). *Theory of library catalogue.*

Madras (India): Madras Library Association.

-. (1955). *Heading and canons: comparative study of five catalogue codes*. Madras (India): S. Viswanathan.

-.(1976). *Prolegomena to library classification*. 3rd ed. Bombay: Asia Publishing House.

-. (1988). *Classified catalogue code: with additional rules for dictionary catalogue code.5th ed.* Bangalore: Sarada Ranganathan Endowment for Library Science.

Read, Jane M. (2003). *Cataloguing Without Tears: Managing Knowledge in the Information Society*. Oxford: Chandos

Rees, L. B. and Clancy, B. A.(1998). Cataloging Electronic Journals: Learning to Weave the Web. *Internet Reference Services Quarterly, 3* (3), 29-43.

Richmond, Phyllis A. (1977). Mr. Dewey's Classification, Mr Cutter's Catalogue and Dr. Hitchcock's Chickens. *Library Resources Technical Services, 21*(2), 107-119.

Riva, Pat. (2003). Defining the boundaries: FRBR, AACR and the serial. *Serials Librarian, 45* (3),15-21.

Rogers, D. (1997). Cataloguing Internet Resources: the Evolution of the Dublin Core Metadata Set. *Cataloguing Australia, 23* (1/2),17-22.

Sardo, Lucia. (2004). Functional Requirements for Authority Records: a Conceptual Model. *Bollettino AIB, 44* (4), 455-470.

Seikel, Michele. (2013). General Notes in Catalog Records Versus FRBR User Tasks. *Cataloging & Classification Quarterly, 51* (4), 420-427.

Shera, J. H & Egan M. E. (1956) *The Classified Catalogue.* Chicago: American Library Association.

Shera, J.H. (1950). Review of 1949 code. *Library Quarterly, 20,*147-150.

Spalding C. Sumner. (1980). The life and death (?) of corporate authorship. *Library Resources and Technical Services, 24* (3), 195-208.

Spalding, C. S. (1973). ISBD: its Origin, Rationale: and Implications. *Library Journal, 98* (2), 121-123.

Stibbe, H. L. P. (1999). Cataloguing Cartographic Materials in Archives. *Cataloging and Classification Quarterly, 27* (3/4), 443-63.

Stokes, Helen. (1989). AACR2 9 (1988 revision). *Cataloguing Australia, 15* (2), 62-64.

Strauss, Barbara J. (2009). Understanding FRBR: What it is and How it will Affect our Retrieval Tools. *Technical Services Quarterly, 26* (2), 170-172.

Strout, Ruth Frence (1956). Development of the Catalog and Cataloguing Codes. *Library Quarterly, 26*(4), 254-275.

Strutt, Sally E. (1997). Cataloguing and the Internet: considerations at the British Library. *Library Review, 46* (7), 490-499.

Subhramanium, V.K. (1994). Dr. S.R. Ranganathan in Anglo-American Cataloguing Rules, 2nd Edition: a Survey and Observations. *Library Science, 31*(3), 135-151.

Tait, James A. and Anderson, Douglas (1971). *Descriptive Cataloguing: a students' introduction to the Anglo-American cataloguing rules*. 2nd. revd. & enl. ed. London: Clive Bingley

Talmaes, K. (1989). Cataloguing and the needs of an Academic Library. *Cataloguing Australia, 15* (4), 109-113.

Taniguchi, Shoichi. (2013). Event-aware FRBR and FRAD models: are they useful? *Journal of Documentation, 69* (3), 452-472.

Tarulli, Laurel. (2012). Practical Cataloguing: AACR, RDA and MARC21. *Library Review, 61* (7). 543-544.

Taylor, A G. (1999). Where does AACR2 fall short for Internet resources? *Journal of Internet Cataloging, 2* (2), 43-50.

Taylor, Arlene G. (2007).*Introduction to cataloguing and classification*. New Delhi: Atlantic Publishers.

Taylor, Wendy. (Jan 2009). The Ho' Debates in Cataloguing. *Library Information Updat:*, 27.

Tessier, Judith A. (1992). Cataloging Instruction: Development of a Hyper Card Implementation of AACR2, Chapter 21. *Journal of Education for Library and Information Science, 33* (3), 195-211.

Thomas, Paule Rolland. (1983). AACR2: one step towards an International Code. *Cataloging and Classification Quarterly, 3* (4), 45-49.

Thompson, Elizabeth H.(comp.). (1943). *A.L.A. Glossary* of *Library Terms*. Chicago, ALA, 1943, p. 45.

Thompson, James Westfall. (1957). *The Medieval Library*. New York: Hafner Club

Tillett, Barbara B.(1995). Cataloguing Rules and Conceptual Models for the Electronic Environment. *Cataloguing Australia, 21* (3-4), 67-103.

-. (2004). *What is FRBR? A conceptual model for the bibliographic universe*. Retrieved on December 2, 2007, from http://www.ifla.org/VII/s13/frbr/frbr.pdf

-. (2011). Keeping Libraries Relevant in the Semantic Web with Resource Description and Access (RDA). *Serials, 24* (3), 266-272.

Tosaka, Yuji and Park, Jung-ran (2013). RDA: Resource description & access-a survey of the current state of the art. *Journal of the American Society for Information Science and Technology, 64* (4), 651–662.

Trainor, J. (1995). Cataloguing in World 1. *Cataloguing Australia, 21* (3-4), 162-175.

Underwood, Peter G. (2011). Introducing RDA: a Guide to the Basics. *Journal of Librarianship and Information Science, 43* (3), 196-197.

U.S. RDA Test Coordinating Committee. (2011). *Full Report*. Retrieved on August 2, 2011 from http://www.loc.gov/bibliographic-future/rda/rdatesting-finalreport-20june2011.pdf

U.S. RDA Test Coordinating Committee. (2012). *First Quarterly updates.* Retrieved on February 25, 2012 from http://www.loc.gov/aba/rda/pdf/RDA_updates_16jan12.pdf

Verona, Eva. (1959). Literary unit versus bibliographical unit. *Libri. 9*(2), 79-104.

Viswanathan, C.G. (1990). *Cataloguing theory and practice.* 6th ed. New Delhi: Ess Ess Publications.

Weber, Mary Beth and Austin, Fay Angela. (2011). *Describing electronic, digital, and other media using AACR2 and RDA: a How-to-do-it manual and CD-ROM for librarians.* London: Facet Publishing.

Weiks, Jean. (1987). AACR 2: a practical approach. *Journal of Educational Media and Library Sciences, 24* (3), 255-260.

Weiss, Paul and Shadle, Steve. (2006). FRBR in the real world. *The Serials Librarian, 52* (1-2), 91-104.

Welsh, Anne. (2011). Teaching RDA in 2010-11. Catalogue and Index. June(163), 5-8.

Welsh, Anne and Batley, Sue. (2012). *Practical cataloguing : AACR, RDA and MARC 21.* London: Facet Publishing.

Weng, Cathy and Mi, Jia.(2006). Towards Accessibility to Digital Cultural Materials: a FRBRized Approach. *OCLC Systems & Services: International Digital Library Perspectives, 22* (3), 217-232.

Willer, Mirna. (1999). Formats and cataloguing rules: developments for cataloguing electronic resources. *Program, 33* (1), 41–55.

-. (2012). Introducing RDA: A Guide to the Basics. *Cataloging & Classification Quarterly50* (4), 337-341.

Wynar, Bohdan S. (1967). *Introduction to Cataloguing and Classification.* Colorado: Libraries Unlimited.

Yee, Martha M. (1983). Integration of Nonbook materials in AACR2. *Cataloging and Classification Quarterly, 3* (4), 1-18.

-. (2005). FRBRization: a method for turning online public finding lists into online public catalogs. *Information Technology and Libraries,* 24 (2), 77-95.

Young, Naomi Kietzke. (2002). Thinking amphibiously: integrating resources in AACR2. *Library Collections, Acquisitions & Technical Services, 26,* 167–171.

Zhang, Yin and Salaba Athena. (2009). What Is Next for Functional Requirements for Bibliographic Records? A Delphi Study. *The Library Quarterly, 79* (2), 233-255.

Index